WHITE COLLAR CRIME

IN A NUTSHELL

SECOND EDITION

By

ELLEN S. PODGOR

Professor of Law
Georgia State University College of Law

JEROLD H. ISRAEL

Ed Rood Eminent Scholar in Trial
Advocacy and Procedure,
University of Florida College of Law
Alene and Allan F. Smith Professor
of Law Emeritus,
University of Michigan Law School

WEST
GROUP

ST. PAUL, MINN.
1997

COPYRIGHT © 1993 WEST PUBLISHING CO.

COPYRIGHT © 1997 By WEST GROUP
610 Opperman Drive
P.O. Box 64526
St. Paul, MN 55164–0526
1–800–328–9352

Library of Congress Cataloging-in-Publication Data

Podgor, Ellen S., 1952–
    White collar crime in a nutshell / by Ellen S. Podgor, Jerold H.
Israel. — 2nd ed.
        p.   cm. — (Nutshell series)
    Includes index.
    ISBN 0–314–21163–2 (pbk.)
    1. White collar crimes—United States.   I. Israel, Jerold H.,
1934–   . II. Title.   III. Series.
KF9350.Z9P63   1997
345.73'0268—dc21

ISBN 0–314–21163–2

Dedicated to our parents:

Yetta & Benjamin Podgor
Florence & Harry Israel

*

PREFACE

White collar crime is a relatively new concept, having first achieved recognition in 1939. Despite its short life, white collar crime has quickly grown to its present status of being a major focus of the Department of Justice. This nutshell is intended to provide to students a general overview of this growing area. It is hoped that this book will assist in providing a structure to a basically unstructured body of law.

Because of the general focus of this book, it is not recommended as a source for deciding a specific legal issue. Cases were selected for this book to be illustrative, rather than comprehensive of each area being discussed. Specific crimes were selected to provide a sampling of the wide array of crimes encompassed within this enormous body of law. This book focuses on white collar crime in the federal criminal context, and does not delve into developments at the state and local level.

This second edition adds the expertise of Jerold Israel, resulting in its substantial expansion of the coverage of procedural issues that impact white collar crime.

It is important to note that the study of white collar crime is a continuing study, with ever changing rules and precedent. Many of the issues within white collar crime, as noted throughout this book, have yet to be resolved.

Thanks go to those who assisted with the first edition, specifically Susan Rappa Bain, Sara Sun Beale, Mark E. Budnitz, Anne S. Emanuel, Marjorie L. Girth, Melissa Harrison, Marjorie Fine Knowles, Eli Lederman, Alfred R. Light, David J. Maleski, Ira Mickenberg, Patricia T. Morgan, Betty Turner, Steve Wermiel, Jack Williams, and Deborah Young. Thanks also go to those who assisted with the second edition, specifically Paul Borman, Victor Flatt, Marjorie Girth, Marjorie Fine Knowles, Eli Lederman, Patricia T. Morgan, and Myrtle Smith.

ELLEN S. PODGOR
JEROLD H. ISRAEL

May, 1997

OUTLINE

Page

PREFACE --- V
TABLE OF CASES --- XVII

PART ONE. GENERAL PRINCIPLES

Chapter One. Scope of White Collar Crime ------------------------------------- 1
Sec.
1.01 Introduction -- 1
1.02 Scope of Federal Criminal Law ----------- 3
1.03 State and/or Federal Prosecution -------- 6
1.04 Federal Influence in International Prosecutions ---------------------------------- 8
1.05 Application of General Principles of Criminal Law ----------------------------- 10
1.06 Defenses --- 11

Chapter Two. Corporate Criminal Liability -- 16
2.01 Overview of Corporate Criminal Liability --- 16
2.02 Standards of Imputing Corporate Criminal Liability ---------------------- 19
2.03 Collective Knowledge ------------------------ 27

Page

Sec.

2.04 Dead Corporations and Noncorporate Entity Liability 29

2.05 Overview of Personal Liability of Corporate Agents 30

2.06 Responsible Corporate Officer 32

PART TWO.   SPECIFIC OFFENSES

Chapter Three.   Conspiracy 37

3.01 Introduction 37
3.02 Agreement 40
3.03 Plurality 41
3.04 Unlawful Object of Conspiracy 46
3.05 Knowledge and Intent 48
3.06 Overt Act 50
3.07 Single or Multiple Conspiracies 50
3.08 Pinkerton Rule 52
3.09 Antitrust Conspiracies 54

Chapter Four.   Mail, Wire and Bank Fraud 57

4.01 Introduction 57
4.02 Scheme to Defraud 59
4.03 Intangible Rights 61
4.04 Intangible Property 64
4.05 Use of the Mails in Furtherance 65
4.06 Limitations to "In Furtherance" 66
4.07 The New "In Furtherance" Test 70
4.08 Wire Fraud 71
4.09 Bank Fraud 72
4.10 Mail Fraud and Other Crimes 73

		Page
Chapter Five. Securities Fraud		76
Sec.		
5.01	Introduction	76
5.02	Mens Rea	79
5.03	Insider Trading	82
5.04	Development of the Misappropriation Theory	86
Chapter Six. Obstruction of Justice		91
6.01	Introduction	91
6.02	Overview of Section 1503	97
6.03	Corruptly or by Threats or Force—Section 1503	98
6.04	Endeavors—Section 1503	101
6.05	To Influence, Obstruct or Impede the Due Administration of Justice—Section 1503	103
6.06	Section 1503 as it Relates to Other Obstruction Statutes	106
Chapter Seven. Bribery and Extortion		110
7.01	Introduction	110
7.02	Overview of Bribery	111
7.03	Bribery—Things of Value	113
7.04	Bribery—Public Official	113
7.05	Bribery—Corruptly to Influence Official Acts	115
7.06	Overview of Hobbs Act	118
7.07	Hobbs Act—Interstate Commerce	119

Sec.   **Page**

7.08   Hobbs Act—Robbery or Extortion 123

7.09   Hobbs Act—"Under Color of Official Right" 125

7.10   Travel Act 128

Chapter Eight. Racketeer Influenced and Corrupt Organizations (RICO) 132

8.01   Introduction 132

8.02   Enterprise 134

8.03   Interstate Commerce 138

8.04   Pattern of Racketeering Activity 139

8.05   Nexus Between Pattern of Racketeering and Enterprise 143

8.06   RICO Conspiracy 144

8.07   Forfeiture 145

8.08   Civil RICO 147

Chapter Nine. False Statements 149

9.01   Introduction 149

9.02   Statements 151

9.03   Exculpatory "No's" 151

9.04   Falsity 154

9.05   Knowledge and Intent 155

9.06   Materiality 158

9.07   Matters Within the Jurisdiction of the Executive, Legislative, or Judicial Branch 159

9.08   Other Crimes 161

Page

Chapter Ten. Perjury and False Declarations 164

Sec.

10.01 Introduction 164
10.02 Oath 167
10.03 Within Tribunals and Proceedings 170
10.04 Falsity 171
10.05 Materiality 174
10.06 Knowledge and Willfulness 175
10.07 Two Witness Rule 175
10.08 Recantation 177

Chapter Eleven. Tax Crimes 181
11.01 Introduction 181
11.02 Willfulness 183
11.03 Tax Evasion 189
11.04 Methods of Proof 191
11.05 Failure to File a Return or Pay a Tax 193
11.06 False Returns 194

Chapter Twelve. Currency Reporting Crimes 198
12.01 Introduction 198
12.02 Bank Secrecy Act 199
12.03 Domestic Financial Institutions 203
12.04 Recordkeeping and Reporting Requirements 205
12.05 Knowledge and Willfulness 208
12.06 Section 6050I 209

Page

Chapter Thirteen. Bankruptcy Crimes --- 213
Sec.
13.01 Introduction ----------------------------------- 213
13.02 Bankruptcy Fraud ----------------------- 216
13.03 Concealment and False Oath ------------- 217
13.04 Knowingly and Fraudulently ------------- 220

Chapter Fourteen. Environmental Crimes ----------------------------------- 223
14.01 Introduction ----------------------------------- 223
14.02 Mens Rea ----------------------------------- 225
14.03 Refuse Act ----------------------------------- 227
14.04 Water Pollution Control Act -------------- 228
14.05 Resource Conservation and Recovery
       Act (RCRA) ----------------------------- 231

Chapter Fifteen. Computer Crimes ------- 236
15.01 Overview ----------------------------------- 236
15.02 Section 1030 ----------------------------- 237

PART THREE. PROCEDURAL AND EVIDENTIARY ISSUES

Chapter Sixteen. Grand Jury Investigations ----------------------------------- 243
16.01 Investigative Advantages ------------------ 243
16.02 Rule 17 Subpoenas------------------------ 246
16.03 The Fourth Amendment's Over-
       breadth Prohibition ---------------------- 247
16.04 Applying the Overbreadth Prohibition 251

Sec. **Page**

16.05 Other Fourth Amendment Objections .. 253
16.06 Rule 17(c) Objections 257
16.07 "Chilling Effect" Objections 261
16.08 Misuse Objections 264
16.09 Challenging Secrecy Violations 268
16.10 Challenges to the Indictment 273
16.11 Assistance of Counsel 278

Chapter Seventeen. Administrative Agency Investigations 282
17.01 Administrative Subpoenas 282
17.02 Fourth Amendment Overbreadth 283
17.03 The *Powell* Prerequisites 285
17.04 Legitimate Purpose Challenges 288
17.05 Criminal Referrals and Continuing In-
        vestigations 290
17.06 Staff Misconduct 293
17.07 The Role of Counsel 295

Chapter Eighteen. Parallel Proceedings 298
18.01 Introduction 298
18.02 Prosecution Discovery From Parallel
        Proceedings 300
18.03 Delaying the Parallel Civil or Adminis-
        trative Proceeding 303
18.04 Asserting the Self–Incrimination Privi-
        lege 306
18.05 Grand Jury Matter 308
18.06 The "Preliminary To" Requirement 311
18.07 Particularized Need 313

Page

Sec.

18.08 Collateral Estoppel............................ 317

Chapter Nineteen. The Self–incrimination Privilege: Testimony 320

19.01 Applicability of the Privilege 320

19.02 Potential for Incrimination 321

19.03 Incrimination Under the Laws of Another Sovereign 325

19.04 Compelling the Grand Jury Target to Appear.. 327

19.05 Invocation of the Privilege 329

19.06 Advice as to Right.............................. 330

19.07 Separate Proceedings 334

19.08 Scope of the Testimonial Forfeiture..... 334

19.09 Penalties and Burdens........................ 336

19.10 Immunity: Constitutional Grounding... 340

19.11 The Constitutionally Required Scope of the Immunity 341

19.12 The Federal Immunity Provisions: 18 U.S.C. 6000–6005 344

19.13 Prosecuting the Immunized Witness.... 347

19.14 Immunity Agreements.......................... 350

Chapter Twenty. The Self–incrimination Privilege: Documents 352

20.01 *Boyd v. United States* and "Content Protection".................................. 352

20.02 The Act–Of–Production Doctrine 357

20.03 Act of Production Immunity................. 363

20.04 Requiring Non–Testimonial Writings... 366

Sec.   **Page**

20.05 Third Party Production 366

20.06 Required Records 368

20.7 The Entity Exception 369

20.08 The Entity Agent 373

Chapter Twenty–One. Searches 377

21.01 Overview 377

21.02 Fourth Amendment Principles 378

21.03 Law Office Searches 381

21.04 Regulatory Inspections 381

Chapter Twenty–Two. Attorney–client Privilege and Work Product Doctrine 384

22.01 Overview 384

22.02 Attorney–Client Privilege 385

22.03 Work Product Doctrine 387

22.04 Waiver of Attorney–Client Privilege and Work Product Doctrine 389

22.05 Crime Fraud Exception 392

22.06 Joint Defense Agreements 393

PART FOUR. PUNISHMENT

Chapter Twenty–Three. Sanctions 397

23.01 Introduction 397

23.02 Federal Sentencing Commission 399

23.03 Federal Sentencing Guidelines 401

23.04 Constitutionality of the Guidelines 412

23.05 Criminal and Civil Fines 415

OUTLINE

Sec.   **Page**

23.06 Sentencing Guidelines for Organiza-
      tions --- 417
23.07 Licenses and Program Exclusion --------- 422

INDEX -- 427

TABLE OF CASES

References are to Pages

Aguilar, United States v., 515 U.S. 593, 115 S.Ct. 2357, 132 L.Ed.2d 520 (1995), *104, 105*

Ahmad, United States v., 101 F.3d 386 (5th Cir.1996), *230*

Alamo Bank of Texas, United States v., 880 F.2d 828 (5th Cir.1989), *30*

Albernaz v. United States, 450 U.S. 333, 101 S.Ct. 1137, 67 L.Ed.2d 275 (1981), *52*

Alexander v. United States, 509 U.S. 544, 113 S.Ct. 2766, 125 L.Ed.2d 441 (1993), *146*

Allen, United States v., 409 F.Supp. 562 (E.D.Va.1975), aff'd 541 F.2d 278 (4th Cir.1976), *170*

Allied Chemical Corp., United States v., 420 F.Supp. 122 (E.D.Va.1976), *228*

Alvarez, United States v., 755 F.2d 830 (11th Cir.1985), *53, 54*

Anderson, United States v., 790 F.Supp. 231 (W.D.Wash.1992), *395*

Andresen v. Maryland, 427 U.S. 463, 96 S.Ct. 2737, 49 L.Ed.2d 627 (1976), *354, 379*

Apex Oil Co. v. United States, 530 F.2d 1291 (8th Cir.1976), *230*

Apfelbaum, United States v., 445 U.S. 115, 100 S.Ct. 948, 63 L.Ed.2d 250 (1980), *167*

A & P Trucking Co., United States v., 358 U.S. 121, 79 S.Ct. 203, 3 L.Ed.2d 165 (1958), *30*

Arroyo, United States v., 581 F.2d 649 (7th Cir.1978), *117*

Avelino, United States v., 967 F.2d 815 (2nd Cir.1992), *162*

Badders v. United States, 240 U.S. 391, 36 S.Ct. 367, 60 L.Ed. 706 (1916), *58*

Baggot, United States v., 463 U.S. 476, 103 S.Ct. 3164, 77 L.Ed.2d 785 (1983), *312, 313*

XVII

Bank of New England, N.A., United States v., 821 F.2d 844 (1st Cir.1987), *28, 209*

Bank of Nova Scotia v. United States, 487 U.S. 250, 108 S.Ct. 2369, 101 L.Ed.2d 228 (1988), *275*

Barrett, United States v., 837 F.2d 1341 (5th Cir.1988), *294*

Barry v. United States, 865 F.2d 1317, 275 U.S.App.D.C. 218 (D.C.Cir.1989), *271, 272*

Bates, United States v., 840 F.2d 858 (11th Cir.1988), *131*

Baxter v. Palmigiano, 425 U.S. 308, 96 S.Ct. 1551, 47 L.Ed.2d 810 (1976), *338, 339*

Beall, United States v., 126 F.Supp. 363 (N.D.Cal.1954), *68*

Bednar, United States v., 728 F.2d 1043 (8th Cir.1984), *174*

Bedore, United States v., 455 F.2d 1109 (9th Cir.1972), *153*

Beery, United States v., 678 F.2d 856 (10th Cir.1982), *220*

Belcher, United States v., 927 F.2d 1182 (11th Cir.1991), *207*

Bellis v. United States, 417 U.S. 85, 94 S.Ct. 2179, 40 L.Ed.2d 678 (1974), *372*

Beneficial Finance Co., Commonwealth v., 360 Mass. 188, 275 N.E.2d 33 (Mass.1971), *24*

Bevill, Bresler & Schulman Asset Management Corp., Matter of, 805 F.2d 120 (3rd Cir.1986), *394*

Bilzerian, United States v., 926 F.2d 1285 (2nd Cir.1991), *48, 81, 389*

Bishop, United States v., 412 U.S. 346, 93 S.Ct. 2008, 36 L.Ed.2d 941 (1973), *183, 184, 185*

Biswell, United States v., 406 U.S. 311, 92 S.Ct. 1593, 32 L.Ed.2d 87 (1972), *382*

Blackmon, United States v., 839 F.2d 900 (2nd Cir.1988), *73*

Blair v. United States, 250 U.S. 273, 39 S.Ct. 468, 63 L.Ed. 979 (1919), *264, 265*

Blandford, United States v., 33 F.3d 685 (6th Cir.1994), *128*

Bledsoe, United States v., 674 F.2d 647 (8th Cir.1982), *136, 137*

Blumenthal v. United States, 332 U.S. 539, 68 S.Ct. 248, 92 L.Ed. 154 (1947), *41, 52*

Boots, United States v., 80 F.3d 580 (1st Cir.1996), *9*

Borowski, United States v., 977 F.2d 27 (1st Cir.1992), *229*

Bourgeois v. Commonwealth, 217 Va. 268, 227 S.E.2d 714 (Va. 1976), *32*

Bowman, United States v., 260 U.S. 94, 43 S.Ct. 39, 67 L.Ed. 149 (1922), *9*

TABLE OF CASES

Boyd v. United States, 116 U.S. 616, 6 S.Ct. 524, 29 L.Ed. 746 (1886), *247, 248, 249, 352, 353, 354, 355, 356, 369, 370*

Boyer, United States v., 694 F.2d 58 (3rd Cir.1982), *79*

Bramblett, United States v., 348 U.S. 503, 75 S.Ct. 504, 99 L.Ed. 594 (1955), *160, 161*

Brand, United States v., 775 F.2d 1460 (11th Cir.1985), *99, 102*

Branzburg v. Hayes, 408 U.S. 665, 92 S.Ct. 2646, 33 L.Ed.2d 626 (1972), *261, 262, 263, 270*

Braswell v. United States, 487 U.S. 99, 108 S.Ct. 2284, 101 L.Ed.2d 98 (1988), *374, 375*

Braverman v. United States, 317 U.S. 49, 63 S.Ct. 99, 87 L.Ed. 23 (1942), *52*

Brewster, United States v., 408 U.S. 501, 92 S.Ct. 2531, 33 L.Ed.2d 507 (1972), *115*

Brittain, United States v., 931 F.2d 1413 (10th Cir.1991), *230*

Brogan v. United States, ___ U.S. ___, 117 S.Ct. 2430, 138 L.Ed.2d 192 (1997), *154*

Bronston v. United States, 409 U.S. 352, 93 S.Ct. 595, 34 L.Ed.2d 568 (1973), *172, 218*

Brown, United States v., 79 F.3d 1550 (11th Cir.1996), *59*

Brown v. Walker, 161 U.S. 591, 16 S.Ct. 644, 40 L.Ed. 819 (1896), *321, 340, 342*

Bryant, United States v., 766 F.2d 370 (8th Cir.1985), *71*

Bucey, United States v., 876 F.2d 1297 (7th Cir.1989), *204*

Buckley, United States v., 934 F.2d 84 (6th Cir.1991), *227, 233*

Bucuvalas, United States v., 909 F.2d 593 (1st Cir.1990), *43*

Burton, United States v., 737 F.2d 439 (5th Cir.1984), *189*

Byrd, United States v., 765 F.2d 1524 (11th Cir.1985), *349*

Caceres, United States v., 440 U.S. 741, 99 S.Ct. 1465, 59 L.Ed.2d 733 (1979), *295*

Cady, Roberts & Co., 40 S.E.C. 907 (1961), *84*

Calandra, United States v., 414 U.S. 338, 94 S.Ct. 613, 38 L.Ed.2d 561 (1974), *256*

California Bankers Ass'n v. Shultz, 416 U.S. 21, 94 S.Ct. 1494, 39 L.Ed.2d 812 (1974), *200, 201*

Callanan v. United States, 223 F.2d 171 (8th Cir.1955), *124*

Camara v. Municipal Court of City and County of San Francisco, 387 U.S. 523, 87 S.Ct. 1727, 18 L.Ed.2d 930 (1967), *382*

Capo, United States v., 817 F.2d 947 (2nd Cir.1987), *124*

Caporale, United States v., 806 F.2d 1487 (11th Cir.1986), *146*

Cargo Service Stations, Inc., United States v., 657 F.2d 676 (5th Cir.1981), *56*

Carpenter v. United States, 484 U.S. 19, 108 S.Ct. 316, 98 L.Ed.2d 275 (1987), *64, 65, 88*

Carpenter, United States v., 791 F.2d 1024 (2nd Cir.1986), *88, 89*

Carrion, United States v., 809 F.2d 1120 (5th Cir.1987), *131*

Castle, United States v., 925 F.2d 831 (5th Cir.1991), *9*

Central Bank of Denver, N.A. v. First Interstate Bank of Denver, N.A., 511 U.S. 164, 114 S.Ct. 1439, 128 L.Ed.2d 119 (1994), *76*

Chapman v. California, 386 U.S. 18, 87 S.Ct. 824, 17 L.Ed.2d 705 (1967), *276*

Chapman Dodge Center, Inc., State v., 428 So.2d 413 (La.1983), *23*

Cheek, United States v., 3 F.3d 1057 (7th Cir.1993), *188*

Cheek v. United States, 498 U.S. 192, 111 S.Ct. 604, 112 L.Ed.2d 617 (1991), *186, 187*

Chiarella v. United States, 445 U.S. 222, 100 S.Ct. 1108, 63 L.Ed.2d 348 (1980), *84, 85, 86, 87*

Christy Pontiac–GMC, Inc., State v., 354 N.W.2d 17 (Minn.1984), *24*

Clizer, United States v., 464 F.2d 121 (9th Cir.1972), *166*

Cogdell, United States v., 844 F.2d 179 (4th Cir.1988), *153*

Coghlan v. United States, 147 F.2d 233 (8th Cir.1945), *217, 218*

Cohen, United States v., 202 F.Supp. 587 (D.Conn.1962), *99*

Cole v. United States, 329 F.2d 437 (9th Cir.1964), *101*

Colonnade Catering Corp. v. United States, 397 U.S. 72, 90 S.Ct. 774, 25 L.Ed.2d 60 (1970), *382*

Commonwealth v. _____ (see opposing party)

Computer Sciences Corp., United States v., 689 F.2d 1181 (4th Cir.1982), *73*

Continental Oil Co. v. United States, 330 F.2d 347 (9th Cir. 1964), *394*

Cooper v. United States, 471 U.S. 1130, 105 S.Ct. 2664, 86 L.Ed.2d 281 (1985), *108*

Copperweld Corp. v. Independence Tube Corp., 467 U.S. 752, 104 S.Ct. 2731, 81 L.Ed.2d 628 (1984), *54, 55*

Couch v. United States, 409 U.S. 322, 93 S.Ct. 611, 34 L.Ed.2d 548 (1973), *366, 367*

Counselman v. Hitchcock, 142 U.S. 547, 12 S.Ct. 195, 35 L.Ed. 1110 (1892), *320, 321, 341, 342, 343*

Culbert, United States v., 435 U.S. 371, 98 S.Ct. 1112, 55 L.Ed.2d 349 (1978), *118*

Curcio v. United States, 354 U.S. 118, 77 S.Ct. 1145, 1 L.Ed.2d 1225 (1957), *373*

Curtis, United States v., 782 F.2d 593 (6th Cir.1986), *189*

D'Amato, United States v., 39 F.3d 1249 (2nd Cir.1994), *60*

Davis, United States v., 548 F.2d 840 (9th Cir.1977), *176*

Dean, United States v., 969 F.2d 187 (6th Cir.1992), *234*

Debrow, United States v., 346 U.S. 374, 74 S.Ct. 113, 98 L.Ed. 92 (1953), *168*

Dee, United States v., 912 F.2d 741 (4th Cir.1990), *232, 234*

Dennis v. United States, 384 U.S. 855, 86 S.Ct. 1840, 16 L.Ed.2d 973 (1966), *47*

Diaz, United States v., 841 F.2d 1 (1st Cir.1988), *380*

DiCarlantonio, United States v., 870 F.2d 1058 (6th Cir.1989), *122*

Diggs, United States v., 560 F.2d 266 (7th Cir.1977), *177*

Dionisio, United States v., 410 U.S. 1, 93 S.Ct. 764, 35 L.Ed.2d 67 (1973), *253, 254, 255, 258, 328*

DiRico, United States v., 78 F.3d 732 (1st Cir.1996), *196*

Dirks v. S.E.C., 463 U.S. 646, 103 S.Ct. 3255, 77 L.Ed.2d 911 (1983), *85, 86*

DiVarco, United States v., 484 F.2d 670 (7th Cir.1973), *195*

Dixon, United States v., 536 F.2d 1388 (2nd Cir.1976), *81*

Dixson v. United States, 465 U.S. 482, 104 S.Ct. 1172, 79 L.Ed.2d 458 (1984), *111, 113*

Doe v. United States, 487 U.S. 201, 108 S.Ct. 2341, 101 L.Ed.2d 184 (1988), *366*

Doe, United States v., 465 U.S. 605, 104 S.Ct. 1237, 79 L.Ed.2d 552 (1984), *354, 356, 359, 361, 362, 363*

Doe, United States v., 455 F.2d 1270 (1st Cir.1972), *267*

Donovan v. Dewey, 452 U.S. 594, 101 S.Ct. 2534, 69 L.Ed.2d 262 (1981), *382*

Dotterweich, United States v., 320 U.S. 277, 64 S.Ct. 134, 88 L.Ed. 48 (1943), *33, 34, 35, 235*

Douglas Oil Co. of California v. Petrol Stops Northwest, 441 U.S. 211, 99 S.Ct. 1667, 60 L.Ed.2d 156 (1979), *314, 315*

Dreier v. United States, 221 U.S. 394, 31 S.Ct. 550, 55 L.Ed. 784 (1911), *371*

Dunn v. United States, 442 U.S. 100, 99 S.Ct. 2190, 60 L.Ed.2d 743 (1979), *165, 171*

Dunnigan, United States v., 507 U.S. 87, 113 S.Ct. 1111, 122 L.Ed.2d 445 (1993), *405*

Durland v. United States, 161 U.S. 306, 16 S.Ct. 508, 40 L.Ed. 709 (1896), *57*

Dynavac, Inc., United States v., 6 F.3d 1407 (9th Cir.1993), *311*

Educational Development Network Corp., United States v., 884 F.2d 737 (3rd Cir.1989), *293, 310*

Edwards v. United States, 312 U.S. 473, 61 S.Ct. 669, 85 L.Ed. 957 (1941), *74*

Eisenberg v. Gagnon, 766 F.2d 770 (3rd Cir.1985), *394*

Eisenberg, United States v., 711 F.2d 959 (11th Cir.1983), *270*

Eisenstein, United States v., 731 F.2d 1540 (11th Cir.1984), *205*

Elders, United States v., 569 F.2d 1020 (7th Cir.1978), *120, 121*

Elliott, United States v., 571 F.2d 880 (5th Cir.1978), *142*

Endicott Johnson Corp. v. Perkins, 317 U.S. 501, 63 S.Ct. 339, 87 L.Ed. 424 (1943), *285*

Engler, United States v., 806 F.2d 425 (3rd Cir.1986), *226*

Essex, United States v., 407 F.2d 214 (6th Cir.1969), *97, 104*

Evans v. United States, 504 U.S. 255, 112 S.Ct. 1881, 119 L.Ed.2d 57 (1992), *110, 125, 127, 128*

Fasolino, United States v., 586 F.2d 939 (2nd Cir.1978), *101*

Fasulo v. United States, 272 U.S. 620, 47 S.Ct. 200, 71 L.Ed. 443 (1926), *59*

Fausek v. White, 965 F.2d 126 (6th Cir.1992), *387*

Fayer, United States v., 523 F.2d 661 (2nd Cir.1975), *101*

Federal Trade Commission v. American Tobacco Co., 264 U.S. 298, 44 S.Ct. 336, 68 L.Ed. 696 (1924), *284*

Fein, United States v., 504 F.2d 1170 (2nd Cir.1974), *170*

Felix, United States v., 503 U.S. 378, 112 S.Ct. 1377, 118 L.Ed.2d 25 (1992), *40*

Feola, United States v., 420 U.S. 671, 95 S.Ct. 1255, 43 L.Ed.2d 541 (1975), *49*

Fields, United States v., 838 F.2d 1571 (11th Cir.1988), *102*

Fields, United States v., 592 F.2d 638 (2nd Cir.1978), *302*

Fisher v. United States, 425 U.S. 391, 96 S.Ct. 1569, 48 L.Ed.2d 39 (1976), *355, 356, 357, 358, 359, 360, 361, 362, 364, 365, 366, 367, 373, 374*

Fornaro, United States v., 894 F.2d 508 (2nd Cir.1990), *175, 179*

Forrest, United States v., 639 F.2d 1224 (5th Cir.1981), *177*

Foster v. United States, 265 F.2d 183 (2nd Cir.1959), *286*

Franks v. Delaware, 438 U.S. 154, 98 S.Ct. 2674, 57 L.Ed.2d 667 (1978), *380*

Frezzo Bros., Inc., United States v., 461 F.Supp. 266 (E.D.Pa. 1978), aff'd 602 F.2d 1123 (3rd Cir.1979), rev. in other respects 642 F.2d 59 (1981), on remand 546 F.Supp. 713 (1972), aff'd 703 F.2d 62 (1983), *230*

Fund for Constitutional Government v. National Archives and Records Service, 656 F.2d 856, 211 U.S.App.D.C. 267 (D.C.Cir.1981), *309*

Garber, United States v., 607 F.2d 92 (5th Cir.1979), *188, 189*

Gardner v. Broderick, 392 U.S. 273, 88 S.Ct. 1913, 20 L.Ed.2d 1082 (1968), *338*

Garner, United States v., 837 F.2d 1404 (7th Cir.1987), *140*

Garner v. United States, 424 U.S. 648, 96 S.Ct. 1178, 47 L.Ed.2d 370 (1976), *329*

Garner v. Wolfinbarger, 430 F.2d 1093 (5th Cir.1970), *387*

Garrity v. New Jersey, 385 U.S. 493, 87 S.Ct. 616, 17 L.Ed.2d 562 (1967), *339*

Gaudin, United States v., 515 U.S. 506, 115 S.Ct. 2310, 132 L.Ed.2d 444 (1995), *159, 196*

Gelbard v. United States, 408 U.S. 41, 92 S.Ct. 2357, 33 L.Ed.2d 179 (1972), *257*

Gel Spice Co., Inc., United States v., 773 F.2d 427 (2nd Cir.1985), *381*

George, United States v., 477 F.2d 508 (7th Cir.1973), *62*

Gertner, United States v., 65 F.3d 963 (1st Cir.1995), *212, 288, 289*

Giancola, United States v., 783 F.2d 1549 (11th Cir.1986), *204*

Gillespie, United States v., 974 F.2d 796 (7th Cir.1992), *333*

Goetz v. United States, 59 F.2d 511 (7th Cir.1932), *218*

Gold, United States v., 743 F.2d 800 (11th Cir.1984), *32*

Goldberg, United States v., 756 F.2d 949 (2nd Cir.1985), *204*

Goldberger & Dubin, P.C., United States v., 935 F.2d 501 (2nd Cir.1991), *210, 211*

Goldblatt, United States v., 813 F.2d 619 (3rd Cir.1987), *73*

Gollott, United States v., 939 F.2d 255 (5th Cir.1991), *203*

Goodstein, United States v., 883 F.2d 1362 (7th Cir.1989), *221*

Gorman, United States v., 807 F.2d 1299 (6th Cir.1986), *113*

Grand Jury 89–4–72, In re, 932 F.2d 481 (6th Cir.1991), *313*

Grand Jury 87–3 Subpoena Duces Tecum, In re, 955 F.2d 229 (4th Cir.1992), *263*

Grand Jury Investigation, In re, 842 F.2d 1223 (11th Cir.1987), *393*

Grand Jury Investigation, In re, 610 F.2d 202 (5th Cir.1980), *270*

Grand Jury Investigation (90–3–2), Matter of, 748 F.Supp. 1188 (E.D.Mich.1990), *271*

Grand Jury Investigation No. 83–2–35, In re, 723 F.2d 447 (6th Cir.1983), *386*

Grand Jury Proceedings, In re, 87 F.3d 377 (9th Cir.1996), *392*

Grand Jury Proceedings, In re, 814 F.2d 61 (1st Cir.1987), *266, 273*

Grand Jury Proceedings, In re, 576 F.2d 703 (6th Cir.1978), *372*

Grand Jury Proceedings, In re, v. Under Seal, 102 F.3d 748 (4th Cir.1996), *388*

Grand Jury Proceedings (Manges), In re, 745 F.2d 1250 (9th Cir.1984), *368*

Grand Jury Proceedings of Dec., 1989, Matter of, 903 F.2d 1167 (7th Cir.1990), *346*

Grand Jury Proceedings United States, In re, 626 F.2d 1051 (1st Cir.1980), *366*

Grand Jury Subpoena, In re, 920 F.2d 235 (4th Cir.1990), *310*

Grand Jury Subpoena Duces Tecum Dated November 16, 1974, Matter of, 406 F.Supp. 381 (S.D.N.Y.1975), *395*

Grand Jury Subpoena Duces Tecum Dated Oct. 29, 1992, In re, 1 F.3d 87 (2nd Cir.1993), *357*

Grand Jury Subpoena Duces Tecum (Doe), In re, 605 F.Supp. 174 (E.D.N.Y.1985), *372*

Grand Jury Subpoenas, 89–3 and 89–4, John Doe 89–129, In re, 902 F.2d 244 (4th Cir.1990), *395*

Grand Jury Subpoena Served on Meserve, Mumper & Hughes, In re, 62 F.3d 1222 (9th Cir.1995), *301*

Grand Jury Subpoena Served Upon Doe, In re, 781 F.2d 238 (2nd Cir.1986), *264*

Granite Const. Co. v. Superior Court of Fresno County, 149 Cal.App.3d 465, 197 Cal.Rptr. 3 (Cal.App. 5 Dist.1983), *18*

Green, United States v., 745 F.2d 1205 (9th Cir.1984), *157*

Greenberg, United States v., 735 F.2d 29 (2nd Cir.1984), *195*

Greene v. Sullivan, 731 F.Supp. 835 (E.D.Tenn.1990), *425*

Gremillion, United States v., 464 F.2d 901 (5th Cir.1972), *174*

Griffin v. California, 380 U.S. 609, 5 Ohio Misc. 127, 85 S.Ct. 1229, 14 L.Ed.2d 106 (1965), *336, 337, 339*

Griffin v. United States, 502 U.S. 46, 112 S.Ct. 466, 116 L.Ed.2d 371 (1991), *40*

Groban, Petition of, 352 U.S. 330, 77 S.Ct. 510, 1 L.Ed.2d 376, 3 O.O.2d 127 (1957), *278*

Grosso v. United States, 390 U.S. 62, 88 S.Ct. 709, 19 L.Ed.2d 906 (1968), *368, 369*

Grunewald v. United States, 353 U.S. 391, 77 S.Ct. 963, 1 L.Ed.2d 931 (1957), *336*

Guiliano, United States v., 644 F.2d 85 (2nd Cir.1981), *221, 222*

Gurule, United States v., 437 F.2d 239 (10th Cir.1970), *252*

Gutierrez–Rodriguez v. Cartagena, 882 F.2d 553 (1st Cir.1989), *308*

Guzzino, United States v., 810 F.2d 687 (7th Cir.1987), *106*

Haas v. Henkel, 216 U.S. 462, 30 S.Ct. 249, 54 L.Ed. 569 (1910), *47*

Hale v. Henkel, 201 U.S. 43, 26 S.Ct. 370, 50 L.Ed. 652 (1906), *248, 249, 250, 251, 353, 369, 370, 371*

Haley v. United States, 394 F.Supp. 1022 (W.D.Mo.1975), *8*

Halper, United States v., 490 U.S. 435, 109 S.Ct. 1892, 104 L.Ed.2d 487 (1989), *415, 416, 417*

Hammer v. United States, 271 U.S. 620, 46 S.Ct. 603, 70 L.Ed. 1118 (1926), *175*

Hammerschmidt v. United States, 265 U.S. 182, 44 S.Ct. 511, 68 L.Ed. 968 (1924), *47, 59*

Harrington, United States v., 947 F.2d 956, 292 U.S.App.D.C. 90 (D.C.Cir.1991), *412*

Harrison v. United States, 7 F.2d 259 (2nd Cir.1925), *38*

Hartley, United States v., 678 F.2d 961 (11th Cir.1982), *44, 138*

Hayes Intern. Corp., United States v., 786 F.2d 1499 (11th Cir.1986), *233*

Helmsley, United States v., 941 F.2d 71 (2nd Cir.1991), *182, 348*

Henderson, United States v., 386 F.Supp. 1048 (S.D.N.Y.1974), *74*

Hernandez, United States v., 921 F.2d 1569 (11th Cir.1991), *414*

Hernandez, United States v., 730 F.2d 895 (2nd Cir.1984), *107, 108, 109*

Hickman v. Taylor, 329 U.S. 495, 67 S.Ct. 385, 91 L.Ed. 451 (1947), *387, 388*

Hilton Hotels Corp., United States v., 467 F.2d 1000 (9th Cir. 1972), *27*

Hintze v. I.R.S., 879 F.2d 121 (4th Cir.1989), *290*

H.J. Inc. v. Northwestern Bell Telephone Co., 492 U.S. 229, 109 S.Ct. 2893, 106 L.Ed.2d 195 (1989), *141, 142*

Hoffman v. United States, 341 U.S. 479, 71 S.Ct. 814, 95 L.Ed. 1118 (1951), *321, 322, 323*

Hoflin, United States v., 880 F.2d 1033 (9th Cir.1989), *234*

Holland v. United States, 348 U.S. 121, 75 S.Ct. 127, 99 L.Ed. 150 (1954), *192*

Holmes v. Securities Investor Protection Corp., 503 U.S. 258, 112 S.Ct. 1311, 117 L.Ed.2d 532 (1992), *147*

Horn, United States v., 811 F.Supp. 739 (D.N.H.1992), rev. in part 29 F.3d 754 (1st Cir.1994), *391*

Hubbard v. United States, 514 U.S. 695, 115 S.Ct. 1754, 131 L.Ed.2d 779 (1995), *161*

Hudson v. United States, 272 U.S. 451, 47 S.Ct. 127, 71 L.Ed. 347 (1926), *318*

Iannelli v. United States, 420 U.S. 770, 95 S.Ct. 1284, 43 L.Ed.2d 616 (1975), *40, 45*

Illinois v. Abbott & Associates, Inc., 460 U.S. 557, 103 S.Ct. 1356, 75 L.Ed.2d 281 (1983), *316*

Illinois v. Gates, 462 U.S. 213, 103 S.Ct. 2317, 76 L.Ed.2d 527 (1983), *378*

Ingram v. United States, 360 U.S. 672, 79 S.Ct. 1314, 3 L.Ed.2d 1503 (1959), *49*

In re (see name of party)

International Minerals & Chemical Corp., United States v., 402 U.S. 558, 91 S.Ct. 1697, 29 L.Ed.2d 178 (1971), *226*

Irwin, United States v., 654 F.2d 671 (10th Cir.1981), *151*

Jacobson v. United States, 503 U.S. 540, 112 S.Ct. 1535, 118 L.Ed.2d 174 (1992), *12, 13*

James v. United States, 366 U.S. 213, 81 S.Ct. 1052, 6 L.Ed.2d 246 (1961), *188*

Jenkins, United States v., 943 F.2d 167 (2nd Cir.1991), *131*

John Doe, Inc. I, United States v., 481 U.S. 102, 107 S.Ct. 1656, 95 L.Ed.2d 94 (1987), *316, 317*

Johnson & Towers, Inc., United States v., 741 F.2d 662 (3rd Cir.1984), *33, 231, 232, 233, 234*

Kahn, United States v., 472 F.2d 272 (2nd Cir.1973), *178*

Kann v. United States, 323 U.S. 88, 65 S.Ct. 148, 89 L.Ed. 88 (1944), *68, 69, 70*

Kastigar v. United States, 406 U.S. 441, 92 S.Ct. 1653, 32 L.Ed.2d 212 (1972), *343, 344, 347, 348, 349*

Kenny, United States v., 973 F.2d 339 (4th Cir.1992), *109*

Klausner, United States v., 80 F.3d 55 (2nd Cir.1996), *196*

Koenig, United States v., 388 F.Supp. 670 (S.D.N.Y.1974), *83*

Koon v. United States, ___ U.S. ___, 116 S.Ct. 2035, 135 L.Ed.2d 392 (1996), *408, 409*

Kordel, United States v., 397 U.S. 1, 90 S.Ct. 763, 25 L.Ed.2d 1 (1970), *303, 304*

Kotteakos v. United States, 328 U.S. 750, 66 S.Ct. 1239, 90 L.Ed. 1557 (1946), *51*

Kraig, United States v., 99 F.3d 1361 (6th Cir.1996), *48*

Kungys v. United States, 485 U.S. 759, 108 S.Ct. 1537, 99 L.Ed.2d 839 (1988), *158*

Kuta, United States v., 518 F.2d 947 (7th Cir.1975), *122*

Lane, United States v., 474 U.S. 438, 106 S.Ct. 725, 88 L.Ed.2d 814 (1986), *69*

Langford, United States v., 946 F.2d 798 (11th Cir.1991), *80*

Lanza, United States v., 260 U.S. 377, 43 S.Ct. 141, 67 L.Ed. 314 (1922), *7*

Larranaga, United States v., 787 F.2d 489 (10th Cir.1986), *175*

LaSalle Nat. Bank, United States v., 437 U.S. 298, 98 S.Ct. 2357, 57 L.Ed.2d 221 (1978), *290, 292*

Lattimore, United States v., 127 F.Supp. 405 (D.D.C.1955), aff'd 232 F.2d 334, 98 U.S.App.D.C. 77 (D.C.Cir.1955), *173*

Lefkowitz v. Cunningham, 431 U.S. 801, 97 S.Ct. 2132, 53 L.Ed.2d 1 (1977), *338*

Lefkowitz v. Turley, 414 U.S. 70, 94 S.Ct. 316, 38 L.Ed.2d 274 (1973), *338*

Leon, United States v., 468 U.S. 897, 104 S.Ct. 3405, 82 L.Ed.2d 677 (1984), *379, 380*

Lester, United States v., 749 F.2d 1288 (9th Cir.1984), *107, 108*

Lighte, United States v., 782 F.2d 367 (2nd Cir.1986), *173*

Lilley, United States v., 291 F.Supp. 989 (S.D.Tex.1968), *82*

Lindholm, United States v., 24 F.3d 1078 (9th Cir.1994), *219*

Local 807 of International Broth. of Teamsters, Chauffeurs, Stablemen and Helpers of America, United States v., 315 U.S. 521, 62 S.Ct. 642, 86 L.Ed. 1004 (1942), *118*

Lopez, United States v., 514 U.S. 549, 115 S.Ct. 1624, 131 L.Ed.2d 626 (1995), *5, 6, 119*

Louisiana Power and Light Co. v. United Gas Pipe Line Co., 493 So.2d 1149 (La.1986), *55*

Lynch, United States v., 180 F.2d 696 (7th Cir.1950), *218*

MacDonald & Watson Waste Oil Co., United States v., 933 F.2d 35 (1st Cir.1991), *33, 235*

Maddox, United States v., 492 F.2d 104 (5th Cir.1974), *13*

Malloy v. Hogan, 378 U.S. 1, 84 S.Ct. 1489, 12 L.Ed.2d 653 (1964), *323, 336*

Mandel, United States v., 415 F.Supp. 997 (D.Md.1976), *132*

Mandel, United States v., 296 F.Supp. 1038 (S.D.N.Y.1969), *82*

Mandujano, United States v., 425 U.S. 564, 96 S.Ct. 1768, 48 L.Ed.2d 212 (1976), *278, 279, 330, 332*

Mara, United States v., 410 U.S. 19, 93 S.Ct. 774, 35 L.Ed.2d 99 (1973), *253*

Marashi, United States v., 913 F.2d 724 (9th Cir.1990), *190*

Mariano, United States v., 983 F.2d 1150 (1st Cir.1993), *408*

Marshall v. Barlow's, Inc., 436 U.S. 307, 98 S.Ct. 1816, 56 L.Ed.2d 305 (1978), *382*

Martindell v. International Tel. and Tel. Corp., 594 F.2d 291 (2nd Cir.1979), *301*

Masterpol, United States v., 940 F.2d 760 (2nd Cir.1991), *109*

Mathews v. United States, 485 U.S. 58, 108 S.Ct. 883, 99 L.Ed.2d 54 (1988), *13, 14*

Matter of (see name of party)

Maze, United States v., 414 U.S. 395, 94 S.Ct. 645, 38 L.Ed.2d 603 (1974), *58, 67, 69, 70*

Mazzei, United States v., 521 F.2d 639 (3rd Cir.1975), *118*

McCormick v. United States, 500 U.S. 257, 111 S.Ct. 1807, 114 L.Ed.2d 307 (1991), *125, 126, 128*

McCullough v. Suter, 757 F.2d 142 (7th Cir.1985), *138*

McDaniel, United States v., 482 F.2d 305 (8th Cir.1973), *349*

McNally v. United States, 483 U.S. 350, 107 S.Ct. 2875, 97 L.Ed.2d 292 (1987), *62, 63, 64, 65*

TABLE OF CASES

Mechanik, United States v., 475 U.S. 66, 106 S.Ct. 938, 89 L.Ed.2d 50 (1986), *276, 277*

Medina de Perez, United States v., 799 F.2d 540 (9th Cir.1986), *153*

Melendez v. United States, ___ U.S. ___, 116 S.Ct. 2057, 135 L.Ed.2d 427 (1996), *409*

Melrose Distillers, Inc. v. United States, 359 U.S. 271, 79 S.Ct. 763, 3 L.Ed.2d 800 (1959), *29*

Merolla, United States v., 523 F.2d 51 (2nd Cir.1975), *122*

Metheany v. United States, 365 F.2d 90 (9th Cir.1966), *219*

Miller, United States v., 425 U.S. 435, 96 S.Ct. 1619, 48 L.Ed.2d 71 (1976), *201*

Miller, United States v., 904 F.2d 65, 284 U.S.App.D.C. 245 (D.C.Cir.1990), *334*

Minarik, United States v., 875 F.2d 1186 (6th Cir.1989), *48*

Minnesota v. Murphy, 465 U.S. 420, 104 S.Ct. 1136, 79 L.Ed.2d 409 (1984), *331*

Miranda v. Arizona, 384 U.S. 436, 86 S.Ct. 1602, 16 L.Ed.2d 694 (1966), *278, 279, 330, 331, 332*

Mistretta v. United States, 488 U.S. 361, 109 S.Ct. 647, 102 L.Ed.2d 714 (1989), *398, 412, 414*

Mittelman, United States v., 999 F.2d 440 (9th Cir.1993), *381*

Molinares, United States v., 700 F.2d 647 (11th Cir.1983), *168, 169*

Monia, United States v., 317 U.S. 424, 63 S.Ct. 409, 87 L.Ed. 376 (1943), *329, 330, 331*

Moore, United States v., 613 F.2d 1029, 198 U.S.App.D.C. 296 (D.C.Cir.1979), *178, 179*

Morganroth, In re, 718 F.2d 161 (6th Cir.1983), *324*

Morris, United States v., 928 F.2d 504 (2nd Cir.1991), *241*

Morton Salt Co., United States v., 338 U.S. 632, 70 S.Ct. 357, 94 L.Ed. 401 (1950), *284*

Moss, United States v., 9 F.3d 543 (6th Cir.1993), *394*

Muldoon, United States v., 931 F.2d 282 (4th Cir.1991), *117*

Muntain, United States v., 610 F.2d 964, 198 U.S.App.D.C. 22 (D.C.Cir.1979), *116*

Murdock, United States v., 290 U.S. 389, 54 S.Ct. 223, 78 L.Ed. 381 (1933), *184*

Murphy v. Waterfront Commission of New York Harbor, 378 U.S. 52, 84 S.Ct. 1594, 12 L.Ed.2d 678 (1964), *325, 327, 342, 343*

Myers, United States v., 692 F.2d 823 (2nd Cir.1982), *117*

National Commodity and Barter Ass'n v. United States, 951 F.2d 1172 (10th Cir.1991), *262*

National Organization for Women, Inc. v. Scheidler, 510 U.S. 249, 114 S.Ct. 798, 127 L.Ed.2d 99 (1994), *135*

Nedley, United States v., 255 F.2d 350 (3rd Cir.1958), *123*

Nelson Radio & Supply Co. v. Motorola, Inc., 200 F.2d 911 (5th Cir.1952), *44, 55*

Newman, United States v., 664 F.2d 12 (2nd Cir.1981), *87, 89*

New York v. Burger, 482 U.S. 691, 107 S.Ct. 2636, 96 L.Ed.2d 601 (1987), *383*

New York Cent. & H.R.R. Co. v. United States, 212 U.S. 481, 29 S.Ct. 304, 53 L.Ed. 613 (1909), *17, 18, 27*

Nobles, United States v., 422 U.S. 225, 95 S.Ct. 2160, 45 L.Ed.2d 141 (1975), *391*

North, United States v., 910 F.2d 843, 285 U.S.App.D.C. 343 (D.C.Cir.1990), *347, 349*

O'Donnell, United States v., 539 F.2d 1233 (9th Cir.1976), *219*

Ogle, United States v., 613 F.2d 233 (10th Cir.1979), *99*

O'Hagan, United States v., ___ U.S. ___, 117 S.Ct. 759, 136 L.Ed.2d 695 (1997), *89, 90*

Oklahoma Press Pub. Co. v. Walling, 327 U.S. 186, 66 S.Ct. 494, 90 L.Ed. 614 (1946), *251, 284*

One Assortment of 89 Firearms, United States v., 465 U.S. 354, 104 S.Ct. 1099, 79 L.Ed.2d 361 (1984), *318*

Pacific Hide & Fur Depot, Inc., United States v., 768 F.2d 1096 (9th Cir.1985), *226*

Park, United States v., 421 U.S. 658, 95 S.Ct. 1903, 44 L.Ed.2d 489 (1975), *34, 35, 235*

Parr v. United States, 363 U.S. 370, 80 S.Ct. 1171, 4 L.Ed.2d 1277 (1960), *67, 68, 69, 78*

Pascucci, United States v., 943 F.2d 1032 (9th Cir.1991), *119*

Paternostro v. United States, 311 F.2d 298 (5th Cir.1962), *152*

Pelletier, United States v., 898 F.2d 297 (2nd Cir.1990), *350, 351*

Peltz, United States v., 433 F.2d 48 (2nd Cir.1970), *79*

Pereira v. United States, 347 U.S. 1, 74 S.Ct. 358, 98 L.Ed. 435 (1954), *58, 66*

TABLE OF CASES

Perez v. United States, 402 U.S. 146, 91 S.Ct. 1357, 28 L.Ed.2d 686 (1971), *5*

Perholtz, United States v., 842 F.2d 343, 268 U.S.App.D.C. 347 (D.C.Cir.1988), *137*

Perrin v. United States, 444 U.S. 37, 100 S.Ct. 311, 62 L.Ed.2d 199 (1979), *129, 130*

Petition of (see name of party)

Pettibone v. United States, 148 U.S. 197, 13 S.Ct. 542, 37 L.Ed. 419 (1893), *105*

Phillips, United States v., 606 F.2d 884 (9th Cir.1979), *219*

Pickel v. United States, 746 F.2d 176 (3rd Cir.1984), *292*

Pillsbury Co. v. Conboy, 459 U.S. 248, 103 S.Ct. 608, 74 L.Ed.2d 430 (1983), *346*

Pinkerton v. United States, 328 U.S. 640, 66 S.Ct. 1180, 90 L.Ed. 1489 (1946), *52, 53*

Poindexter, United States v., 951 F.2d 369, 292 U.S.App.D.C. 389 (D.C.Cir.1991), *92*

Polakoff, United States v., 121 F.2d 333 (2nd Cir.1941), *100*

Pomponio, United States v., 429 U.S. 10, 97 S.Ct. 22, 50 L.Ed.2d 12 (1976), *185*

Porter, United States v., 711 F.2d 1397 (7th Cir.1983), *365*

Powell, United States v., 469 U.S. 57, 105 S.Ct. 471, 83 L.Ed.2d 461 (1984), *43*

Powell, United States v., 379 U.S. 48, 85 S.Ct. 248, 13 L.Ed.2d 112 (1964), *285, 286, 287, 288, 289, 293, 294*

Procter & Gamble Co., United States v., 356 U.S. 677, 78 S.Ct. 983, 2 L.Ed.2d 1077 (1958), *315*

Professional Reactor Operator Soc. v. United States Nuclear Regulatory Com'n, Nuclear Reg. Rep. P 20,535, 939 F.2d 1047, 291 U.S.App.D.C. 219 (D.C.Cir.1991), *297*

Protex Industries, Inc., United States v., 874 F.2d 740 (10th Cir.1989), *232*

Pungitore, United States v., 910 F.2d 1084 (3rd Cir.1990), *140*

Rabbitt, United States v., 583 F.2d 1014 (8th Cir.1978), *119, 125*

Rasheed, United States v., 663 F.2d 843 (9th Cir.1981), *100*

Ratzlaf v. United States, 510 U.S. 135, 114 S.Ct. 655, 126 L.Ed.2d 615 (1994), *208, 209*

Regent Office Supply Co., United States v., 421 F.2d 1174 (2nd Cir.1970), *60*

Reichhold Chemicals, Inc. v. Textron, Inc., 157 F.R.D. 522 (N.D.Fla.1994), *385*

Reina v. United States, 364 U.S. 507, 81 S.Ct. 260, 5 L.Ed.2d 249 (1960), *323*

R. Enterprises, Inc., United States v., 498 U.S. 292, 111 S.Ct. 722, 112 L.Ed.2d 795 (1991), *257, 260, 262, 263*

Reveron Martinez, United States v., 836 F.2d 684 (1st Cir.1988), *175*

Reves v. Ernst & Young, 507 U.S. 170, 113 S.Ct. 1163, 122 L.Ed.2d 525 (1993), *143*

Rewis v. United States, 401 U.S. 808, 91 S.Ct. 1056, 28 L.Ed.2d 493 (1971), *130*

Richard Knutson, Inc., State v., 196 Wis.2d 86, 537 N.W.2d 420 (Wis.App.1995), *19*

Richard Roe, Inc., In re, 68 F.3d 38 (2nd Cir.1995), *392*

Ritchie, United States v., 15 F.3d 592 (6th Cir.1994), *288*

Rivera, United States v., 994 F.2d 942 (1st Cir.1993), *408*

Robertson, United States v., 514 U.S. 669, 115 S.Ct. 1732, 131 L.Ed.2d 714 (1995), *138*

Robinson v. Cheney, 876 F.2d 152, 277 U.S.App.D.C. 393 (D.C.Cir.1989), *424*

Rodgers, United States v., 466 U.S. 475, 104 S.Ct. 1942, 80 L.Ed.2d 492 (1984), *159*

Rodriguez–Rios, United States v., 14 F.3d 1040 (5th Cir.1994), *152*

Rogers v. United States, 340 U.S. 367, 71 S.Ct. 438, 95 L.Ed. 344 (1951), *321, 334, 335, 336*

Rubin, United States v., 559 F.2d 975 (5th Cir.1977), *146*

Russello v. United States, 464 U.S. 16, 104 S.Ct. 296, 78 L.Ed.2d 17 (1983), *145*

Ryan, United States v., 455 F.2d 728 (9th Cir.1971), *100*

Rylander, United States v., 460 U.S. 752, 103 S.Ct. 1548, 75 L.Ed.2d 521 (1983), *373*

Sablan, United States v., 92 F.3d 865 (9th Cir.1996), *242*

Salinas v. United States, ___ U.S. ___, 117 S.Ct. 1079, 137 L.Ed.2d 214 (1997), *145*

Sampson, United States v., 371 U.S. 75, 83 S.Ct. 173, 9 L.Ed.2d 136 (1962), *69*

Sansone v. United States, 380 U.S. 343, 85 S.Ct. 1004, 13 L.Ed.2d 882 (1965), *184, 191*

Santa Rita Store Co., United States v., 16 N.M. 3, 113 P. 620 (N.M.1911), *44*

Schafrick, United States v., 871 F.2d 300 (2nd Cir.1989), *219*

Schmerber v. California, 384 U.S. 757, 86 S.Ct. 1826, 16 L.Ed.2d 908 (1966), *354, 355*

Schmidt, United States v., 947 F.2d 362 (9th Cir.1991), *46*

Schmuck v. United States, 489 U.S. 705, 109 S.Ct. 1443, 103 L.Ed.2d 734 (1989), *70, 71*

Schofield v. First Commodity Corp. of Boston, 793 F.2d 28 (1st Cir.1986), *137*

Schwimmer v. United States, 232 F.2d 855 (8th Cir.1956), *253*

Scott, United States v., 660 F.2d 1145 (7th Cir.1981), *193*

S.E.C. v. Graystone Nash, Inc., 25 F.3d 187 (3rd Cir.1994), *307*

Securities and Exchange Commission v. Dresser Industries, Inc., 628 F.2d 1368, 202 U.S.App.D.C. 345 (D.C.Cir.1980), *292*

Securities and Exchange Commission v. ESM Government Securities, Inc., 645 F.2d 310 (5th Cir.1981), *293, 294*

Securities and Exchange Commission v. Materia, 745 F.2d 197 (2nd Cir.1984), *88, 89*

Securities and Exchange Commission v. Texas Gulf Sulphur Co., 401 F.2d 833 (2nd Cir.1968), *83*

Securities and Exchange Commission v. Wheeling–Pittsburgh Steel Corp., 648 F.2d 118 (3rd Cir.1981), *289*

Sedima, S.P.R.L. v. Imrex Co., Inc., 473 U.S. 479, 105 S.Ct. 3275, 87 L.Ed.2d 346 (1985), *147*

Shapiro v. United States, 335 U.S. 1, 68 S.Ct. 1375, 92 L.Ed. 1787 (1948), *368*

Shepherd Const. Co., Inc., State v., 248 Ga. 1, 281 S.E.2d 151 (Ga.1981), *21, 22*

Shortt Accountancy Corp., United States v., 785 F.2d 1448 (9th Cir.1986), *196, 197*

Silverman, United States v., 745 F.2d 1386 (11th Cir.1984), *102*

Simmons, United States v., 591 F.2d 206 (3rd Cir.1979), *104*

Sindel, United States v., 53 F.3d 874 (8th Cir.1995), *211*

Smith, United States v., 35 F.3d 344 (8th Cir.1994), *179*

Smith v. United States, 363 F.2d 143 (5th Cir.1966), *168*

Smull, United States v., 236 U.S. 405, 35 S.Ct. 349, 59 L.Ed. 641 (1915), *164*

Socony–Vacuum Oil Co., United States v., 310 U.S. 150, 60 S.Ct. 811, 84 L.Ed. 1129 (1940), *56*

Sorrells v. United States, 287 U.S. 435, 53 S.Ct. 210, 77 L.Ed. 413 (1932), *12*

Special September 1978 Grand Jury (II), In re, 640 F.2d 49 (7th Cir.1980), *393*

Spevack v. Klein, 385 U.S. 511, 87 S.Ct. 625, 17 L.Ed.2d 574 (1967), *337, 338*

Spies v. United States, 317 U.S. 492, 63 S.Ct. 364, 87 L.Ed. 418 (1943), *184, 184, 189, 190, 191*

Standard Oil Co., United States v., 384 U.S. 224, 86 S.Ct. 1427, 16 L.Ed.2d 492 (1966), *228*

Standard Oil Co. of Tex. v. United States, 307 F.2d 120 (5th Cir.1962), *26*

State v. _____ (see opposing party)

Stavroulakis, United States v., 952 F.2d 686 (2nd Cir.1992), *41*

Steinberg, In re, 837 F.2d 527 (1st Cir.1988), *357*

Steinhardt Partners, L.P., In re, 9 F.3d 230 (2nd Cir.1993), *390*

Stevens, United States v., 909 F.2d 431 (11th Cir.1990), *44*

Tanner v. United States, 483 U.S. 107, 107 S.Ct. 2739, 97 L.Ed.2d 90 (1987), *47*

Taylor, United States v., 798 F.2d 1337 (10th Cir.1986), *277*

Texas Heart Institute, United States v., 755 F.2d 469 (5th Cir.1985), *287, 289*

The President Coolidge (Dollar Steamship Co. v. United States), 101 F.2d 638 (9th Cir.1939), *27*

Thomas, United States v., 8 F.3d 1552 (11th Cir.1993), *123*

Thomas, United States v., 916 F.2d 647 (11th Cir.1990), *100, 103, 104*

Thompson, United States v., 685 F.2d 993 (6th Cir.1982), *136*

Tilton, United States v., 610 F.2d 302 (5th Cir.1980), *54*

Tobias, United States v., 863 F.2d 685 (9th Cir.1988), *180*

Touche Ross & Co. v. S.E.C., 609 F.2d 570 (2nd Cir.1979), *423*

Traitz, United States v., 871 F.2d 368 (3rd Cir.1989), *117*

Turkette, United States v., 452 U.S. 576, 101 S.Ct. 2524, 69 L.Ed.2d 246 (1981), *135, 137*

Ullmann v. United States, 350 U.S. 422, 76 S.Ct. 497, 100 L.Ed. 511 (1956), *321*

(Under Seal), United States v., 794 F.2d 920 (4th Cir.1986), *327*

TABLE OF CASES

Uniformed Sanitation Men Ass'n v. Commissioner of Sanitation of City of New York, 392 U.S. 280, 88 S.Ct. 1917, 20 L.Ed.2d 1089 (1968), *338*

United States v. _____ (see opposing party)

United States Gypsum Co., United States v., 438 U.S. 422, 98 S.Ct. 2864, 57 L.Ed.2d 854 (1978), *56*

United States Steel Corp., United States v., 328 F.Supp. 354 (N.D.Ind.1970), *228*

Upjohn Co. v. United States, 449 U.S. 383, 101 S.Ct. 677, 66 L.Ed.2d 584 (1981), *385, 387, 389*

Ursery, United States v., ___ U.S. ___, 116 S.Ct. 2135, 135 L.Ed.2d 549 (1996), *417*

Wade v. United States, 504 U.S. 181, 112 S.Ct. 1840, 118 L.Ed.2d 524 (1992), *407*

Washington, United States v., 431 U.S. 181, 97 S.Ct. 1814, 52 L.Ed.2d 238 (1977), *332*

Watts, United States v., ___ U.S. ___, 117 S.Ct. 633, 136 L.Ed.2d 554 (1997), *402*

Weiler v. United States, 323 U.S. 606, 65 S.Ct. 548, 89 L.Ed. 495 (1945), *176*

Weiner, United States v., 578 F.2d 757 (9th Cir.1978), *80*

Wells, United States v., ___ U.S. ___, 117 S.Ct. 921, 137 L.Ed.2d 107 (1997), *159*

Wheat v. United States, 486 U.S. 153, 108 S.Ct. 1692, 100 L.Ed.2d 140 (1988), *280, 281*

White, United States v., 322 U.S. 694, 64 S.Ct. 1248, 88 L.Ed. 1542 (1944), *353, 371*

White, United States v., 766 F.Supp. 873 (E.D.Wash.1991), *230*

White, United States v., 124 F.2d 181 (2nd Cir.1941), *80*

White Fuel Corp., United States v., 498 F.2d 619 (1st Cir.1974), *228*

Wiener, United States v., 96 F.3d 35 (2nd Cir.1996), *152*

Williams, United States v., 504 U.S. 36, 112 S.Ct. 1735, 118 L.Ed.2d 352 (1992), *274*

Williams, United States v., 341 U.S. 58, 71 S.Ct. 595, 95 L.Ed. 747 (1951), *170*

Williams, United States v., 705 F.2d 603 (2nd Cir.1983), *14, 15, 113*

Williams v. United States, 503 U.S. 193, 112 S.Ct. 1112, 117 L.Ed.2d 341 (1992), *410*

Wilson v. United States, 221 U.S. 361, 31 S.Ct. 538, 55 L.Ed. 771 (1911), *370, 371, 373*

Winter, United States v., 663 F.2d 1120 (1st Cir.1981), *351*

Wise, United States v., 370 U.S. 405, 82 S.Ct. 1354, 8 L.Ed.2d 590 (1962), *31*

Woodward, United States v., 469 U.S. 105, 105 S.Ct. 611, 83 L.Ed.2d 518 (1985), *162*

Wulff, United States v., 758 F.2d 1121 (6th Cir.1985), *226*

Yagow, United States v., 953 F.2d 427 (8th Cir.1992), *219, 220*

Yellow Cab Co., United States v., 332 U.S. 218, 67 S.Ct. 1560, 91 L.Ed. 2010 (1947), *54*

Yermian, United States v., 468 U.S. 63, 104 S.Ct. 2936, 82 L.Ed.2d 53 (1984), *156, 157*

Zicarelli v. New Jersey State Commission of Investigation, 406 U.S. 472, 92 S.Ct. 1670, 32 L.Ed.2d 234 (1972), *326, 327*

Zolin, United States v., 491 U.S. 554, 109 S.Ct. 2619, 105 L.Ed.2d 469 (1989), *295, 393*

WHITE COLLAR CRIME
IN A NUTSHELL
SECOND EDITION

*

PART ONE
GENERAL PRINCIPLES

CHAPTER ONE

SCOPE OF WHITE COLLAR CRIME

§ 1.01 Introduction

Sociologist Edwin Sutherland is noted for having coined the phrase "White Collar Crime." The term appeared in a speech he gave to the American Sociological Society in 1939. In his speech, Sutherland openly attacked criminologists whose theories considered crime to be a result of poverty or psychopathic and sociopathic conditions. His criticism was in part based upon their failure to consider white collar criminals. Sutherland saw improper business practices of individuals in powerful positions as criminal offenses and not simply civil wrongs. He saw this as a significant issue for society's consideration.

In his book *White Collar Crime*, Sutherland defined the term white collar crime as "crime committed by a person of respectability and high social status in the course of his occupation." His definition concentrated on the offender's social status and occupation, although his focus tended to be more narrowly confined to crimes committed by large corporate enterprises.

Although white collar crime has been subject to varying definitions, a definition that focuses on the offense rather than the offender is prevalent today. In the 1983 Annual Report of the Attorney General, white collar crimes were defined as:

> ... illegal acts that use deceit and concealment—rather than the application or threat of physical force or violence—to obtain money, property, or service; to avoid the payment or loss of money; or to secure a business or professional advantage. White collar criminals occupy positions of responsibility and trust in government, industry, the professions and civic organizations.

Even when one adopts an offense approach in defining white collar crime, the scope of the term remains uncertain in that there is no list of included and excluded offenses.

Although there are no set categories of offenses that make up white collar crime, there are several federal statutes that continually appear in this context. Some of these federal offenses are not limited solely to white collar crime, but have been used to prosecute street and property crimes as well. These statutes are often used for white collar criminality due to the broad interpretation given to them by the courts. For example, many white collar offenses are prosecuted as mail fraud (18 U.S.C. § 1341), wire fraud (18 U.S.C. § 1343), conspiracy (18 U.S.C. § 371), racketeering (18 U.S.C. §§ 1961–1963), bribery (18 U.S.C. § 201), false statements (18 U.S.C. § 1001), obstruction of justice (18 U.S.C. §§ 1501–1518) and tax crimes (26 U.S.C. §§ 7201–7206). There are other statutes that are used almost exclusively for white collar offenses. For example, criminal acts involving bank fraud (18 U.S.C. § 1344) and false claims (18 U.S.C. § 287) usually fit the white collar crime category.

These lists of offenses are by no means exhaustive. White collar crime includes corporate offenses and most offenses involving public corruption. Many white collar crime prosecutions have employed statutes relating to securities fraud and antitrust violations. Encompassed by the term in recent years are criminal acts prohibited by environmental, health, and computer laws.

Although white collar crime is a relatively new concept, it has grown extensively during its short life. Key areas within white collar crime that the Department of Justice has recently focused on are financial institution fraud, defense procurement fraud, health care fraud, computer crime, international fraud, and telemarketing fraud. The Department of Justice has also continued its efforts in combating antitrust violations, public corruption, and money laundering.

§ 1.02   Scope of Federal Criminal Law

Clearly a prosecutor needs a statutory base for prosecuting white collar criminal conduct. In the realm of the federal criminal law system, this conduct can be based on a vast array of statutory offenses. In recent years there has been a growth of statutes added to the federal criminal code that specifically pertain to white collar criminal conduct. This has been noticeable in provisions added to combat financial frauds.

It is necessary that Congress, in enacting these statutes, remain within the bounds of the Constitution. Article I, Section 8 of the United States Constitution sets forth the congressional powers, including provisions that grant Congress postal, taxing, and commerce powers.

Federal criminal law's use of Congress' postal power is best evidenced by the mail fraud statute. (18 U.S.C. § 1341). This pervasive statute has been extensively used in the realm of white collar crime.

The taxing power granted Congress serves as the jurisdictional base for many tax offenses. (26 U.S.C. §§ 7601–7606). Before 1970 it also served to criminalize many drug offenses. Drug statutes today usually employ the commerce powers.

The most widely used jurisdictional base for criminalizing federal offenses is the commerce power. The Constitution of the United States gives Congress the power "to regulate Commerce with Foreign Nations, and among the several States, and with the Indian Tribes." "Congress may regulate the use of the channels of interstate commerce," "regulate and protect the instrumentalities of interstate commerce, or persons or things in interstate commerce, even though the threat may come only from intrastate activities," and "regulate those activities having a substantial relation to interstate commerce, i.e., those activities that substantially affect interstate commerce." *United States v. Lopez* (S.Ct.1995).

Many federal statutes used in the prosecution of white collar crime employ the commerce clause as the jurisdictional basis. For example, wire fraud (18 U.S.C. § 1343) requires interstate commerce. A racketeering prosecution requires an "enterprise which is engaged in, or the activities of which affect, interstate or foreign commerce." (18 U.S.C. § 1962). Likewise, the Hobbs Act requires that the robbery or extortion affect commerce.

The conduct itself, under certain federal criminal statutes, can be purely local and yet be prosecuted as a federal offense. These local activities are part of a class of activities that Congress determines warrants congressional intervention because of their impact on commerce. In *Perez v. United States* the Supreme Court affirmed a conviction under the Consumer Credit Protection Act. (18 U.S.C. § 891 et seq.). The Court found that although petitioner's loan sharking may have been intrastate, he was a member of a class that engaged in "extortionate credit transactions" that affected commerce. The Court found that "loan sharking in its national setting is one way organized crime holds its guns to the heads of the poor and the rich alike and syphons funds from numerous localities to finance its national operations."

Most federal criminal statutes using the commerce clause as its jurisdictional base predicate the action on direct transportation in interstate commerce or conduct that actually affects interstate commerce. In *United States v. Lopez* the Supreme Court held that the Gun–Free School Zone Act, prohibiting possession of a weapon in the vicinity of a school, exceeded Congress' Commerce Clause authority in that it involved intrastate activity not involved in commerce and not economic activity.

§ 1.03   State and/or Federal Prosecution

Of the roughly 1.5 million felony prosecutions brought in the United States each year, less than 50,000 are brought in the federal system. Prosecutions against white collar crimes are, likewise, not limited to the federal system in that many state statutes focus on conduct that meets accepted definitions of white collar crime. The same white collar criminal offenses often can be prosecuted by both the federal and state systems. For example, the RICO statute uses nine state crimes as predicates for a racketeering charge. (18 U.S.C. § 1961). These predicate acts can be prosecuted as state crimes.

When criminal conduct fits the definition of both the federal and state jurisdictions a joint decision is often made as to which body will proceed with the prosecution. Factors considered in choosing the jurisdiction include the available investigative and prosecutorial resources, the jurisdiction with the law that best supports the government, the location with the maximum possible penalty and the place where the criminality best fits the policy priorities of that jurisdiction. Efficiency factors such as the jurisdiction with greater expertise and experience, the better ability to handle the case within their caseload and present location of the suspects can play a part in determining who will proceed with the action. In many instances the conduct is subject to state prosecution but has been ignored by the state prosecutor or local police for political reasons. The use of the federal system in these instances offers a neutral forum for proceeding.

Under the dual sovereignty rule, there is no restriction to both the state and federal jurisdiction prosecuting the defendant for what is basically the same conduct. Since the state and federal governments are separate entities each may determine its own offenses. *United States v. Lanza* (S.Ct.1922). Some states, however, by statute or case law prohibit a state prosecution following a federal trial. Additionally, some federal statutes prohibit a federal prosecution when the same act or acts previously resulted in a conviction or acquittal on the merits under state law. For example, the federal statute that criminalizes certain acts involving the interstate or foreign shipments by carrier, expressly prohibits a federal prosecution under the statute where there has been a conviction or acquittal on the merits under the laws of any state. (18 U.S.C. § 659).

Often the issue of dual prosecution is resolved by examination of the policies of the respective government prosecutors. For example, the Department of

Justice has a policy against duplicative federal and state prosecutions. Known as the *Petite* policy, it "precludes the initiation or continuation of a federal prosecution, following a prior state or federal prosecution based on substantially the same act(s) or transaction(s), unless:" the matter involves a "substantial federal interest," the prior prosecution left the interest "demonstrably unvindicated," and the "defendant(s)' conduct constitutes a federal offense" with admissible evidence "sufficient to obtain and sustain a conviction." The prosecution must also "be approved by the appropriate Assistant Attorney General." Where the government fails to abide by the *Petite* policy, cases have found that there is no legal basis for overturning the defendant's conviction. *Haley v. United States* (W.D.Mo.1975).

Besides overlapping prosecutions within the federal and state system, white collar offenses often find themselves the subject of parallel proceedings in regulatory bodies and civil courts. Procedural questions related to collateral estoppel, staying of proceedings, effect upon fifth amendment rights, and use of grand jury materials are questions that have merited resolution in this context (see chap. 18).

§ 1.04 Federal Influence in International Prosecutions

Federal prosecutions may also be premised upon conduct occurring outside the United States. In some instances the federal statute will specifically contain a provision providing for extraterritoriality. (18 U.S.C. § 1512). Other instances require courts to ascertain whether an extraterritorial application should be permitted. *United States v. Bowman* (S.Ct.1922). Several courts have allowed white collar prosecutions where the conduct occurred outside the United States. Recently, however, in *United States v. Boots* (1st Cir.1996), the First Circuit reversed wire fraud convictions where the object of the scheme to defraud was a foreign government.

Some federal statutes are specifically focused on conduct occurring outside the United States. For example, the Foreign Corrupt Practices Act (FCPA) was implemented to combat bribery of foreign officials by United States companies (see § 7.01).

In *United States v. Castle* (5th Cir. 1991), the Fifth Circuit held that since "foreign officials" were excluded from prosecution under the FCPA, the United States government could not prosecute foreign officials "under 18 U.S.C. § 371, for conspiracy to violate the FCPA." The court noted the "legislative policy to leave unpunished a well-defined group of persons [foreign officials] who were necessary parties to the acts constituting a violation of the substantive law." "Most likely Congress made this choice because United States businesses were perceived to be the aggressors and the efforts expended in resolving the diplomatic, jurisdictional, and enforcement difficulties that would arise upon the prosecution of foreign officials was not worth the minimal deterrent value of such prosecutions." The court also noted that "many foreign nations already prohibited the receipt of a bribe by an official."

§ 1.05 Application of General Principles of Criminal Law

White collar crimes, like other crimes, are subject to general principles of criminal law. These principles emanate from the United States Constitution, federal and state statutes, and court interpretations. They are affected in some instances by the procedures provided by administrative regulations and rulings. Although there is no specific principle that is altered when applied in the white collar crime setting, there are certain statutory principles and criminal defenses that routinely appear and others that are seldom dominating forces. For example, it is common to see an entrapment defense in a white collar crime case. It is rare, however, to see an insanity defense.

General principles relative to actus reus, mens rea, and causation are placed in the perspective of the specific federal statute as it is examined within this book. Many of these statutes include attempts to commit the offense within the statutory terms. Additionally, conspiracy is discussed (18 U.S.C. § 371) as both a separate federal offense premised on a conspiracy to defraud the United States and as it relates to other statutes as a conspiracy to commit any offense against the United States. Punishment of white collar offenders, although now subject to the federal sentencing guidelines, provides unique considerations that merit separate examination.

In addition to the general adoption of criminal law principles relative to white collar offenses, it is also important to note that federal law includes general provisions regarding principals and accessories. In 18 U.S.C. § 2 a principal is defined as one who "commits an offense against the United States or aids, abets, counsels, commands, induces or procures its commission." A second provision of this same statute incorporates the agency theory that one is a principal if they willfully cause an act to be done that if performed by that person or another would be a criminal offense.

Accessories after the fact are the subject of a separate federal statute. 18 U.S.C. § 3 criminalizes and defines accessories after the fact and also provides a lesser penalty for the accessory then would be received by the principal. The application of these provisions appears to be no different in the context of white collar crimes then with other types of crime.

§ 1.06 Defenses

Defenses available to white collar defendants are, likewise, no different from those available to the nonwhite collar defendants. Limitations to responsibility premised upon infancy, insanity, or intoxication have equal applicability in white collar crime cases as in other types of crime. Principles relating to duress and necessity remain unmodified when applied to white collar offenses. Defenses such as alibi, self defense, or defense of property, although available, seldom constitute an issue in the white collar case.

Prominent in white collar cases is the entrapment defense. Entrapment arises from individual instances of the government enticing a defendant to commit acts of criminality as well as elaborate government sting operations that attempt to net central figures and groups of individuals engaged in criminal activity.

For the last several decades, differing views have appeared in the law as to whether entrapment should be judged from an objective or subjective perspective. The objective view concentrated on the government conduct while the subjective view looked to the defendant's predisposition to commit the offense. The majority view today adopts a test that is predominantly a subjective approach. This view has been adhered to in federal courts.

"Where the Government has induced an individual to break the law and the defense of entrapment is at issue, . . ., the prosecution must prove beyond reasonable doubt that the defendant was disposed to commit the criminal act prior to first being approached by Government agents." *Jacobson v. United States* (S.Ct.1992). Government officials may not originate a criminal design, "implant in the mind of an innocent person the disposition to commit the alleged offense and induce its commission in order that they may prosecute." *Sorrells v. United States* (S.Ct.1932).

Entrapment first requires a showing of government inducement. A private party, unrelated to the government, who induces the defendant does not provide a basis for invoking an entrapment defense. Where defendants were convicted of conspiracy for knowingly transporting stolen shirts in interstate commerce, an entrapment defense was properly denied where the alleged entrapment was by a shirt manufacturer who used private investigators to locate the individuals suspected of taking the shirts. The Fifth Circuit held that "entrapment does not extend to inducement by private citizens." *United States v. Maddox* (5th Cir.1974).

In addition to government inducement, entrapment requires a lack of predisposition by the defendant to engage in criminal conduct. Recently, in reversing a conviction for an alleged violation of the Child Protection Act (18 U.S.C. § 2252), the Supreme Court in *Jacobson v. United States* stated that "[w]hen the Government's quest for convictions leads to the apprehension of an otherwise law-abiding citizen who, if left to his own devices, likely would have never run afoul of the law, the courts should intervene."

There is no requirement in federal criminal law that a defendant admit all the elements of the crime in order to proceed with an entrapment defense. Where the facts support an entrapment defense, an instruction on entrapment should be submitted to the jury, despite inconsistent defenses being offered by the defendant. *Mathews v. United States* (S.Ct. 1988).

In *Mathews*, an employee of the Small Business Administration (SBA) was convicted of accepting a gratuity in exchange for an official act. (18 U.S.C. § 201 (g)). The defendant was alleged to have accepted loans in return for cooperation in SBA matters. The district court refused defendant's request for an entrapment jury instruction finding that the instruction should not be given where the defendant failed to admit the elements of the offense. The Supreme Court reversed and remanded this case, noting the permissibility of inconsistent defenses but also finding it necessary for the lower court to consider whether there was sufficient evidence to support the giving of an entrapment instruction.

The use, although unsuccessfully, of the entrapment defense in the context of white collar crime prosecutions is seen in examining cases resulting from Operation Abscam. One such case is *United States v. Williams* (2d Cir.1983).

In *Williams*, Senator Harrison Williams was convicted of charges, including bribery, as part of Operation Abscam. His defense was based alternatively upon no crime being committed and entrapment. On appeal the Second Circuit rejected defendant's argument that there was insufficient evidence to support the jury's conclusion that the defendant was predisposed to commit the crime. The Senator had argued that he initially rejected the criminal conduct and that it was performed as a result of the government's persistence "in persuading [him] to commit the crimes that [he was] not ready and willing to commit." Although the court in *Williams* found strong evidence of government persuasion, it likewise found that the totality of the evidence provided a sufficient basis for the jury's finding that the defendant was " 'ready and willing' to commit the crimes charged as soon as the opportunity was first presented."

In *Williams* the defendant also argued that the "government's agents in developing the case against them exceeded an outer limit of fairness mandated by the Due Process Clause." Outrageous government conduct differs from an entrapment defense in that the focus of a claim is on the government's improper conduct as opposed to whether the defendant is predisposed to commit the offense. In examining a claim of outrageous government conduct one looks at the government conduct to decide whether there is a constitutional due process violation. In *Williams* the Second Circuit rejected this claim as it had in other Abscam cases. Despite the enormity of the inducement offered Senator Williams, the court did not consider it "unconstitutional when offered to a person with the experience and sophistication of a United States Senator."

CHAPTER TWO

CORPORATE CRIMINAL LIABILITY

§ 2.01 Overview of Corporate Criminal Liability

The initial common law view was that a corporation could not be held criminally liable, although the individual members of the corporation could. Lacking a mind, the corporation could not form the mens rea necessary for criminality. Not having physical attributes, there was no actus reus. Additionally, even if convicted of an offense, the corporation could not be imprisoned for the crime.

The development toward corporate criminal liability emerged in response to corporate violations involving acts of omission with respect to regulatory nuisance type offenses. Since these strict liability offenses did not require a mens rea, lacked an affirmative act, and had punishment in the form of fines, the acceptance of corporate criminal liability for these crimes was in keeping with accepted doctrine.

The barriers to corporate criminal liability further disintegrated by the extension of criminality to acts of misfeasance. Although still applicable only to the strict liability offenses, courts found no rationale for differentiating between acts of nonfeasance and those of misfeasance.

Eventually, corporate criminal liability expanded beyond the strict liability arena and grew to encompass crimes with an intent element. Pivotal in this development of corporate criminal liability was the Supreme Court's ruling in *New York Central & Hudson River Railroad Co. v. United States* (S.Ct. 1909).

In *New York Central*, the railroad company and its assistant traffic manager were convicted for violations of the Elkins Act. The Elkins Act prohibited a person or corporation from granting or receiving rebates with respect to the transportation of property in interstate commerce by common carrier. The act was not limited to conduct amounting to an omission, but included affirmative acts by "any director or officer thereof, or any receiver, trustee, lessee, agent or person acting for or employed by such corporation." Defendants were accused of paying rebates to companies shipping sugar as well as to the consignees of the sugar. The corporate defendant questioned the constitutionality of subjecting a corporation to criminal prosecution, alleging a violation of the Due Process Clause. The corporation argued that punishing a corporation would in effect be punishing innocent stockholders. Since the corporation's board of directors and stockholders could not authorize an illegal act, the corporation could not be found criminally liable. The corporation also argued that the statute deprived the corporation of the due process right to a presumption of innocence.

In affirming the applicability of the Elkins Act to a corporation, the Supreme Court authorized prosecutions against corporations for certain specific intent crimes. The Court employed a tort theory of liability and applied it in this criminal context, finding that acts of an agent, done for the benefit of the principal and within the scope of the employment, are imputed to the principal. To effectuate a public policy, the Court determined it was proper, with respect to the Elkins Act, that the corporation could be "held responsible for and charged with the knowledge and purposes of their agents, acting within the authority conferred upon them."

Although *New York Central* provides a firm basis in the law for finding a corporation guilty of an offense with an intent element, there has been significant criticism of corporate criminal liability. Critics question whether there is any deterrent effect in punishing a corporation and whether the innocent shareholders and eventual consumers will, in fact, bear the ultimate cost. Despite this criticism, it is apparent that corporate criminal liability is an accepted and growing body of law.

Legislatures do not always limit corporate criminal liability to property offenses. Crimes "against the person" have been successfully prosecuted. For example, in *Granite Construction Co. v. Superior Court of Fresno County* (Cal.App.1983), a California Appellate Court permitted a corporation to be prosecuted for manslaughter. The court chose to uphold the legislative language found in the California Penal Code, which defined "person" to include corporations. The court noted that "[i]f corporations are liable for crimes of specific intent, then they should be equally liable for crimes of negligence or recklessness."

Although corporate criminal liability has been extended to a vast array of criminal offenses, some jurisdictions have refused to extend liability to corporations for acts, like manslaughter, that are against the person. The statutory language defining the crime, as relating to human beings only, has been the determining factor for rejecting corporate criminal liability. Most courts, however, interpret the term "person" to include corporations. For example, in *State v. Richard Knutson, Inc.* (Wis.Ct. App.1995), the Wisconsin Court of Appeals found that a corporation could be prosecuted for negligent homicide by vehicle in that it was "within the class of perpetrators covered by the statute."

Corporate criminal liability has recently played a significant role in the prosecution of environmental crimes (see chap.14). Corporations can also be prosecuted for workplace deaths resulting from a willful disregard of an Occupational Health and Safety Administration (OSHA) standard. The increased penalties mandated under the federal sentencing guidelines for organizations can impact the prosecution and sentencing of corporations. (see § 23.06).

§ 2.02 Standards of Imputing Corporate Criminal Liability

The criminal liability of a corporation is predicated upon acts or omissions of its agents. Two standards have developed as to when liability should be imputed to the corporation. These can best be expressed by reference to the Model Penal Code Rule and the common law doctrine of respondeat superior.

Section 2.07 of the Model Penal Code offers a somewhat restrictive approach to corporate criminal liability. Corporate liability can only be found in one of three ways: (1) for violations (minor offenses not classified as crimes that are punishable by fine only) or offenses defined by statute outside the criminal code where the legislature has clearly imposed liability on the corporation "and the conduct is performed by an agent acting in behalf of the corporation within the scope of his office or employment;" (2) where there is an omission of a specific duty of affirmative performance imposed on corporations by law; or (3) where the offense was authorized, performed, or recklessly tolerated by the board of directors or by a high managerial agent acting in behalf of the corporation within the scope of employment.

Although this code provision restricts liability to three categories, it does not limit the criminal liability exclusively to corporations. Rather, it extends its realm to unincorporated associations. An association can be liable when there is a "specific duty of affirmative performance imposed on associations by law," or the offense is defined by statute outside the criminal code and the legislature has clearly imposed liability on the association, "and the conduct is performed by an agent of the association acting in behalf of the association within the scope of his office or employment." The exception to finding liability in this circumstance, for both the corporation and unincorporated association, is where the legislature has designated an accountable agent or has specified the circumstances of accountability. In these latter instances the legislature's designation will control.

Where the Model Penal Code restricts corporate criminal liability to three categories and provides deference only to clear legislative language for liability, it also assumes the imputation of liability to the corporation where the offense is a strict liability prohibition. Absent a clear legislative intent to reject strict liability to the corporation, offenses of this nature will be assumed to apply to corporations.

The Model Penal Code addresses individual liability for the conduct of corporate agents acting on behalf of the corporation (see § 2.05). It also provides a defense to the corporation where, absent a contrary legislative purpose, there is proof "by a preponderance of the evidence that the high managerial agent having supervisory responsibility over the subject matter of the offense employed due diligence to prevent its commission."

States that have incorporated a Model Penal Code-type provision within their statutes have experienced controversies on a variety of issues. For example, in *State v. Shepherd Construction Co.* (Ga. 1981), the corporate defendant was charged with a violation of a Georgia statute that prohibited conspiracies "in restraint of free and open competition in transactions with the State." The corporation argued that the statutory provision under which they were charged only provided for imprisonment. Since a corporation was incapable of being imprisoned, the defendant argued, the legislature did not intend to include corporations.

The Georgia Supreme Court, in rejecting this argument in the *Shepherd* case, noted that the state code defined "person" to include corporations and also provided courts with the power to suspend a prison sentence and impose a fine of up to ten thousand dollars. By reading the conspiracy statute in light of existing definition sections of the state code, the court determined that it was in keeping with legislative intent to prosecute corporations for violations of this statute.

A forceful dissent in *Shepherd* by Justice Smith objected to the majority's finding of a legislative intent based upon these facts. Although supportive of corporate criminal liability, this dissent stated, "the determination that corporations are to be held accountable is for the legislature."

The Model Penal Code's application of corporate criminal liability when the offense is committed, authorized, or recklessly tolerated by "a high managerial agent acting in behalf of the corporation within the scope of his office or employment," raises questions as to (1) who is a "high managerial agent," and (2) when is that individual acting in behalf of the corporation. Although "high managerial agent" is defined in the Model Penal Code, the definition is far from being a bright line determinant. The definition provides that the agent is one "having duties of such responsibility that his conduct may fairly be assumed to represent the policy of the corporation or association."

One court refused to find a corporation liable for the acts of its managers and employees where there was no finding of complicity by the officers or directors of the corporation. In order to assess liability against the corporation, it was necessary to have evidence of criminal intent. Evidence of intent is apparent when the crime results from direct authorization of the board of directors. Where, however, the criminal act is committed by an employee and no authorization or knowledge by the corporation is presented, the criminal intent element of the statute is not met. Despite the fact that the manager handled the operations of the automobile dealership, the court found that the corporation was not subject to liability in that the president had no real knowledge and control of the day-to-day business operations. The dealership in this case was owned by a corporation that was the subsidiary of another corporation which in turn was owned by the president. *State v. Chapman Dodge Center, Inc.* (La. 1983).

Another court found corporate criminal liability for conduct involving a rebate scheme in an automobile dealership where the individual directly accused of having committed the criminal acts was a salesperson and fleet manager. The Minnesota Supreme Court, finding corporate criminal liability,

noted that the individual "was acting in furtherance of the corporation's business interests." The
corporation, and not the individual, would be receiving the benefit of the rebate. This coupled with
participation by a corporate officer and acknowl-
edgement of the problem by the president, provided
sufficient evidence to support finding the corporation criminally liable. *State v. Christy Pontiac–
GMC, Inc.* (Minn.1984).

Federal courts apply the common law rule of
respondeat superior in assessing whether it is proper to impute the acts of an agent to the corporation.
In contrast to the Model Penal Code, which concentrates on whether the individual who committed the
acts is a "high managerial agent," a court employing respondeat superior would only examine whether the agent was acting within the scope of his or
her authority and on behalf of the corporation. The
doctrine of respondeat superior therefore does not
limit corporate criminal liability to the upper eche-
lon of the corporation, but rather permits liability
to be found when the criminal actions are the result
of any employee acting within the scope of employment in behalf of the corporation.

In *Commonwealth v. Beneficial Finance Co.*
(Mass.1971), the Massachusetts Supreme Court was
presented with the question of whether the Model
Penal Code or a trial court's jury instructions correctly reflected the law in that jurisdiction. The
corporate defendants argued that acts of a "high
managerial agent" were required for imposing criminal liability on the corporation. In contrast, the

Commonwealth argued for the trial court's standard that stated, "[i]t isn't the name of the office that counts, but it's the position in which the corporation placed that person with relation to its business, with regard to the powers and duties and responsibilities and authority which it gave to him which counts." The court's instructions concentrated on whether the "acts and the intent of the individuals were the acts and intent of the corporation."

The Massachusetts Supreme Court adopted the trial court's view that a standard similar to the rule of respondeat superior should be employed. "The Commonwealth must prove that the individual for whose conduct it seeks to charge the corporation criminally was placed in a position by the corporation where he had enough power, duty, responsibility and authority to act for and in behalf of the corporation to handle the particular business or operation or project of the corporation in which he was engaged at the time that he committed the criminal act, with power of decision as to what he would or would not do while acting for the corporation, and that he was acting for and in behalf of the corporation in the accomplishment of that particular business or operation or project, and that he committed a criminal act while so acting." This approach to corporate criminal liability seemed more appropriate to the court in light of the evidentiary deficiencies of the Model Penal Code approach.

Use of both the Model Penal Code and respondeat superior standards raise the issue as to when an agent is acting on behalf of a corporation. According to the Fifth Circuit, corporate criminal liability requires that the conduct be for the benefit of the corporation. It does not, however, mandate that the corporation actually receive a benefit. In *Standard Oil Co. of Texas v. United States* (5th Cir.1962), the Fifth Circuit reversed convictions where the statute required the conduct to be a knowing violation. Since the individuals from whom the government was imputing knowledge to the corporation were acting to further their own criminal enterprise and not the corporations, the court found it improper to hold the corporation liable. The court stated, "[u]nder a statute requiring that there be 'a specific wrongful intent,' ... the corporation does not acquire that knowledge or possess the requisite 'state of mind essential for responsibility' through the activities of unfaithful servants whose conduct was undertaken to advance the interests of parties other than their corporate employer." Other jurisdictions have ruled in accord with this Fifth Circuit view.

The issue of when an agent is acting on behalf of a corporation is further complicated when the agent acts directly against orders given by the corporation. Courts have liberally interpreted the phrase "acting on behalf of a corporation," finding liability despite the action being contrary to a corporation's instructions. Where the offense is a regulatory nuisance offense, such as a prohibition against throwing garbage from a ship into navigable waters, the corporation can be held liable despite the fact that personnel were told not to engage in these acts. *The*

President Coolidge (Dollar Steamship Co. v. United States) (9th Cir.1939).

In *United States v. Hilton Hotels Corp.* (9th Cir. 1972), the Ninth Circuit concluded "that as a general rule a corporation is liable under the Sherman Act for the acts of its agents in the scope of their employment, even though contrary to general corporate policy and express instructions to the agent." The *Hilton* case involved a purchasing agent who participated in a boycott by threatening a supplier with loss of the hotel's business if the supplier refused to pay a fee to an association organized to attract conventions to the city. The agent's conduct was in direct opposition to corporate policy and instructions. The court, in imputing liability to the corporation, noted that agents are pressured to maximize profits for a corporation and that violations of the Sherman Act result in profit to the corporation and not the individual. The court also stressed the difficulty the government would have in identifying the particular agent responsible for the violation. The court believed that punishment of the agent would not likely be a deterrent, while punishment of the corporation would be an effective deterrent.

§ 2.03 Collective Knowledge

Where corporate criminal liability was once applicable only to strict liability offenses, as noted in the *New York Central* case, it now can apply to offenses with an intent element. As a result of this extension, the issue has arisen as to what level of culpability is required for corporate liability. Where an individual agent possesses sufficient intent, the issue becomes whether that agent's knowledge can be imputed to the corporation. As noted, the resolution of this question may depend upon whether the jurisdiction applies a respondeat superior rule or adopts a model penal code approach. More difficult is where no one corporate agent possesses the necessary intent, but rather the intent is formed as a result of collective knowledge.

In *United States v. Bank of New England, N.A.* (1st Cir.1987) the First Circuit examined the propriety of jury instructions that permitted the imputation of knowledge to the corporation by use of collective knowledge. The Bank of New England was convicted of thirty-one violations of the Currency Transaction Reporting Act in failing to report transactions in excess of ten thousand dollars by a customer who used multiple checks that were each under ten thousand dollars. The customer had presented these checks to a single bank teller. One of several arguments raised on appeal contested the trial court's instructions to the jury on "willfulness," which here require knowledge of the reporting requirements.

The trial court had instructed the jury that it could "look at the bank as an institution." Its knowledge, the district court stated, "is the sum of all of the employees." In finding these instructions proper, the First Circuit noted that a collective knowledge instruction is appropriate when applied in the context of corporate criminal liability. The court stated, "[c]orporations compartmentalize knowledge, subdividing the elements of specific duties and operations into smaller components." One department or individual may be unaware of the operations of another unit of the corporation. The court noted that "[s]ince the Bank had the compartmentalized structure common to all large corporations, the court's collective knowledge instruction was not only proper but necessary."

§ 2.04   Dead Corporations and Noncorporate Entity Liability

Dissolved corporations can be the subject of a criminal prosecution when a state provides for the continuation of the entity after dissolution. In *Melrose Distillers, Inc. v. United States* (S.Ct.1959), the Supreme Court permitted a criminal action against a corporation that had dissolved. The Court predicated its decision on the fact that the applicable state statutes of Maryland and Delaware continued the corporations to make them "existing" corporations for the purposes of section eight of the Sherman Act. The Court stated, "[i]n this situation there is no more reason for allowing them to escape criminal penalties than damages in civil suits." The *Melrose* case has been used by courts to extend liability to defunct corporations when the specific statute involved contains a survival clause or permits the corporation to exist for a purpose.

Cases have also applied criminal liability to corporations despite a merger. For example, a bank was found criminally liable for failing to file currency transaction reports despite its merger with another bank. The court stated that the bank could not escape punishment by merging with another bank and assuming that bank's "corporate persona." *United States v. Alamo Bank of Texas* (5th Cir. 1989).

Courts have not limited entity liability exclusively to the corporate body. In *United States v. A & P Trucking Company* (S.Ct.1958), the Supreme Court reversed the dismissal of informations charging a partnership with violations of Interstate Commerce Commission regulations and the Motor Carrier Act. The Court noted that the Motor Carrier Act defined "person" to include partnerships. The Interstate Commerce Commission regulation used the term "whoever," which the Court considered defined by the "Rules of Construction" definition of "person." (1 U.S.C. § 1). The Court stated that "it certainly makes no difference whether the carrier which commits the infraction is organized as a corporation, a joint stock company, a partnership, or an individual proprietorship. The mischief is the same, and we think that Congress intended to make the consequences of infraction the same." Thus, despite language of "knowingly and willfully" in the regulations, the Court held that partnerships can be prosecuted for violations of these statutes.

§ 2.05 Overview of Personal Liability of Corporate Agents

Where corporate criminal liability evolved over time, historically corporate agents have always been held personally liable for their criminal conduct. The fact that an agent may be acting on behalf of a corporation does not release the agent from being held criminally accountable.

This principle of personal liability of a corporate agent was reinforced in the Supreme Court case of *United States v. Wise* (S.Ct.1962), where the government contested on direct appeal a district court's dismissal of an indictment against a corporate officer for violations of the Sherman Act. The District Court's rationale was that the Sherman Act was inapplicable to corporate officers who act in their representative capacity. In reversing this lower court decision, the Supreme Court noted that the Sherman Act's inclusion of corporations in its definition of "persons" did not serve to exclude prosecutions against individuals who have a responsible share in the criminal conduct.

The Model Penal Code (§ 2.07 (6)) imposes individual liability on the corporate agent for conduct performed on behalf of the corporation "to the same extent as if it were performed in his own name or behalf." Where there is an affirmative duty to act, the agent "having primary responsibility for the discharge of the duty is legally accountable for a reckless omission to perform the required act to the same extent as if the duty were imposed by law directly upon himself."

Where the criminal conduct is performed directly by the agent of the corporation, courts have had little difficulty in imposing liability. Even when the agent is not an officer, director, or manager, liability has been found for the criminal acts committed. Liability has been extended to agents as well as independent contractors. There have been occasional instances in which it is argued that a subordinate should not be held liable for the criminal act in that the individual was acting under the orders of a superior. In *United States v. Gold* (11th Cir.1984), the Eleventh Circuit found "that 'following orders' can only be a defense where a defendant has no idea that his conduct is criminal." There is, however, no consistent body of law endorsing the position taken in the *Gold* case.

When the offense involves an element of criminal intent, courts generally require that the corporate agent have personally performed, had knowledge of the acts, or have had direction or control over the conduct. For example, in *Bourgeois v. Commonwealth* (Va.1976), the Virginia Supreme Court ruled that despite the fact that the individual charged with the crime was the president of the corporation, it was necessary for the state to present evidence that this individual controlled the circumstances of the illegal acts. Absent evidence of participation in the criminal conduct or knowledge imputed from the business procedures of the corporation or the personnel, the Court found that there was no basis for imputing knowledge of wrongdoing to the president.

§ 2.06 Responsible Corporate Officer

Responsible corporate officers have been held criminally liable by a statute with a "knowing" element, despite the fact that they had no actual knowledge of the criminal conduct. *United States v. Johnson & Towers, Inc.* (3d Cir.1984). Willful blindness to the criminal conduct can be used to support the element of knowledge. The mere fact that one is in the position of official responsibility does not, however, constitute knowledge. *United States v. MacDonald & Watson Waste Oil Co.* (1st Cir.1991). However, where knowledge is an element of the offense, it often can be inferred from circumstantial evidence. This evidence may include the position and responsibilities of the corporate officer.

When the offense is a strict liability offense, there is no need to concentrate on the level of knowledge held by the indicted corporate agent. The offense is imputed via the "responsible corporate officer" doctrine. This doctrine originates from the Supreme Court decision in *United States v. Dotterweich* (S.Ct. 1943).

Dotterweich, along with the Buffalo Pharmacal Company, Inc., was charged with violating the Federal Food, Drug and Cosmetic Act. As president and general manager of the corporation, he was accused of violations involving the shipping in interstate commerce of adulterated and misbranded drugs. The drugs had been purchased from the manufacturer, repacked under the Buffalo Pharmacal Company name, and shipped in interstate commerce. Only Dotterweich was convicted after a jury trial.

Justice Frankfurter, writing for the majority, found that Dotterweich was a "person" punishable for violations of the Federal Food, Drug, and Cosmetic Act. The Court recognized the offense as a strict liability crime, thus eliminating any requirement for the government to show knowledge on the part of Dotterweich. Liability, the court found, rests upon whether the individual has a "responsible share in the furtherance of the transaction." The Court declined in this opinion to define the term "responsible share," leaving the definition to "the good sense of prosecutors, the wise guidance of trial judges, and the ultimate judgment of juries."

In a dissent written by Justice Murphy, and joined by three members of the court, it was noted that guilt was being "imputed to the respondent solely on the basis of his authority and responsibility as president and general manager of the corporation." The dissent objected to this imputation of criminality, absent clear statutory authority, and found it "inconsistent with established canons of criminal law to rest liability on an act in which the accused did not participate and of which he had no personal knowledge."

The Supreme Court elaborated on the *Dotterweich* case thirty-two years later in the case of *United States v. Park* (S.Ct.1975). Park, the chief executive officer of a national retail food chain, was charged with violations of the Federal Food, Drug, and Cosmetic Act. His office was located in Philadelphia, Pennsylvania while the warehouse contaminated with rodents, from which there were interstate food shipments, was located in Baltimore, Maryland. Park had been advised that steps were being taken to remedy the conditions in the warehouse. In finding defendant Park criminally liable, the Supreme Court reiterated its holding in *Dotterweich*. The Court emphasized that those who have a "responsible relationship" have a duty under the Act not only "to seek out and remedy violations" but also a duty "to implement measures that will insure that violations will not occur." A defendant is afforded the defense, and has the burden of proof if offered, of showing that he or she is " 'powerless' to prevent or correct the violation." The government is only required to show "that the defendant had, by reason of his position in the corporation, responsibility and authority either to prevent in the first instance, or promptly to correct, the violation complained of, and that he failed to do so."

The Court in *Park* examined the trial court's instructions and determined that taken as a whole they properly reflected this legal standard. The instructions did not permit a finding of guilt strictly upon Park's position in the corporation. Rather, the instructions "advised the jury that to find guilt it must find respondent 'had a responsible relation to the situation,' and 'by virtue of his position ... had ... authority and responsibility' to deal with the situation."

Three members of the Court dissenting in Park agreed with what it termed "the language of negligence" of the majority. The dissent, however, felt that the instructions used in the case had failed to adhere to the standard set by the Court. Whether strict liability has been abandoned for a negligence standard in applying the "responsible officer" doctrine is a subject of legal debate.

Corporate executives and employees indicted for alleged acts committed in their corporate capacity have sought reimbursement from the corporation for their attorney fees and other expenses. Likewise, if the corporate executive or employee is convicted, reimbursement has been sought for fines assessed against them. Courts have resolved issues premised upon indemnification in a variety of contexts with varying results. Executives seeking indemnification have proceeded using statutory authority, corporate policy, or an implied or express agreement between the corporation and the executive. Indemnification or payment of current expenses has been sought directly from the corporation, or alternatively pursuant to a Directors and Officers Liability Insurance Policy.

PART TWO
SPECIFIC OFFENSES

CHAPTER THREE
CONSPIRACY

§ 3.01 Introduction

Throughout the United States Code there are specific conspiracy statutes. Some of these statutes appear within the criminal code. [i.e., conspiracy against rights of citizens (18 U.S.C. § 241)]. Other conspiracy statutes exist outside Title 18. [i.e., conspiracy in restraint of trade (15 U.S.C. § 1); conspiracy to monopolize trade (15 U.S.C. § 2)]. In some instances conspiracy provisions are incorporated within the terms of a statute. [i.e., racketeering conspiracies (18 U.S.C. § 1962 (d)); conspiracy in bribery in sporting contests (18 U.S.C. § 224)]. The one general federal conspiracy statute, 18 U.S.C. § 371, criminalizes conspiracies to commit any offense against the United States as well as conspiracies to defraud the United States or its agencies.

Judge Learned Hand referred to conspiracy as "that darling of the modern prosecutor's nursery."

Harrison v. United States (2d Cir.1925). This is especially true when placed in the context of white collar crime. Although individual acts of white collar crime are abundant, an overwhelming number of white collar criminal acts are group related. In recent years conspiracy charges have sometimes resulted in megatrials that involve many defendants and lengthy trials.

Conspiracy is an inchoate crime. One of the essential aims of conspiracy is to protect against concerted criminal activity. Conspiracy is punished as a crime to attack the special dangers resulting from group activity. ("In union there is strength").

Conspiracy charges offer prosecutors several advantages. As an inchoate crime, it provides a legal basis for stopping the effects of criminality prior to it reaching full fruition. A federal conspiracy charge under 18 U.S.C. § 371 can be filed when there is an agreement and an overt act. It is unnecessary to wait until the criminal conduct is complete to proceed with conspiracy charges.

The conspiracy offense also offers prosecutors procedural advantages. For example, a charge of conspiracy permits joinder of the co-conspirators for trial. From a practical perspective this enhances the likelihood of conviction in that the evidence to the jury will not be limited to the acts of one individual. Guilt by association can be fostered when the prosecutor presents, in the same trial, evidence of criminal conduct by those associated with the defendant.

Another procedural advantage to the prosecutor in charging conspiracy is found in the broader selection offered in choosing the forum where the case will be heard. The venue of conspiracy charges is in the location where the conspiracy was formed or where any of the overt acts took place. With several defendants and possibly several overt acts, prosecutorial discretion with respect to venue is enhanced by charging conspiracy under section 371.

The conspiracy statute also can have evidentiary advantages for the prosecutor. Hearsay evidence is not permitted at trial unless it meets an exception to the hearsay rule. Federal evidence rules provide as one of the exceptions to hearsay "a statement by a co-conspirator of a party during the course and in furtherance of the conspiracy." (Federal Rules of Evidence, Rule 801(d)(2)(E)). Thus, in a conspiracy trial, statements of a co-conspirator made during the conspiracy may possibly be admitted despite the fact that the statement is hearsay. Relevant evidence also may be expanded by the presence of multiple co-conspirators and possibly several overt acts. Since many conspiracies are proved through circumstantial evidence, the increase in admissible evidence can benefit the prosecutor.

Prosecutors also have an advantage should the evidence at trial be deficient on one of several objects of a conspiracy. A general verdict on a multiple object conspiracy is proper even though the evidence on one of the objects of the conspiracy may be inadequate to support a conviction. When the inadequacy relates to inadequate evidence as opposed to being a "legal error," due process does not require setting aside the verdict. *Griffin v. United States* (S.Ct.1991).

The main federal conspiracy statute, 18 U.S.C. § 371, requires proof of the following elements: (1) an agreement, (2) an unlawful object, (3) knowledge and intent, and (4) an overt act. The statute provides for a penalty of up to five years imprisonment and a fine. If the unlawful object of the conspiracy is a misdemeanor then the punishment is limited to the maximum punishment provided for that misdemeanor. There is no double jeopardy violation when a defendant is prosecuted for both the substantive crime and conspiracy to commit that crime under section 371. Conspiracy to commit a crime is a separate and distinct offense from the crime itself. *United States v. Felix* (S.Ct.1992).

§ 3.02 Agreement

At the heart of the crime of conspiracy is the agreement. The agreement does not have to be written, oral, or explicit. It can be inferred from the "facts and circumstances of the case." *Iannelli v. United States* (S.Ct.1975). If the minds of the parties meet and an understanding is reached to achieve a common purpose, there is an agreement. Mere knowledge, without agreement, does not meet this element of the offense.

Incumbent to forming an agreement is, however, some knowledge. The conspirators must know of the conspiracy's purpose and must knowingly participate in it. Conspirators do not have to agree to every step of the conspiracy. An overall agreement to carry out the objectives of the conspiracy suffices.

Although it is necessary to have evidence beyond a reasonable doubt that the conspirators agreed on the "essential nature of the plan," it is not necessary to prove that all conspirators had knowledge of all the plan's details or even of the participation of all others in the conspiracy. *Blumenthal v. United States* (S.Ct.1947). For example, a conspiracy conviction was affirmed despite the fact that the defendant convicted of conspiracy to violate the money laundering statute (18 U.S.C. § 1956) believed the money was from narcotics trafficking and the co-conspirator believed the money came from gambling. Since the conspirators agreed on the essential scheme, to launder money, the agreement element of the conspiracy was satisfied. *United States v. Stavroulakis* (2d Cir.1992). The agreement must be to achieve an unlawful objective. (see § 3.04).

A defense to a conspiracy charge may be premised upon a defendant's withdrawal from the conspiracy. The defendant arguing withdrawal must prove an affirmative act of withdrawal. This can be shown through action communicated to co-conspirators that disavows or defeats the purpose of the conspiracy.

§ 3.03 Plurality

Conspiracy requires two or more parties forming the agreement. This plurality requirement does not necessitate that the government charge all members of the conspiracy. It is common to see a con-

spiracy case proceed against one defendant with
unindicted co-conspirators mentioned in the charging document.

With plurality required, the issue arises as to
whether there are in fact two or more persons to
the agreement when one defendant is acquitted and
another is convicted. For many years case law relative to conspiracy prohibited inconsistent verdicts.
Thus, if one defendant of a two person conspiracy
was acquitted, then the other defendant's conviction could not stand. Further, if all but one of the
defendants of a multiple party conspiracy were acquitted, then the remaining defendant would have
to be acquitted. Since the essence of a conspiracy is
the agreement between two or more individuals, the
elimination by acquittal of all those with whom the
defendant could have conspired precluded a conspiracy conviction for the remaining defendant.

The rule prohibiting inconsistent verdicts did not
apply where one defendant was tried and convicted
and the other defendant was not charged with the
crime. It likewise did not apply to the situation
where two defendants were convicted but one was
acquitted. As long as an agreement could be shown,
there was no inconsistency in the verdicts. Additionally, some courts refused to extend the rule
prohibiting inconsistent verdicts to situations where
the defendants were tried separately. These courts
only allowed for the reversal of inconsistent verdicts
where the verdicts resulted from the same trial.

Many courts have now departed from the rule of
prohibiting inconsistent verdicts. Reference is often

made to the case of *United States v. Powell* (S.Ct. 1984) which held that inconsistency alone is not a basis for reversing a conviction. In *Powell* the Supreme Court found it acceptable to have a defendant's conviction for the crime of using the telephone to facilitate the offense when there is an acquittal of the offense itself. (The charges were conspiracy to possess cocaine and possession of cocaine). *Powell*, however, did not directly address the issue of inconsistency in conspiracy verdicts between co-conspirators.

In *United States v. Bucuvalas* (1st Cir.1990) the First Circuit found that jury verdicts acquitting one alleged conspirator and convicting the sole other alleged conspirator at the same trial on the same count did not require a reversal of the appellant's conviction. The court noted that justice is met in that the appellate tribunal reviews the evidence to determine its sufficiency to support the jury's decision. In applying *Powell* to inconsistent verdicts between two alleged conspirators, the court found the "rule of consistency" no longer viable. Not all courts, however, apply *Powell* to inconsistent verdicts between alleged conspirators. Some courts see the rule of consistency between co-conspirators in a conspiracy case as an exception to *Powell*.

The requirement of plurality also raises issues of whether two parties are forming an agreement when both parties are corporations or the agreement is between a corporation and its employees. Courts have found that two corporations can form a conspiracy where the indictment involves two corporations and an individual associated with each. Plurality, likewise, exists if the conspiracy involves a corporation and one of its officers with a third party. Plurality, however, has been found not to exist when a single agent acts for both corporations. *United States v. Santa Rita Store Co.* (N.M.1911).

When the corporation conspires with its own officers, agents, and employees, prosecutions under 18 U.S.C. § 371 have generally been found permissible. *United States v. Hartley* (11th Cir.1982). Intracorporate conspiracies, however, have generally not been upheld in the context of charges of violating antitrust laws. *Nelson Radio & Supply Co. v. Motorola, Inc.* (5th Cir.1952).

Intracorporate conspiracies have also been rejected when only one human actor is involved. In *United States v. Stevens* (11th Cir.1990), the Eleventh Circuit reversed a conspiracy conviction where the defendant, accused of conspiring with a corporation, had been convicted of conspiracy to defraud the government pursuant to 18 U.S.C. § 371. In *Stevens* the defendant was the sole stockholder of the corporation and acted as its sole agent. The court acknowledged that outside the context of antitrust violations, corporations can be criminally liable under section 371 for conspiracies involving its officers or employees. Where, however, the conspiracy involves only one human actor, as in *Stevens*, than the crime of conspiracy is improper.

The existence of plurality also can become an issue when the offense, by its very nature, requires two individuals. For example, crimes of bribery, adultery, incest or bigamy necessitate a minimum of two individuals to achieve the substantive offense. Historically, Wharton's Rule prohibited conspiracy prosecutions "when the crime is of such a nature as to necessarily require the participation of two persons for its commission."

Wharton's Rule has been significantly limited over time. If more than the minimum number of offenders participate in the offense, the rule has been found inapplicable. Further, Wharton's Rule cannot be used if the statute only criminalizes the conduct of one of the parties to the crime. The Model Penal Code does not endorse Wharton's Rule.

The Supreme Court held in *Iannelli v. United States* (S.Ct.1975), that in federal court, Wharton's Rule only acts "as a judicial presumption, to be applied in the absence of legislative intent to the contrary." According to this case, Wharton's Rule requires not only that the parties to the agreement be the only parties to participate in the commission of the offense, but also that "the immediate consequences of the crime rest on the parties themselves rather than on society at large." In *Iannelli*, Wharton's Rule was held not to apply to an alleged gambling conspiracy, in that the offense, a violation of 18 U.S.C. § 1955, differed from the traditional Wharton Rule offenses. Further, the court found that the harm emanating from large gambling activities was not limited to the parties but rather sought to include the participation of additional individuals who, in the case of bettors, were not a party to the conspiracy or to the substantive offense.

Plurality will not be found where a statute specifically protects one party to the offense. Where a party is legislatively protected, it is improper for the government to charge conspiracy. Clearly victims of a crime should not be prosecuted for conspiracy for their unwilling participation in a crime.

Plurality is seriously jeopardized when one of the parties to the conspiracy is a government agent. Courts have found that there is no agreement unless there is at "least one bona fide co-conspirator." *United States v. Schmidt* (9th Cir.1991). If the only person that the defendant conspires with is a government agent, there is no true agreement nor a meeting of the minds. If, however, the agreement includes a government agent coupled with other individuals, then a conspiracy can exist.

§ 3.04 Unlawful Object of Conspiracy

18 U.S.C. § 371 can be subdivided as follows: (1) conspiracies to commit any **offense** against the United States, or (2) conspiracies to **defraud** the United States or its agencies. The offense and defraud clauses of this statute offer alternative methods of charging under section 371.

Under the **offense** provision, the conspiracy has as its object the violation of other civil and criminal statutes. For example, a conspiracy to commit mail fraud (18 U.S.C. § 1341) and conspiracy to obstruct justice (18 U.S.C. § 1503) would be violations of 18 U.S.C. § 371.

In contrast the **defraud** provision focuses not on specific offense activity, but rather on conduct that defrauds the United States. A conspiracy to defraud the United States requires a showing that the accused either cheated the government out of property or money, or interfered with or obstructed a lawful government function by "deceit, craft or trickery or at least by means that are dishonest." *Hammerschmidt v. United States* (S.Ct.1924). It is not incumbent that there be an actual financial or property loss where there is an obstruction or impairment of a lawful function of a department of the government. Thus, even though the charges against the defendant did not allege that the government suffered any monetary loss, the defraud clause was applicable where a release of a cotton crop report to select market speculators obstructed or impaired the lawful delivery of the information by the government. *Haas v. Henkel* (S.Ct.1910).

The scope of the scheme to defraud in section 371 is broad in that the very language of the statute states a defrauding of the United States "in any manner or for any purpose." Courts, however, are bound to scrutinize criminal conspiracy charges carefully to make certain that its wide net does not "ensnare the innocent as well as the culpable." *Dennis v. United States* (S.Ct.1966). Lenity is to be used in resolving ambiguities as to the scope of the defraud clause. *Tanner v. United States* (S.Ct.1987).

The relationship between the offense and defraud clause of section 371 has been the subject of recent

controversies. One view is that although the government can prosecute a defendant under both the
offense and defraud clauses of section 371, only one
conviction and one punishment is possible. *United
States v. Bilzerian* (2d Cir.1991).

In *United States v. Minarik* (6th Cir.1989), however, the Sixth Circuit held that the government
should be limited to the offense clause of section
371, as opposed to using the defraud clause, in
those instances where Congress specifically enacted
a statute that covers the wrongful conduct. The
court noted that to hold otherwise would allow
prosecutors to circumvent a misdemeanor penalty.
By charging the offense as the felony of conspiracy
to defraud the United States, the government could
effectively obtain a felony punishment where the
specific offense is only a misdemeanor.

More recent decisions in the Sixth Circuit limit
Minarik to the facts presented in the case. Where
the alleged conduct violates more than one specific
offense, fits within the defraud clause, and the
indictment provides adequate notice to the defendant of the alleged charges, the court does not
require that the conspiracy be charged under the
offense clause rather than the defraud clause of the
conspiracy statute. *United States v. Kraig* (6th Cir.
1996).

§ 3.05   Knowledge and Intent

Conspiracy requires both knowledge and specific
intent. As previously noted, the defendant must

agree to the conspiracy. This requires knowledge of the conspiracy's existence, as well as knowledge of the objective of the conspiracy. It does not, however, require knowledge by the accused of all the details of the conspiracy (see § 3.02).

In addition to knowledge, the defendant must also intend to participate in the conspiracy. The degree of mens rea required for the conspiracy is dependent upon the level of intent required for the underlying specific offense. Conspiracy to commit a specific offense only exists when there is sufficient evidence of at least the degree of criminal intent required for the substantive offense. *Ingram v. United States* (S.Ct.1959).

Although knowledge and intent are required, in almost all instances it is not necessary that there be knowledge of a jurisdictional element. "The concept of criminal intent does not extend so far as to require that the actor understand not only the nature of his act but also its consequence for the choice of a judicial forum." *United States v. Feola* (S.Ct.1975). Only in the rare circumstance where the parties need to have knowledge to establish the existence of federal jurisdiction, will it be required that there be knowledge of the federal jurisdiction for the conspiracy offense. In almost all instances, knowledge by the defendant of the existence of federal jurisdiction is not required for the substantive offense, and therefore, will not be required for a conspiracy.

§ 3.06 Overt Act

Although many state jurisdictions and some specific federal conspiracy statutes find the actus reus of a conspiracy charge to be solely the agreement, section 371 requires both an agreement and an overt act in furtherance of the agreement. The overt act does not have to be a criminal act. Further, it does not have to be performed by the individual accused of the crime of conspiracy. As long as one member of the conspiracy committed an overt act in furtherance of the conspiracy, the element is met.

The overt act must take place during the conspiracy. For purposes of the statute of limitations for a conspiracy prosecution, the time does not commence to run until the commission of the last overt act in furtherance of the conspiracy as alleged in the charging document. It is incumbent that the government prove an overt act within the statute of limitations.

§ 3.07 Single or Multiple Conspiracies

Whether the parties are properly joined in one conspiracy and whether the acts of the parties constitute a single or multiple conspiracy, are issues raised in some conspiracy cases. The substantive, procedural, and evidentiary advantages afforded a prosecutor in charging conspiracy can be further enhanced by including in one prosecution multiple defendants and multiple acts. As a result, the government often finds itself arguing that the parties formed one general conspiracy as opposed to several smaller conspiracies, and that the acts of these parties are part of a single conspiracy as opposed to multiple conspiracies.

Although it is necessary to have one overall agreement between the parties to charge conspiracy, it is not necessary to have every participant of the conspiracy know the other individuals involved or know the specific details of every aspect of the conspiracy. When there are more than two members of a conspiracy, the question arises whether in fact all are part of the same conspiracy or perhaps some are involved in one conspiracy and others involved in a different conspiracy.

This issue arose in the case of *Kotteakos v. United States* (S.Ct.1946) where defendants were convicted of a conspiracy to obtain loans under the National Housing Act. One individual, Brown, conspired with many of the defendants and served as the "common and key figure in all the transactions proven." In many cases, however, the defendants did not have any relationship with each other except Brown's connection with each transaction. The Supreme Court rejected this connection as sufficient for a single conspiracy.

The *Kotteakos* court analogized these facts to the hub of a wheel with its spokes. In this case Brown served as the hub of the wheel. The spokes were the individual defendants, who in this case had no relationship to each other. Except for Brown, the individual conspirators were not interested in anything but their own loan. The conspiracies were therefore separate and disconnected with no one overriding plan. Absent a single comprehensive plan, there was no single conspiracy. Rather the defendants were involved in multiple conspiracies with Brown.

The "wheel and spoke" conspiracy has been distinguished from the "chain" conspiracy. In a "chain" conspiracy, the court looks to whether the parties serve as links in a chain. In *Blumenthal v. United States* (S.Ct.1947), the Supreme Court found that the parties had agreed to sell liquor at prices exceeding the ceiling set by regulations of the Office of Price Administration. The Court found that the agreements were steps in the formulation of one larger general conspiracy. By reason of all having knowledge of the plan's general scope and common end, the disposing of the whiskey, they could be drawn together in a single conspiracy.

A single agreement with multiple criminal objectives is one conspiracy, as opposed to several separate conspiracies. It is improper to charge several counts of conspiracy when only one agreement is involved. *Braverman v. United States* (S.Ct.1942). This is not, however, true when there is a single agreement to violate different conspiracy statutes. *Albernaz v. United States* (S.Ct.1981).

§ 3.08 Pinkerton Rule

In *Pinkerton v. United States* (S.Ct.1946), the Supreme Court held that a conspirator can be liable for the substantive offenses of a co-conspirator that are in furtherance of the conspiracy. Defendant

Pinkerton's convictions for violations of the Internal Revenue Code and conspiracy were affirmed despite the fact that there was no evidence that he had directly participated in or had knowledge of the substantive offenses. The evidence showed that defendant's brother committed these substantive offenses while the defendant was in prison. The jury, however, found that these substantive offenses were committed in furtherance of the conspiracy.

Pinkerton requires that to find a conspirator liable for the substantive offense of a co-conspirator, the substantive offense (1) must be within the scope and in furtherance of the conspiracy, (2) be committed by one or more members of the conspiracy, and (3) the individual accused of the substantive offense must be a member of the conspiracy at the time the specific offense was committed. It is within the province of a jury to apply this rule to the facts.

In some instances *Pinkerton* is applied when the substantive crime is a primary goal of the alleged conspiracy. *United States v. Alvarez* (11th Cir.1985). Other cases employ the *Pinkerton* Rule where the substantive crime "facilitates the achievement of one of the primary goals" of the conspiracy.

In *Pinkerton*, the Supreme Court noted that its holding did not encompass cases where the substantive offenses were not reasonably foreseen as a necessary or natural consequence of the unlawful agreement. Some courts have used this language to find liability where the substantive offenses were not the objective of the conspiracy, but were reasonably foreseeable by the conspirators. *United States v. Tilton* (5th Cir.1980). Reasonably foreseeable, but originally unintended, substantive offenses may be limited to where the conspirator "played more than a 'minor' role in the conspiracy, or had actual knowledge of at least some of the circumstances and events culminating in the reasonably foreseeable but originally unintended substantive crime." *United States v. Alvarez* (11th Cir.1985).

§ 3.09 Antitrust Conspiracies

Section One of the Sherman Act addresses conspiracies intended to produce an unreasonable restraint of trade or commerce. It requires plurality as well as an interstate nexus. In contrast, section two of the Sherman Act can be met absent plurality in that it prohibits "every person" from monopolizing any part of trade or commerce. Issues raised in prosecutions under section one have included whether plurality exists when there is an intra-enterprise or intra-corporate conspiracy. Alleged violators of section one have also contested the level of intent necessary for the prosecution.

Historically intra-enterprise conspiracies were subject to the Sherman Act. As early as 1947, the Supreme Court rejected arguments that a Sherman Act conspiracy could not be premised upon affiliated corporations. *United States v. Yellow Cab Co.* (S.Ct. 1947). This position was significantly altered by the United States in 1984 when the Court issued its decision in *Copperweld Corp. v. Independence Tube Corp.* (S.Ct.1984).

In *Copperweld*, the Supreme Court held that a parent corporation and its wholly owned subsidiary were incapable of conspiring with each other for purposes of section one of the Sherman Act. Officers and employees of the same company lack the necessary plurality of actors needed for a section one conspiracy. The Court found that section one did not reach conduct that was "wholly unilateral."

The Court did not, however, resolve whether this prohibition should be extended to intra-enterprise conspiracies where the parent corporation is accused of conspiring with an affiliated corporation that it does not completely own. A Louisiana court interpreting a state antitrust statute declined to adopt the *Copperweld* position, noting that it departed from the Supreme Court's own precedent and from a prevailing decision of the Louisiana Court. *Louisiana Power and Light Company v. United Gas Pipe Line Co.* (La.1986).

Plurality does not exist when the parties are part of the same corporation. Unlike the general conspiracy provision found in section 371, section one of the Sherman Act does not permit intra-corporate conspiracies. "A corporation cannot conspire with itself any more than a private individual can, and it is the general rule that the acts of the agent are the acts of the corporation." *Nelson Radio & Supply Co. v. Motorola, Inc.* (5th Cir.1952).

When the defendant is accused of a violation of section one of the Sherman Act, and the conduct is not per se illegal, it is necessary for the government to prove intent. In *United States v. United States Gypsum Co.* (S.Ct.1978), the Supreme Court held that a mens rea is the rule rather than the exception in criminal law. The trial court in *Gypsum* had erred in instructing the jury that "if the effect of the exchanges of pricing information was to raise, fix, maintain, and stabilize prices, then the parties to them are presumed, *as a matter of law*, to have intended that result." The Court found that "action undertaken with knowledge of its probable consequences and having the requisite anticompetitive effects can be a sufficient predicate for a finding of criminal liability under antitrust laws."

If the offense is a per se violation, courts have found that there is no requirement to show that the accused intended to restrain trade. Showing that the defendant knowingly engaged in conduct that violated the law suffices. *United States v. Cargo Service Stations, Inc.* (5th Cir.1981). Agreements to fix prices are unlawful per se under the Sherman Act. *United States v. Socony–Vacuum Oil Co., Inc.* (S.Ct.1940).

CHAPTER FOUR

MAIL, WIRE AND BANK FRAUD

§ 4.01 Introduction

The mail fraud statute was one of 327 sections of the 1872 recodification of the Postal Act. Its initial emphasis was on the misuse of the postal system by way of a counterfeit scheme.

In its infancy there was a disparity of interpretation of this criminal offense with some courts reading the mail fraud statute to include any scheme that misused the postal system while others endorsed a more literal reading. Congress clarified the scope of the offense by providing in 1889 a detailed mail fraud statute that listed all imaginable counterfeit schemes that the framers of the Act could envision. Included within the array of schemes outlawed by this congressional revision were schemes dealing with "green articles," "counterfeit money fraud," and "paper goods."

Durland v. United States (S.Ct.1896) set the tone for future mail fraud cases by interpreting this new act broadly. Mail fraud would include "everything designed to defraud by representations as to the past or present, or suggestions and promises as to the future." *Durland's* holding was followed by a 1909 congressional revision that added to the mail fraud statute the language "or for obtaining money or property by means of false or fraudulent pretenses, representations, or promises."

Today, the crime of mail fraud is located in section 1341 of Title 18 of the United States Code. It requires proof of two elements: (1) a scheme devised or intending to defraud or for obtaining money or property by fraudulent means, and (2) use or causing to use the mails (or private carrier) in furtherance of the fraudulent scheme. Unlike its predecessor, the present day offense does not require that the mails be an essential aspect of the scheme to defraud. A mailing that is "incidental to an essential part of the scheme" (*Pereira v. United States* (S.Ct.1954)) or "one step in the plot" (*Badders v. United States* (S.Ct.1916)) suffices.

Due to the breadth of the statute, as well as its simplicity of proof, mail fraud is extensively used by federal prosecutors. Chief Justice Burger termed mail fraud the "stopgap" provision in his dissenting opinion in *United States v. Maze* (S.Ct.1974), finding that the offense served the purpose of providing criminality to new frauds until particularized legislation could be passed. In reality, however, mail fraud often serves as the charged offense despite the existence of a specific statute that criminalizes the conduct.

The felony of mail fraud carries a penalty of not more than five years imprisonment and a fine. Where the mail fraud affects a financial institution, the allowed penalty is increased to imprisonment of not more than thirty years and a fine of up to one million dollars. Enhanced penalties are also provided when the conduct involves telemarketing fraud. (18 U.S.C. § 2326).

§ 4.02 Scheme to Defraud

The scheme to defraud element of the crime of mail fraud encompasses a myriad of frauds. The ever expanding list includes credit card fraud, divorce mill fraud, franchise fraud, insurance fraud, securities fraud, medical drug fraud and fraud premised upon political malfeasance. Rarely is conduct excluded from the bounds of this element.

The scheme to defraud element is not limited by the common law definition of fraud. Conduct characterized by the deprivation of something of value by "trick, deceit, chicane or overreaching" are encompassed within the terms of the statute. *Hammerschmidt v. United States* (S.Ct.1924). Mail fraud does not, however, criminalize "all sharp conduct, manipulative acts, or unethical transactions." *United States v. Brown* (11th Cir. 1996).

Use of extortion does not equate with conduct included within a scheme to defraud. Thus, in *Fasulo v. United States* (S.Ct.1926), the Supreme Court rejected the use of mail fraud for demands of money by threat and coercion through fear and force. The Court found that a scheme premised upon threats of murder and bodily harm was not a "scheme to defraud."

Implicit within the scheme to defraud element is that the defendant have a fraudulent intent. Courts have varied on the degree of fraudulent intent necessary to support a mail fraud conviction. Some require proof of a specific intent to defraud while others have been satisfied when the defendant acts recklessly or with willful blindness. Irrespective of the standard employed, courts often allow the mens rea to be inferred from the evidence.

An intent to deceive does not, however, always coincide with an intent to defraud. For example, in *United States v. Regent Office Supply Co.* (2d Cir. 1970), the Second Circuit rejected the use of mail fraud premised upon use of false pretenses in the preliminary stages of a sales solicitation. The defendant in *Regent* stipulated that its agents used false pretenses and representations in obtaining access to customers of stationary supplies. Argued, however, was that the price and quality of the merchandise to be sold were being honestly portrayed to the customers. The Second Circuit found that false representations which are "not directed to the quality, adequacy or price of goods to be sold or otherwise to the nature of the bargain," do not form a scheme to defraud. Although actual defrauding is not required for conviction, the government does have to show that "some actual harm or injury was contemplated by the schemer."

In *United States v. D'Amato* (2d Cir.1994), the Second Circuit reversed mail fraud convictions finding insufficient evidence of intent on either a "right to control theory" or a "false pretenses theory."

Rejecting the government's use of "right to control theory," the court stated that "[w]here a third party acting upon instructions from a corporate agent is charged with depriving shareholders of their right to control, the government must prove that the third party knew that the concealment would involve" "(i) information available to shareholders as provided by the state of incorporation's laws providing access to corporate books and records," "(ii) information that, if withheld or inaccurate would result in rendering information that is public materially misleading," or "(iii) information that would materially aid shareholders in enforcing management's fiduciary obligations under state law." The court also rejected a "false pretenses" theory, declining "the government's invitation to infer fraudulent intent on the part of an attorney where the government argued that an attorney accepted a retainer agreement and is subsequently not called upon to perform services that the government or trier of fact deems worth to be paid."

§ 4.03 Intangible Rights

Schemes to defraud premised upon the deprivation of intangible rights surfaced in the 1940s and developed in the 1970s and 1980s. Public officials were charged with the crime of mail fraud for depriving the citizenry of the right to good government and honest services. During this period, mail fraud was not limited to cases where a victim suffered monetary or property loss but included breaches of an owed fiduciary duty. Routinely encompassed within the words "any scheme or artifice to defraud" were political malfeasance that deprived citizens of intangible rights. In addition to political malfeasances, the charge of mail fraud was also used in instances when an employee was alleged to have deprived an employer of honest and faithful services. *United States v. George* (7th Cir. 1973).

McNally v. United States (S.Ct.1987) abruptly halted the use of an intangible rights theory. The Supreme Court reversed mail fraud convictions of three defendants who were convicted for participating in a scheme to defraud the citizens and government of Kentucky of their intangible right to have the Commonwealth's affairs conducted honestly.

Defendant Hunt, then chairperson of the state democratic party had been given de facto control over selecting the insurance agencies from which the state would purchase its policies. Hunt, together with codefendants McNally and Gray, were accused of a scheme that extracted commissions from Kentucky's worker's compensation insurance business into agencies in which the defendants had an interest.

Both the government's charge and the jury's instructions in the *McNally* case did not include language of a deprivation of the Commonwealth's money or property. The essence of the action was the fiduciary duty owed by a public official to the public and the misuse of a public office for private gain.

In reversing the convictions, Justice White stated that while the mail fraud statute protected property rights, it did not encompass the intangible right of the citizenry to good government. Absent congressional clarification, allegations of a deprivation of money or property would be required to meet the scheme to defraud element of the mail fraud statute.

Justice Stevens, joined in parts by Justice O'Connor, offered a heavily footnoted dissent in the *McNally* case. He rejected the narrow construction provided by the majority in defining the term "defraud" as contradicting the construction that the federal courts had consistently given the statute, as well as the meaning provided the term in § 371, the prohibition of conspiracies to "defraud the United States."

In 1988, Congress accepted Justice White's invitation in the *McNally* decision for congressional clarification by enacting 18 U.S.C. § 1346. This new provision, applicable to both mail and wire fraud, defines the term "scheme or artifice to defraud" to include "a scheme or artifice to deprive another of the intangible right of honest services." Although a legislative sponsor of this new provision said that the intent was to restore mail fraud to its pre-*McNally* status, it remains to be seen whether courts will find that § 1346 reaches all of the conduct prosecuted as mail fraud prior to *McNally*. Courts have been reluctant to accept challenges of vagueness of § 1346.

§ 4.04 Intangible Property

Within months of the *McNally* decision, the Supreme Court accepted and decided the case of *Carpenter v. United States* (S.Ct.1987). While *McNally* foreclosed the use of mail fraud premised upon intangible **rights** (absent the congressional redefinition in § 1346), *Carpenter* opened new doors by permitting schemes to defraud based upon intangible **property**.

In *Carpenter*, defendant Winans, a reporter for the Wall Street Journal, authored a highly regarded column that offered information on selected stocks and takeovers. The Wall Street Journal had an official policy and practice that before publication, the contents of the "Heard on the Street" column were the confidential information of the newspaper. Defendant Winans revealed this confidential information to co-conspirators Felis and Brant, stockbrokers, who used the advance information to buy and sell stocks based upon the probable impact of the newspaper articles on the market.

Although the contents of the newspaper articles were not altered to increase the potential profits of the conspirators, Felis and Winans were convicted for mail fraud, wire fraud and securities violations. Defendant Carpenter, a roommate of Winans, was convicted for aiding and abetting.

The Supreme Court unanimously affirmed the mail fraud and wire fraud convictions. Justice White, the author of the opinion, commenced his legal analysis of the case by reaffirming the *McNal-*

ly requirement of a deprivation of money or property for upholding mail and wire fraud convictions. He noted that although mail fraud is limited in its scope to the protection of property rights, there is no requirement that these property rights be tangible. The fiduciary obligation owed by Winans to the Wall Street Journal and the breach of that duty by exploiting the confidential business information for a personal benefit, resulted in a scheme to defraud of intangible property.

Carpenter therefore serves to reinforce *McNally's* holding requiring that a charge of mail fraud include a deprivation of "money or property" as opposed to intangible **rights**. It also, however, extends its reach to include both tangible and intangible **property**. In deciding whether a business license is property, several theories have been used by courts with differing results.

§ 4.05   Use of the Mails in Furtherance

Besides the crime of mail fraud requiring a scheme to defraud, it is also necessary that the mails be used in furtherance of the fraudulent scheme. This second element of the offense of mail fraud requires (a) a mailing, (b) by the defendant or caused to be mailed by the defendant, (c) in furtherance of a scheme to defraud.

Historically, the use of the United States Postal System was the jurisdictional object that brought the fraudulent conduct within the bounds of a federal statute. The statute, however, was amended in 1994 to include the language "or deposits or caused to be deposited any matter or thing whatever to be sent or delivered by any private or commercial interstate carrier." Items sent using Federal Express, UPS, or similar carriers may now be subject to prosecution under the mail fraud statute.

It is unnecessary, however, for the defendant to have personally sent a letter. Use of an agent can suffice. In *Pereira v. United States* (S.Ct.1954), the Supreme Court set forth the test to decide whether the defendant had caused the mails to be used. The Court held that "where one does an act with knowledge that the use of the mails will follow in the ordinary course of business, or where such use can reasonably be foreseen, even though not actually intended, then he 'causes' the mails to be used."

In addition to a mailing by the defendant, or caused to be mailed by the defendant, it is also necessary that there be a nexus between the scheme to defraud and the mailing. This is reflected in the requirement that the mailing be "in furtherance" of the scheme to defraud. This latter subpart has been the subject of several controversies presented to courts.

§ 4.06 Limitations to "In Furtherance"

Historically, cases reflected four legal limitations to a mailing being in furtherance of a scheme to defraud. Mailings which conflicted with the scheme, were an imperative command of duty imposed by the state, occurred prior to commencement of the scheme, or occurred after fruition of the scheme, were found not to be in furtherance of the scheme to defraud.

In *United States v. Maze* (S.Ct.1974), the defendant's conviction for mail fraud was reversed in that the mailings were "not sufficiently closely related to the respondent's scheme to bring his conduct within the statute." The defendant was alleged to have stolen his roommate's credit card and used the card for the purchase of food and lodging in his travels to various states. The four counts of mail fraud were based upon the merchant's mailing of the sales slips of purchase to the bank issuing the credit card.

In *Maze*, the Supreme Court rejected the use of mail fraud, finding that the mailing of the credit card slips conflicted with the defendant's purpose and that the mailing occurred after fruition of the scheme to defraud. As a result of *Maze*, mailings that aid in the detection of the fraud or are counterproductive to the scheme to defraud are considered as not within the legal limits of being "in furtherance" of the scheme to defraud.

In *Parr v. United States* (S.Ct.1960), the Supreme Court rejected the use of mail fraud as not being in furtherance of the scheme to defraud because the mailings were an imperative duty to the state. Also alleged was that the mailings in *Parr* were after the scheme to defraud had reached fruition. The twenty count indictment for mail fraud and conspiracy to commit mail fraud in *Parr* was based upon defendant's alleged scheme to defraud a school district of money through misappropriation and embezzlement. The mailings included letters for the assessment and collection of school taxes. The Court rejected the use of mail fraud stating that mailings "under the imperative command of duty imposed by state law" are not criminal for the purposes of mail fraud "even though some of those who are so required to do the mailing for the District plan to steal."

It is rare that courts have supported the legal duty limitation to the "in furtherance" aspect of mail fraud, as enunciated in *Parr*, when there has been no showing of the mailing being dispatched after completion of the scheme to defraud. Thus, charges of mail fraud for the mailing of fraudulent tax returns are for the most part not barred by the "legal duty" limitation.

Mailings prior to commencement of the scheme or after fruition of the scheme, were recognized by courts as not in furtherance of the scheme to defraud. In *United States v. Beall* (N.D.Cal.1954), the Northern District of California Court found mailings of a fund raising campaign for the Infantile Paralysis Foundation to be a part of a lawful fund raising effort. A later misappropriation of the money was therefore embezzlement and not mail fraud. In that the mailing was prior to any fraud, it was not in furtherance of the scheme to defraud.

Kann v. United States (S.Ct.1944) showed the Supreme Court's initial adoption of an after-the-fact mailing not being in furtherance of the scheme to defraud. Defendant Kann, president of a corporation that manufactured munitions, was indicted with fellow workers for allegedly divesting company funds on government contracts for their personal benefit. The mailings that formed the basis of the charges were checks cashed by defendants that were presented to the drawee banks for purposes of collection. The nexus between the mailing and the scheme to defraud was lacking in that the scheme was completed at the time of the mailing.

Like *Kann*, the mailings in *Parr* and *Maze* were also mailings to collect on funds. In all these cases, the scheme had reached fruition and thus the mailings were immaterial to defendants' continuation of the scheme to defraud. *Kann, Parr,* and *Maze* contained forceful dissents by justices of the Supreme Court.

A recognized exception to after the fact mailings being considered "in furtherance" of the scheme is where the mailings serve to "lull" the victims into the defendant's scheme. *United States v. Sampson* (S.Ct.1962). In *United States v. Lane* (S.Ct.1986), the Supreme Court rejected respondent's claim that there was insufficient evidence to support mail fraud convictions based upon insurance claims mailed after fruition of the scheme to defraud. In referring to *Sampson*, the *Lane* Court concluded that the after-the-scheme mailings met the "in furtherance" element in that they "were designed to lull the victims into a false sense of security."

§ 4.07 The New "In Furtherance" Test

In 1989 the Supreme Court in *Schmuck v. United States* (S.Ct.1989) enunciated a new test for determining whether a mailing was in furtherance of a scheme to defraud. The Court stated that a mailing is in furtherance if it "is part of the execution of the scheme as conceived by the perpetrator at the time."

In *Schmuck*, the defendant was convicted of twelve counts of mail fraud in a scheme of selling automobile dealers vehicles with rolled back odometers at prices artificially inflated as a result of the altered low-mileage. The mailings were twelve title applications submitted by the automobile dealers on behalf of their customers to the Wisconsin Department of Transportation.

The Supreme Court, in addition to rejecting defendant's argument that he was entitled to have the jury instructed on the lesser charge of odometer tampering, also rejected defendant's claim that the mailings were not in furtherance of the scheme to defraud.

Justice Blackmun, writing the opinion for the majority noted that the use of the mails need not be an essential element of the scheme. It is, likewise, irrelevant if it is later shown that the mailings were counterproductive to the scheme. Unlike *Kann, Parr,* and *Maze*, the mailings did not resemble postfraud accounting. The Court found that the evidence in the *Schmuck* case supported a rational finding that the mailing was part of the execution as conceived by the defendant at the time. The title application was essential to the successful passage of title to the customers and thus to the continuity of the scheme. A failure in the passage of title would have jeopardized the defendant's "trust and goodwill with the retail dealers upon whose unwitting cooperation" the scheme depended.

A four person dissent criticized the majority in *Schmuck* for discarding precedent and for making mail fraud into a crime of "mail" and "fraud" as opposed to mailings that are in furtherance of the fraud. Whether the decision will create "problems for tomorrow," as predicted by the dissenters, remains to be seen. Likewise uncertain, is the viability of the four limitations to in furtherance previously recognized by courts.

§ 4.08 Wire Fraud

The wire fraud statute, 18 U.S.C. § 1343, was passed in 1952 and operates parallel to mail fraud. Like mail fraud, the emphasis of the crime is on the scheme to defraud as opposed to the means used in effectuating the deception. Wire fraud does, however, require a transmittal in interstate or foreign commerce by means of wire, radio, or television communication of writings, signs, signals, pictures or sounds.

Although there is a requirement of an interstate transmission, there is no requirement that the defendant know or foresee of the transmission going interstate. In *United States v. Bryant* (8th Cir. 1985), defendants sent two telegrams from Kansas

City, Missouri to Bridgetown, Missouri. The telegrams, however, were routed through Middletown,
Virginia. The Eighth Circuit affirmed the defendants' convictions for wire fraud finding that the
defendant need not know or foresee that the communication would be interstate. The necessity for
an interstate transmittal is merely a jurisdictional
requirement to satisfy the constitutional limitation
on congressional acts over intrastate activities pursuant to the Commerce Clause of the United States
Constitution.

§ 4.09   Bank Fraud

In response to the increase in financial frauds,
Congress in 1984 passed the bank fraud statute (18
U.S.C. § 1344). This statute criminalizes the conduct of one who "knowingly executes, or attempts
to execute, a scheme or artifice to defraud a financial institution, or to obtain ... property owned by,
or under the custody or control of, a financial
institution, by means of false or fraudulent pretenses, representations, or promises." Like mail
fraud's provision relative to financial institutions,
bank fraud today carries a penalty of up to thirty
years imprisonment and a maximum fine of one
million dollars.

The term "scheme to defraud" mirrors the term
as seen in the mail and wire fraud statutes. In
interpreting this element in the context of bank
fraud, a court remarked that a scheme to defraud is
incapable of precise definition. It requires case by
case analysis to determine whether the scheme

demonstrates a "departure from fundamental honesty, moral uprightness, or fair play and candid dealings in the general life of the community." *United States v. Goldblatt* (3d Cir.1987). In some cases, check kiting has been found to be a scheme to defraud that can be prosecuted as bank fraud. Courts have not, however, ruled consistently on whether the term "execute" should be interpreted to refer to the entire series of acts or whether multiple counts for each act can be charged.

Where money is legally withdrawn from a bank by victims of a confidence scheme, the bank fraud statute was held to be inapplicable. Despite the existence of a scheme to defraud, the Second Circuit found no violation of section 1344. "Where the victim is not a bank and the fraud does not threaten the financial integrity of a federally controlled or insured bank, there seems no basis in the legislative history for finding coverage under section 1344(a)(2)." *United States v. Blackmon* (2d Cir. 1988). It is not, however, necessary that the financial institution actually suffer a loss.

§ 4.10 Mail Fraud and Other Crimes

Mail fraud is often used in place of or in conjunction with a statute that is specifically tailored to meet the prohibited conduct. It is rare that courts find that it inappropriate to use mail fraud in these scenarios.

For example, in *United States v. Computer Sciences Corp.* (4th Cir.1982), the Fourth Circuit concluded that the district court had erred in dismissing mail and wire fraud charges being prosecuted in conjunction with a charge pursuant to the false claims statute (18 U.S.C. § 287). The court found no language in the statutes that revealed "mutual exclusivity insofar as the prosecution is concerned."

Mail fraud is used in cases where the crimes could be prosecuted under the Bankruptcy Act, Landum–Griffin Act, Jenkins Act, National Stolen Property Act, Truth in Lending Act and the Federal Trade Commission Act. Mail fraud is often an alternative to a securities violation. In *Edwards v. United States* (S.Ct.1941) the Supreme Court rejected the argument that securities laws preempt the use of the mail fraud statute. The Court noted that "[t]he two can exist and be useful, side by side."

A rare instance of finding the use of mail fraud as overcharging by a prosecutor is seen in the case of *United States v. Henderson* (S.D.N.Y.1974). This 1974 decision of the United States District Court of the Southern District of New York involved charges of attempted evasion of taxes and mail fraud for the mailing of the tax returns. The court rejected the joint charges as a "pyramiding of sentences" that was "utterly unrealistic." Use of mail fraud to reach the same conduct prohibited by the Internal Revenue Code was found to be "beyond the intent of Congress."

The *Henderson* court view has been rejected by the majority of courts deciding issues of a similar nature. The Department of Justice did, however, recently add a guideline requiring department approval prior to bringing a mail fraud prosecution that is premised upon mailed tax returns. This guideline provides that authorization for this type of prosecution will only be granted in exceptional circumstances.

Mail fraud has historically been one of several statutes used to prosecute health care fraud. Recently, Congress enacted 18 U.S.C. § 1347, a statute which specifically targets health care fraud. The statute includes the same "scheme or artifice" language found in mail, wire, and bank fraud. It provides for imprisonment of up to ten years, imprisonment of up to twenty years if the violation results in serious bodily injury, and a term of years or life if the violation results in death.

CHAPTER FIVE
SECURITIES FRAUD

§ 5.01 Introduction

An overlap between civil and criminal law is apparent in examining cases involving securities fraud. An individual violating securities statutes can be subject to civil and administrative proceedings, criminal prosecution, or dual civil and criminal actions (see chap. 18). The Supreme Court, however, recently held in *Central Bank of Denver v. First Interstate Bank of Denver* (S.Ct.1994), that a private plaintiff could not use 18 U.S.C. § 2, the aiding and abetting statute, as the basis of their suit under § 10(b) of the Securities Exchange Act. To sustain a criminal prosecution it is necessary that the accused acted willfully.

Securities violations are typically investigated by the Securities and Exchange Commission (SEC). Most often criminal prosecutions arise when the SEC refers the matter to the Department of Justice for criminal prosecution. (15 U.S.C. § 78 u(d)). Selective enforcement of violations occurs both in the referring of matters to the Department of Justice and in their decision of whether to prosecute.

Although securities violations may arise under an array of federal acts, most often prosecutions under securities law emanate from the Securities Act of 1933 and the Securities Exchange Act of 1934. These acts are found in Title 15 of the United States Code.

Section 24 of the Securities Act of 1933 (15 U.S.C. § 77x) provides criminality to willful violations of provisions under the Act or rules and regulations of the Commission. It also prohibits, in a registration statement filed under the Act, the making of any untrue statement of material fact or omitting to state any material fact required to be stated or necessary so as to keep a statement from being misleading. This felony offense authorizes a fine and imprisonment up to five years.

The Securities Exchange Act of 1934, likewise, provides criminality to willful violations of the civil provisions of the Act. A willful violation of a provision of this Act, or rule or regulation thereunder, can result in criminal penalties. Additionally, false or misleading statements of material facts made willfully and knowing in "any application, report, or document required to be filed" by the Act are subject to criminal prosecution. Amendments to the Securities Exchange Act of 1934 authorize stiffer penalties than its predecessor, permitting fines up to one million dollars and imprisonment up to ten years. In the case of persons other than natural persons, the fine may be increased to two million five hundred thousand dollars. The authorized term of imprisonment cannot be imposed if the defendants prove that they had no knowledge of the rule or regulation violated. The penalty provision also differs for a violation of 15 U.S.C. § 78dd–1, the statute pertaining to the prohibited foreign trade practices by issuers.

Prosecutions of securities fraud have concentrated on violations of section 17(a) of the Securities Act of 1933 and section 10(b) of the Securities Exchange Act of 1934 and its accompanying Rule 10b–5. In recent years, prosecutions under these provisions have been the subject of significant publicity with increased government investigations into insider trading. Legislative response to insider trading is seen in the passage of two congressional acts. The Insider Trading Sanctions Act (ITSA) and the Insider Trading and Securities Fraud Enforcement Act (ITSFEA) include provisions that increase the penalties to individuals engaged in improper insider trading.

Other securities sections have also served as the basis of a criminal prosecution. For example, prosecutions have been brought under section 5 of the Securities Act of 1933 for failure to register the sale of securities. Failure to file reports or the filing of false reports are among the prosecutions brought under the Securities Exchange Act of 1934.

Securities fraud, however, has not been exclusively prosecuted under these specific securities statutes. The government uses general criminal provisions, often in conjunction with violations of the Securities Exchange Act, to combat this criminality. For example, when there is a scheme to defraud coupled with a mailing in furtherance of the scheme, mail fraud has been included by prosecutors. Other general criminal statutes that have been employed include wire fraud, false statements, perjury, obstruction of justice, interstate transportation of stolen property, and conspiracy to commit an offense against the United States or to defraud the United States.

§ 5.02 Mens Rea

Willfulness is necessary for a criminal prosecution under the Securities Act and Securities Exchange Act. This mens rea precludes prosecutions when the accused acted through mistake, excusable neglect, or inadvertence. Acts that are deliberate and intentional have been found sufficient to meet the willfulness requirement. Although willfulness does not necessitate that the defendant be aware of the applicable statute or rule, some circuits require that the prosecutor establish "a realization on the defendant's part that he was doing a wrongful act." *United States v. Peltz* (2d Cir.1970).

Although most courts find mere negligent conduct insufficient, reckless indifference has been found to be an intentional misrepresentation. Courts have found it proper to charge a jury "that the specific intent to deceive may be found from a material misrepresentation of fact made with reckless disregard of the facts." *United States v. Boyer* (3d Cir.1982).

One who acts with willful blindness can also be found culpable. When a person standing in a position of authority takes a "hands off" position, it has been found proper for the court to give a "conscious avoidance" instruction. *United States v. Langford* (11th Cir.1991).

Usually willfulness is proven through circumstantial evidence. A jury may infer this intent from the evidence presented. The experience and intellect of the accused, as well as the cumulative effect of all the evidence presented, have been factors used in supporting a jury determination of willfulness. *United States v. White* (2d Cir.1941).

In *United States v. Weiner* (9th Cir.1978), the Ninth Circuit upheld securities convictions entered against auditors of Equity Funding Corporation of America. Defendants argued that they were victims of the fraud perpetrated by Equity Funding officers. In finding sufficient evidence to support these convictions, the court noted the lack of backup documentation to support entries. The court found that either the auditors failed to follow accepted auditing standards or that they cooperated with Equity Funding officials. The amount of fraud involved and the lengthy time period over which it extended could lead to the conclusion that the defendants "were totally inept or, more likely, were at least partly aware of the false inflation of Equity Funding's accounts." The instruction given in *Weiner* advised the jury that good faith constituted a complete defense.

A defendant who asserts a defense premised upon good faith opens themselves to cross-examination as to the basis for their understanding that their actions were legal. In *United States v. Bilzerian* (2d Cir.1991), the defendant made a motion in limine requesting that he be permitted to testify at trial as to his good faith belief in the lawfulness of his conduct, without being subjected to cross-examination on communications with his attorney. The Second Circuit upheld the trial court's declining to rule on the motion in limine in the abstract, finding that the judge's ruling did not preclude the defendant from denying criminal intent and from arguing a good faith defense in opening and closing statements and through the examination of witnesses. The appellate court in *Bilzerian* noted that it lacked a specific factual basis to determine prejudice to the defendant in that he chose not to testify and thus, no privileged communications were admitted into evidence.

A person can be found culpable for willfully violating a statute, rule, or regulation of the Securities Act of 1933 and Securities Exchange Act of 1934 absent knowledge of the existence of the applicable statute, rule, or regulation. Knowledge, however, is required under the Securities Exchange Act of 1934 when the criminal charge is premised upon a false or misleading statement of any material fact in any application, report, or document required to be filed under the Act. *United States v. Dixon* (2d Cir.1976). Thus, the government must prove that the accused acted both willfully and knowingly when proceeding under the second clause of section 32(a) of the Securities Exchange Act of 1934.

When a defendant, convicted under the Securities Exchange Act of 1934, has no knowledge of the violated rule or regulation, the court is precluded by statute from entering a sentence of imprisonment. The defendant, however, has the burden to demonstrate a lack of knowledge. Since the no knowledge proviso is directed toward sentencing, it has been found not to place an unconstitutional burden on the defendant to disprove an element of the offense. *United States v. Mandel* (S.D.N.Y.1969).

A defendant, who plead guilty to a violation of Rule 10b–5, was precluded from obtaining the benefits of the no knowledge proviso in *United States v. Lilley* (S.D.Tex.1968). The court found that the "no knowledge" clause meant that the accused had no knowledge that their conduct was contrary to law. The court stated that it does not mean that the defendant did not know "the precise number or common name of the rule, the book and page where it was to be found, or the date upon which it was promulgated. It does not even mean proof of a lack of knowledge that their conduct was proscribed by rule rather than by statute." The court found that by pleading guilty to securities fraud, the "defendants admitted that they knew securities fraud was prohibited, which is the substance of Rule 10b–5. No more knowledge is required."

§ 5.03 Insider Trading

There is an "expectation of the securities marketplace that all investors trading on impersonal exchanges have relatively equal access to material information." *Securities and Exchange Commission v. Texas Gulf Sulpher Co.* (2d Cir.1968). Insider trading, although not specifically defined by any statute, arises when an insider, with material nonpublic information, trades in securities without first disclosing the material inside information to the public. Issues arise as who is an insider and when it is necessary to disclose nonpublic information. Issues can also arise as to whether the information is material.

Insider trading prosecutions have been at the forefront of white collar crime cases. Investment bankers, lawyers, arbitragers, and financial executives have been among the many that have been indicted and convicted for violations of securities laws. In many instances the individuals reached plea agreements that required government cooperation in further investigations. Significant publicity has surrounded many of the insider trading cases.

Insider trading cases are usually prosecuted under section 10(b) of the Securities Exchange Act of 1934 and its accompanying Rule 10b–5. The government has the burden of proving that the accused willfully employed a scheme to defraud, or misrepresented or failed to disclose a material fact, or engaged in a course of business which operated as a fraud, in connection with the purchase or sale of any security. *United States v. Koenig* (S.D.N.Y. 1974). Federal jurisdiction is attained by showing that the accused used a means or instrumentality of interstate commerce, the mails, or any facility of any national securities exchange.

In *Chiarella v. United States* (S.Ct.1980), the Supreme Court reversed a criminal conviction that was predicated on a violation of Rule 10b–5. Petitioner Chiarella worked as a "markup man" for a financial printer engaged in the printing of announcements of corporate takeover bids. Although the documents delivered to the printer did not initially disclose the names of the target companies, petitioner deduced this information and purchased stock in the target companies prior to this information being disclosed to the public. Chiarella's profits from the purchase and sale of these stocks exceeded thirty thousand dollars.

Justice Powell, writing the opinion for the majority, examined the effect of silence on the part of a person holding nonpublic market information. The Court reaffirmed the position taken in the Securities and Exchange Commission case of *Cady, Roberts & Co.* (1961), which held that a corporate insider must abstain from trading in the shares of the corporation unless the corporate insider has first disclosed all known material inside information. The obligation to disclose, however, rested upon one having the affirmative "duty to disclose arising from a relationship of trust and confidence between parties to a transaction."

Distinguishing petitioner's conduct from this precedent, the Court noted that Chiarella was not a corporate insider and that he had not received confidential information from the target company. The Court found error that the trial court "[i]n effect ... instructed the jury that petitioner owed a duty to everyone; to all sellers, indeed, to the market as a whole." Not being an agent, fiduciary, or person in whom the sellers had placed their trust and confidence petitioner did not have a duty to disclose. To hold otherwise, the Court believed would create a "general duty between all participants in market transactions to forego actions based on material, nonpublic information."

The Court in *Chiarella* refused to speculate on what duty may be owed to anyone other than the seller, in that the issue had not been submitted to the jury. The dissenting opinions, however, addressed this second question finding that the jury instructions properly charged a violation of Section 10(b) and Rule 10b–5. Chief Justice Burger, in his dissenting opinion, expressed the view that Chiarella had "misappropriated—stole to put it bluntly— valuable nonpublic information entrusted to him in the utmost confidence."

The Court expounded upon the ramifications of the disclosure of information in the case of *Dirks v. Securities and Exchange Commission* (S.Ct.1983). Dirks, a securities analyst, received inside information from a former officer of Equity Funding of America. This information, of alleged overstatement of assets by the company as a result of fraudulent corporate practices, was given to Dirks for the purpose of verification and disclosure to the public. Dirks received a censure from the SEC for disclosure of this inside information to clients and investors. The SEC took the position that a tippee "inherits" the duty to disclose the information or abstain whenever the tippee receives the information from an insider. By passing the information to traders the SEC found that Dirks had breached this fiduciary duty.

In reversing the SEC position, that had been upheld by the lower courts, the Supreme Court in a 6–3 decision found that Dirks had no duty to abstain from using this information. Justice Powell, writing the majority opinion, found that "[t]he tippers received no monetary or personal benefit for revealing Equity Funding's secrets, nor was their purpose to make a gift of valuable information to Dirks." Since the motivation was the exposure of the fraud, the Court found no breach of duty to shareholders by the insider. Absent a breach of duty by the insider, there was no derivative breach by Dirks.

§ 5.04 Development of the Misappropriation Theory

In both *Chiarella* and *Dirks* the Court concentrated on the duty owed to shareholders by an insider and by individuals receiving information from the insider. Absent a duty owed, the Court was not willing to extend insider trading liability. Some appellate courts, however, permitted the bounds of insider trading to be extended through the use of a misappropriation theory.

The doctrine of misappropriation arose in Chief Justice Burger's dissenting opinion in the *Chiarella* case. He expressed the view "that a person who has misappropriated nonpublic information has an absolute duty to disclose that information or to refrain from trading." In *United States v. Newman* (2d Cir.1981), the Second Circuit accepted and applied this misappropriation theory. Newman was accused of participating in a scheme to misappropriate confidential information regarding upcoming tender offers. He, along with two co-conspirators, employees of two investment banking firms, were alleged to have gathered and traded on nonpublic information.

The prosecution's indictment in the *Newman* case focused on the issue unresolved in *Chiarella*, that being, duties owed to persons other than the sellers. The government's case specifically rested upon a duty allegedly owing to the defendant's employers and their employers' clients. The court in *Newman* reversed the district court's dismissal of the indictment, finding that Rule 10b–5 contained "no specific requirement that fraud be perpetrated upon the seller or buyer of securities." The court noted that in other areas of the law, deceitful misappropriation of confidential information by a fiduciary, was considered a crime. The court found that this same standard should be applied to conduct under the Securities Acts.

The tenuous status of the misappropriation theory was highlighted by the fact that the *Newman* case was not a unanimous decision. A concurring and dissenting opinion, written by Senior District Judge Dumbauld, noted that "[t]he culprits in the case at bar (as in *Chiarella*) owed no duty to the sellers of the target company securities which they purchased." Despite the deceptive and improper violation of a fiduciary duty to employers and customers of the employers, Judge Dumbauld stated that these parties had not at the time actually purchased or sold any target securities.

Later decisions in the second circuit, however, affirmed the use of the misappropriation theory in the context of an employee misappropriating confidential information. In *Securities and Exchange Commission v. Materia* (2d Cir.1984), the Second Circuit affirmed an injunction and disgorgement of unlawfully obtained profits where an employee of a printing company misappropriated confidential information concerning tender offers and subsequently traded on the information. The court found that the misappropriation of material nonpublic information by an employee, perpetrated a fraud upon the employer that was prohibited by the antifraud provisions of the Securities Exchange Act of 1934.

In *United States v. Carpenter* (2d Cir.1986), the Second Circuit revisited the misappropriation theory in the context of convictions of a newspaper reporter, former newspaper clerk, and stockbroker for violations of section 10(b) of the Securities Exchange Act of 1934 and Rule 10b–5. The Supreme Court accepted certiorari on this case but affirmed the securities violations by an equally divided court. Defendants' convictions for mail and wire fraud were unanimously affirmed in a landmark Supreme Court case that held that the "money or property" clause of the mail fraud statute included both tangible and intangible property (see chap. 4).

In affirming the district court's judgment of conviction on the securities fraud counts, the Second Circuit in *Carpenter* examined the misappropriation theory as applied to an insider trading scheme that misappropriated information from the Wall Street Journal prior to its publication. Although *Newman* and *Materia* involved corporate clients of the employer, the court found that the misappropriation theory "broadly proscribes the conversion by 'insiders' or *others* of material non-public information in connection with the purchase or sale of securities."

The Supreme Court directly addressed and endorsed the misappropriation theory in its recent decision in *United States v. O'Hagan* (S.Ct. 1997). Justice Ginsberg's majority opinion initially distinguishes the "classical theory" from the "misappropriation theory." "The classical theory targets a corporate insider's breach of duty to shareholders with whom the insider transacts, and the misappropriation theory outlaws trading on the basis of nonpublic information by a corporate 'outsider' in breach of a duty owed not to a trading party, but to the source of the information." "In lieu of premising liability on a fiduciary relationship between company insider and purchaser or seller of the company's stock, the misappropriation theory premises liability on a fiduciary turned trader's deception of those who entrusted him with access to confidential information."

Finding "deception" through nondisclosure "central" to a misappropriation theory, the Court noted "if the fiduciary discloses to the source that he plans to trade on the nonpublic information, there is no 'deceptive device' and thus no § 10(b) violation—although the fiduciary turned trader may remain liable under state law for breach of a duty of loyalty." The Court also noted that the element "in connection with the purchase or sale of [a] security" is met "because the fiduciary's fraud is consummated, not when the fiduciary gains the confidential information, but when without disclosure to his principle, he uses the information to purchase or sell securities." *United States v. O'Hagan* (S.Ct. 1997).

CHAPTER SIX

OBSTRUCTION OF JUSTICE

§ 6.01 Introduction

Most of the obstruction of justice offenses are found in chapter 73 of Title 18. Here one finds a conglomerate of specific statutes that protect proceedings in the three branches of government in addition to the individuals connected with these proceedings. There has been a growth and restructuring of these offenses in recent years to increase the protection afforded witnesses, victims, and informants as well as provide smoother federal audits and examinations of financial institutions.

The breadth of protection provided by the obstruction of justice statutes in chapter 73 is seen by examining these specific offenses. Criminalized by specific statutes are obstructive conduct involving an assault on a process server (§ 1501), resistance to an extradition agent (§ 1502), influencing a juror through a writing (§ 1504), theft or alteration of a record or process (§ 1506), picketing, parading, using sound equipment, or demonstrating in or near a courthouse or "a building or residence occupied or used by such judge, juror, witness, or court officer" (§ 1507), "[r]ecording, listening to, or observing proceedings of grand or petit juries while [they are] deliberating or voting" (§ 1508), obstruction relating to court orders (§ 1509), and obstruction pertaining to state and local law enforcement (§ 1511).

Section 1503 has historically served as the focal point of the obstruction charges. Although its original protection was for officers, jurors, and witnesses, the passage of the Victim and Witness Protection Act in 1982 transferred the specific reference to witnesses in section 1503 into new provisions of this chapter. Despite the elimination in section 1503's language of obstruction against witnesses, the section remains a noteworthy provision in that it contains an omnibus clause that prohibits obstruction of the "due administration of justice."

The Victim and Witness Protection Act also modified section 1505. This section pertains to obstruction under the Antitrust Civil Process Act and proceedings before departments, agencies, and committees of the government. This section plays a crucial role in the prosecution of obstructions related to proceedings before Congress and federal agencies. In *United States v. Poindexter* (D.C.Cir. 1991), the District of Columbia held the term "corruptly," as used in section 1505, to be "too vague to provide constitutionally adequate notice that it prohibits lying to the Congress." The court stated that, "neither the legislative history nor the prior judicial interpretation of § 1505 supplies the constitutionally required notice that the statute on its face lacks." Recently Congress added a new provision stating that the term "corruptly" as used in

§ 1505 "means acting with an improper purpose, personally or by influencing another, including making a false or misleading statement, or withholding, concealing, altering, or destroying a document or other information." (18 U.S.C. § 1515(b)).

Originally, section 1505 criminalized obstructive conduct directed against both witnesses and parties. As a result of the Victim and Witness Protection Act, witnesses and parties are now incorporated into the new obstruction statutes. Untouched by the 1982 amendment, however, is the omnibus clause of section 1505 that protects "the due and proper administration of the law under which any pending proceeding is being had before any department or agency of the United States."

Two of the new provisions created by the Victim and Witness Protection Act, sections 1512 and 1513, heighten the scrutiny provided to obstruction involving witnesses, victims, and informants. Section 1512, a section that was modified in 1986 and again in 1988, criminalizes conduct that uses intimidation, physical force, or threats, or conduct that involves corruptly persuading another person to withhold testimony, destroy objects of an official proceeding, evade legal process, or be absent from an official proceeding. This section includes conduct involving attempts to kill and actual killing of a person to prevent that individual from testifying, producing evidence, or communicating information about the commission of a crime or a violation of probation, parole, or release.

Congress made the statute applicable to incidents within the United States, as well as providing extra-territorial federal jurisdiction. Additionally, the government is given discretion to bring an action for violation of this section in either the district of the official proceeding, or alternatively, the location where the alleged offense occurred.

Where section 1512 concentrates on obstruction prior to a proceeding, section 1513 focuses on retaliation against witnesses, victims, and informants. Section 1513 prohibits conduct that causes or threatens to cause "bodily injury to another person" as retaliation for being a witness, providing evidence in an official proceeding, or giving information relating to an offense to a law enforcement officer. Section 1513 also applies to acts both inside and outside the United States.

Also added to the obstruction offenses by the Victim and Witness Protection Act of 1982 is a provision that permits a government attorney to bring a civil action to restrain harassment of a victim or witness. (§ 1514). This section provides for a temporary restraining order and issuance of protective order where "there are reasonable grounds to believe that harassment of an identified victim or witness in a Federal criminal case exists or that such an order is necessary to prevent and restrain an offense under section 1512 of this title, other than an offense consisting of misleading conduct, or under section 1513 of this title."

The statutory language used in sections 1512 and 1513 is defined in section 1515. This section was also added as a result of the passage of the Victim and Witness Protection Act.

Another key provision for the government's prosecution of obstructive conduct is found in section 1510 of title 18. This section prohibits obstruction of criminal investigations by means of bribery. In 1989 Congress expanded the reach of section 1510 to specifically criminalize obstruction of criminal investigations by officers of financial institutions. The section also criminalizes obstruction by those involved in the business of insurance.

This recent focus on financial criminality is reflected not only in section 1510, but also by the addition of two recent obstruction statutes. In 1988, Congress added section 1516, a provision criminalizing obstruction of a federal audit and, in 1990, section 1517 was added making it a criminal offense to obstruct the examination of a financial institution. The recent focus on health care fraud is reflected in the addition of section 1518, a section relating to obstruction of criminal investigations of health care offenses.

Penalties for obstruction of justice vary dependent upon the specific statutory offense employed. A maximum term of imprisonment of six months is provided for violation of section 1504, the statute relating to influencing a juror through use of a writing. Some obstruction of justice offenses are misdemeanors carrying a maximum term of imprisonment of one year (§§ 1501, 1502, 1507, 1508, 1509, 1510(b)(2) and 1512(c)). Other obstruction of justice statutes found within the chapter are felonies carrying a maximum term of five years imprisonment. (§§ 1505, 1506, 1510(a), 1510(b)(1), 1510(d), 1516, 1517 and 1518). The obstruction of justice statutes also permit a court to impose fines.

Penalties for portions of the statutes added by the Victim and Witness Protection Act demonstrate the emphasis Congress intended in this realm. Retaliation offenses pursuant to section 1513 and use of intimidation or physical force, threats or corrupt persuasion as identified in section 1512(b) carry imprisonment of not more than ten years. The maximum penalty under these provisions of sections 1512 and 1513 is increased to twenty years when there is an attempt to kill a witness, victim or informant. (§ 1512(a)(2)(B)). An actual killing can result in a sentence of death. Recently added to §§ 1512 and 1513 are provisions permitting an increase in the maximum sentence to be imposed for jury and witness retaliation and tampering so that it is equivalent to the maximum penalty for the crime being tried in the case that was the object of the obstruction.

Recently, Congress also amended the penalty provisions § 1503, increasing the basic sentence to ten years, with imprisonment of up to twenty years in the case of an attempted killing or where the offense is against a petit jury and a class A or B felony has been charged. An actual killing can result in a sentence of death. Where the offense "occurs in connection with a trial of a criminal case, and the act in violation of this section involves the threat of physical force or physical force, the maximum term of imprisonment which may be imposed for the offense shall be the higher of that otherwise provided by law or the maximum term that could have been imposed for any offense charged in such case."

§ 6.02   Overview of Section 1503

Section 1503 of Title 18 is a contempt statute emanating from the Act of March 2, 1831. Section one of the Act of 1831 pertained to contemptuous conduct occurring in the presence of the court. Section two of this act focused on conduct away from the court. This predecessor statute was eventually split into two distinct offenses with 18 U.S.C. § 401 being obstruction in the court's presence and 18 U.S.C. § 1503 being obstruction away from the court. *United States v. Essex* (1969).

Section 1503 originally served as the focus of obstruction offenses for obstructive acts against witnesses, parties, jurors, or court officers. The Victim and Witness Protection Act removed witnesses and parties from the language of section 1503 making the specific emphasis of the statute on acts occurring against grand and petit jurors and judicial officers. The Victim and Witness Protection Act did not, however, modify the catch-all clause of section 1503 that prohibits obstruction of the "due administration of justice." Thus, today, section 1503 can be divided into two categories; (a) acts of obstruction to jurors or court officers, and (b) obstruction of the "due administration of justice."

Acts of obstruction against jurors or court officers includes **threats or force** that endeavor to "influence, intimidate, or impede any grand or petit juror" or court officer in the discharge of their duties or alternatively, acts of obstruction that **injure** jurors or court officers. "Jurors" has been interpreted to include prospective jurors, and federal district court judges have been found to be included within the category of "officer[s] in or of any court."

The most noteworthy aspect of section 1503 still remains the omnibus clause that covers conduct impeding the "due administration of justice." In order to sustain a conviction under the omnibus clause of section 1503 the government must show that the accused (1) "corruptly or by threats or force," (2) endeavored, (3) "to influence, obstruct, or impede, the due administration of justice." These elements are not always distinct entities, but are often intertwined, with the same evidence being sufficient to meet several aspects of the offense.

§ 6.03 Corruptly or by Threats or Force— Section 1503

Section 1503 requires that the defendant engage in conduct "corruptly, or by threats or force, or by any threatening letter or communication." Courts have generally interpreted these provisions in the alternative finding it only necessary for the government to have evidence of either the accused acting "corruptly" or using some type of "threats or force."

Controversy has existed as to the level of proof required to meet the statutory requisite of "corruptly." Some courts find the term "corruptly" not to be an element of the offense that necessitates specific proof. It can be met by a showing of any attempt to influence a juror or court officer. For example in *United States v. Ogle* (10th Cir.1979) the Tenth Circuit agreed with the trial judge's position that "an endeavor to influence a juror in the performance of his or her duty or to influence, obstruct or impede the due administration of justice is per se unlawful and is tantamount to doing the act corruptly." The court in *Ogle* noted "that the term 'corruptly' does not superimpose a special and additional element on the offense such as a desire to undermine the moral character of a juror." Some courts admit that the term "corruptly" is capable of "different meanings in different connections," but then conclude that as used in section 1503 it includes "any endeavor to influence a witness or to impede or obstruct justice." *United States v. Cohen* (D.Conn.1962).

In contrast, other courts have made "corruptly" a separate element that the government must specifically prove. "The offending conduct must be prompted, at least in part, by a 'corrupt motive'.... and if there is a fair doubt as to whether the defendants' conduct is embraced within the prohibition, the policy of lenity requires that the doubt be resolved in favor of the accused." *United States v.*

Brand (11th Cir.1985). In this context, "corruptly" can require a showing that the accused acted "for an evil or wicked purpose." *United States v. Ryan* (9th Cir.1971). In some instances the "evil or wicked purpose" is met by a showing that the accused acted intentionally or willfully.

In *United States v. Thomas* (11th Cir.1990), the Eleventh Circuit combined some of the varying approaches used in defining the element of "corruptly." The court found "corruptly" to be "the specific intent of the crime," but noted that its meaning can vary with the prosecution. The court stated that, "[g]enerally, the government must show that the defendant knowingly and intentionally undertook an action from which an obstruction of justice was a reasonably foreseeable result.... Although the government is not required to prove that the defendant had the specific purpose of obstructing justice ... it must establish that the conduct was prompted, at least in part, by a 'corrupt motive.'"

A wide assortment of activities have been found to meet the definition of "corruptly." For example "the destruction or concealment of documents can fall within the prohibition of the statute." *United States v. Rasheed* (9th Cir.1981). Although acts of bribery are not required to meet this element of the offense, when there is evidence of bribery, courts have found that there is per se evidence of acting "corruptly." Fraudulent conduct by the accused also can form the basis of this element. As stated in *United States v. Polakoff* (2d Cir.1941), "[i]t is, as 'corrupt' to persuade a public official by lies as by bribes...."

In *Cole v. United States* (9th Cir.1964), the Ninth Circuit discussed the relationship between advising someone to claim the constitutional privilege against self-incrimination and violating section 1503. Although exercising this constitutional right is lawful, where one "bribes, coerces, forces or threatens a witness to claim it, or advises with corrupt motive the witness to take it," it can be found to be an obstruction of justice. In affirming the defendant's conviction in *Cole*, the court noted that the jury had been instructed "that only *corrupt* methods were prohibited; that *corrupt* influence was the only influence prescribed;—that only any act committed *corruptly* was to be considered."

The question of whether a defendant endeavored to influence a witness "corruptly" has been held by one court to be a "mixed question of law and fact, if not one of fact alone." *United States v. Fayer* (2d Cir.1975). Another view is that whether the endeavor was "corrupt" is a question for the jury to determine. *United States v. Fasolino* (2d Cir.1978).

§ 6.04 Endeavors—Section 1503

For the crime of obstruction of justice, an actual obstruction is not required. It is only necessary that the accused "endeavored" to obstruct justice. "[A]n endeavor within the statute ... is very similar to a criminal solicitation statute ... and does not require proof that would support a charge of attempt." *United States v. Fasolino* (2d Cir.1978).

In *United States v. Silverman* (11th Cir.1984), the Eleventh Circuit stated that "endeavor ... describes any effort or assay to accomplish the evil purpose the statute was enacted to prevent.... The government is not required to prove, however, that the defendant harbored the specific purpose of obstructing the due administration of justice; all the government has to establish is that the defendant should have reasonably foreseen that the natural and probable consequence of the success of his scheme would achieve precisely that result." Thus, one does not have to succeed in the endeavor for there to be a successful prosecution for obstruction of justice.

Discussion of whether the defendant endeavored to obstruct justice has occasionally come into play when there is an issue related to the obtaining or giving of a false statement to a court officer. Reversed by the Eleventh Circuit was a conviction where the false statement was not submitted to the prosecutor and it was shown that the false statement never in fact existed. *United States v. Brand* (11th Cir.1985). Where, however, the false statement actually existed, the government relied upon its existence, and there was evidence that it was likely that the statement would be produced in court and justice would be obstructed, it has been found sufficient to satisfy the "endeavor" element. The fact that the false statement was never actually used in court does not bring the conduct outside the purview of the statute. *United States v. Fields* (11th Cir.1988).

§ 6.05   To Influence, Obstruct or Impede the Due Administration of Justice— Section 1503

To meet the element of influencing, obstructing, or impeding the due administration of justice, there must be (1) a pending proceeding, (2) that the accused knew or had notice of, and (3) that the accused intended to influence, obstruct, or impede its administration. Here again, an actual obstruction, although helpful, is not required. The "conduct must be such, however, that its natural and probable effect would be the interference with the due administration of justice." *United States v. Thomas* (11th Cir.1990).

Although a "pending proceeding" is required for application of the omnibus clause of section 1503, courts have liberally construed the term. The term "proceeding" is not limited to an actual court trial. Rather, conduct relating to grand jury proceedings and conduct occurring while a matter is proceeding on appeal have been found sufficient to support an obstruction of justice charge.

Some courts have interpreted "pending proceeding" to include acts occurring after at least a complaint has been filed with the magistrate or a grand jury impaneled. Thus, obstruction of FBI, IRS, or other government agency investigations would not by itself be sufficient to meet the "judicial proceeding" requirement.

Even though a grand jury has been impaneled, however, does not mean that the "pending proceeding" element has always been satisfied. Courts vary on the level of activity required by the grand jury to meet this element. Where an impaneled grand jury has issued no subpoenas, has not been apprised of the alleged criminal conduct, and there has been no showing that the defendant has knowledge of the federal grand jury proceeding, it has been found there was insufficient activity to meet the pending judicial proceeding element. In contrast, where subpoenas have been issued by the Assistant United States Attorney, even though the grand jury has no knowledge of the subpoena or criminal conduct, there was activity sufficient to form the basis of an obstruction charge. *United States v. Simmons* (3d Cir.1979). If the subpoena, however, is merely to furnish documents for an agency investigation, as opposed to an actual grand jury investigation, it has been found insufficient to meet the requirement of a proceeding for purposes of section 1503.

Most courts find that perjury and false statements alone do not constitute an obstruction of justice. *United States v. Essex* (6th Cir.1969). "To show an obstruction of justice based on false testimony, the government must establish a nexus between the false statements and the obstruction of the administration of justice." *United States v. Thomas* (11th Cir.1990).

Recently, in *United States v. Aguilar* (S.Ct.1995), the Supreme Court reexamined the "nexis" required between the act and the judicial proceeding, finding that the "act must have a relationship in time, causation or logic with the judicial proceedings." The Court rejected use of § 1503 where the evidence was limited to "uttering false statements to an investigating agent ... who might or might not testify before a grand jury." The Court stated that, "[w]hat use will be made of false testimony given to an investigating agent who has not been subpoenaed or otherwise directed to appear before the grand jury is far more speculative." The Court in *Aguilar* found this could not "be said to have the 'natural and probable effect' of interfering with the due administration of justice."

Besides there being a pending judicial proceeding, it is incumbent that the accused have knowledge or notice of that fact. In *Pettibone v. United States* (S.Ct.1893), a case involving a conspiracy to obstruct the due administration of justice, the Court stated that " ... a person is not sufficiently charged with obstruction or impeding the due administration of justice in a court unless it appears that he knew or had notice that justice was being administered in such court."

Cases after *Pettibone* have held that there is no requirement that there be direct evidence of knowledge. Information or a reasonably founded belief can be sufficient. Further, knowledge can be inferred from the evidence. Although knowledge is required, the government does not have to prove that the defendant knew that it was a federal proceeding.

Knowledge or notice of the pending proceeding must be accompanied by an intent to impede its administration. *United States v. Guzzino* (7th Cir. 1987). Although a specific intent to impede the administration of justice is an essential element of the offense, direct evidence of this intent is not required. A jury may use circumstantial evidence and may infer the intent from the evidence provided. The level of intent necessary may depend upon what definition a court gives to the term "corruptly."

§ 6.06 Section 1503 as it Relates to Other Obstruction Statutes

Along with the passage of the Victim and Witness Protection Act also came a restructuring of some of the obstruction offenses found in chapter 73. Removed from section 1503 was specific language relating to witnesses and parties. This excluded language formed the basis for the new offenses found in sections 1512 and 1513. As a result of this reorganization, courts have found it necessary to resolve controversies pertaining to the use of the omnibus clause of section 1503 when the new statutes might more specifically criminalize the conduct. In examining the existing cases that have resolved this issue, it is evident that there is a jurisdictional dichotomy. Some courts take the position that section 1503 can be charged alternatively or in conjunction with section 1512 when the conduct involves obstruction against a witness. Others take the position that the general obstruction charge of section 1503 is overridden by the specific victim and witness protection provided in section

1512. There is an added complexity to this issue as a result of an additional modification made to the statute in 1988 by Congress that added the word "corruptly" to section 1512(b).

In *United States v. Lester* (9th Cir.1984), the Ninth Circuit examined the propriety of the government charging a violation of both section 1503 and 1512. The defendant questioned the use of section 1503 for witness tampering in light of the enactment of the Victim and Witness Protection Act. The government contended that despite the passage of a new statute, section 1503's omnibus clause remained intact for conduct that "endeavors to influence, obstruct, or impede, the due administration of justice."

In accepting the government's position, the *Lester* court dissected section 1503 into two parts; the part originally established to protect witnesses and the latter portion used to prevent a miscarriage of justice by corrupt methods. Reading the omnibus clause as a separate aspect to this statute, the court determined "that Congress enacted section 1512 to prohibit specific conduct comprising various forms of coercion of witnesses, leaving the omnibus provision of section 1503 to handle more imaginative forms of criminal behavior, including forms of witness tampering, that defy enumeration."

The *Lester* court mentioned in the decision that it believed this position was in harmony with the view expounded by the Second Circuit in *United States v. Hernandez* (2d Cir.1984). The *Hernandez* case, however, had held that it was improper to use section 1503 with section 1512 conduct in that "congress affirmatively intended to remove witnesses entirely from the scope of section 1503." The *Hernandez* decision also stated that "by enacting [the Act] in 1982, Congress intended that *intimidation and harassment* of witnesses should thenceforth be prosecuted under § 1512 and no longer under § 1503." Using this latter sentence from *Hernandez*, the *Lester* court reconciled its position by finding that section 1503 was still operative with respect to witnesses when the conduct was outside the realm of "intimidation and harassment of witness." Since *Lester* involved conduct that was not on its face an intimidation or harassment of witnesses, but was directed toward the administration of justice, it was proper to use the omnibus clause of section 1503.

Initially the weight of authority appeared to express the view taken by *Lester*, allowing prosecutions under section 1503 when the conduct involved witness tampering. Left for the minority was the more restrictive approach expressed by the Second Circuit in *Hernandez*. In 1985 the Supreme Court denied certiorari in a case that could have resolved this jurisdictional dichotomy. Three justices dissenting on the denial of the petition for writ of certiorari remarked how two large circuits, the fifth and second, had "contrary interpretations" of this statute. *Cooper v. United States* (S.Ct.1985).

This issue takes on a new dimension with the passage of a 1988 amendment to section 1512(b) adding the word "corruptly." This permits a section

1512(b) prosecution when the conduct is noncoercive witness tampering. The Second Circuit in *United States v. Masterpol* (2d Cir.1991) found this statutory addition further support for the *Hernandez* view that Congress, in adding section 1512, "affirmatively intended to remove witnesses entirely from the scope of § 1503." Most circuits, however, reject the position taken by the Second Circuit finding that "[t]he fact that § 1512 more specifically addresses improper conduct involving a witness does not preclude application of § 1503." *United States v. Kenny* (4th Cir.1992).

CHAPTER SEVEN
BRIBERY AND EXTORTION

§ 7.01 Introduction

Official corruption is often prosecuted by charges premised upon the statutory offenses of Bribery of Public Officials and Witnesses (18 U.S.C. § 201), the Hobbs Act (18 U.S.C. § 1951) or the Travel Act (18 U.S.C. § 1952). Although federal offenses, these three statutes are often used in corruption cases involving state and local officials. As one might suspect, this use has raised arguments of the implications on federalism.

The line between each of these three offenses is not always discernible and often a prosecutor has a choice in deciding what statute to use in prosecuting specific conduct. In the recent United States Supreme Court decision of *Evans v. United States* (S.Ct.1992), Justice Thomas, joined by Chief Justice Rehnquist and Justice Scalia, cautioned in their dissent that "[b]y stretching the bounds of extortion to make it encompass bribery, the Court today blurs the traditional distinction between the crimes." Permitting Hobbs Act charges when the conduct is in essence bribery serves to provide federal jurisdiction for what otherwise might be a state

110

crime. Courts have found that bribery and extortion are not mutually exclusive.

The Foreign Corrupt Practices Act (FCPA) serves to combat bribery of foreign officials. The Act, originally passed in 1977, is incorporated into provisions of the Securities Exchange Act of 1934. Under the FCPA, certain corporations are subject to accounting requirements that include the keeping of records "in reasonable detail [to] accurately and fairly reflect the transactions and disposition of the assets of the issuer." (15 U.S.C. § 78 m(b)(2)(A)). The crux of the FCPA provides for the prosecution of those who bribe foreign officials. (15 U.S.C. § 78 dd–1 et. seq.) (see § 1.04).

§ 7.02 Overview of Bribery

The first federal bribery statute of general application was passed in 1853 and titled "An Act to Prevent Frauds Upon the Treasury of the United States." Although today there are many federal bribery offenses in the federal criminal law, the most prominent is section 201 of Title 18. This statute pertains to bribery (§ 201 (b)) and gratuities (§ 201 (c)).

Congress enacted section 201 in 1962 "as part of an effort to reformulate and rationalize all federal criminal statutes dealing with the integrity of government." *Dixson v. United States* (S.Ct.1984). The statute focuses on criminalizing conduct of those who improperly seek preferential treatment from government officials and also those who improperly use their public office for their personal gain. The statute also covers bribes and gratuities given to witnesses for influencing their testimony or absenting themselves from a proceeding. Section 201 criminalizes the conduct of the person giving the bribe as well as the person who receives it.

Bribery (§ 201 (b)(1)) requires the government to show that (1) something of value was given, offered, or promised (2) to a federal public official (3) corruptly to influence an official act. Subsection two of this provision concerns those instances when the offender committing the bribery is the public official. The remaining two subsections of part (b) criminalize conduct of bribing a witness in a federal proceeding or seeking or accepting a bribe as such a witness.

Subsection (c) of section 201 pertains to gratuities. When one is the public official charged with demanding or accepting a gratuity, it is incumbent for there to be a showing that the public official personally sought or accepted something of value. A distinguishing factor separating bribery from gratuities is the level of intent. The gratuity statute does not require proof of a quid pro quo. It is sufficient if the act is "otherwise than as provided by law for the proper discharge of official duty."

Bribery carries a maximum penalty of fifteen years imprisonment and a fine. Additionally it permits disqualification from public office. In contrast, the gratuities provision of this statute provides for a maximum imprisonment of two years.

§ 7.03   Bribery—Things of Value

A liberal construction has been given to the requirement of the bribery payment being "anything of value." Actual commercial value is not necessary. It is the "value which the defendant subjectively attaches to the items received," which controls. Thus, loans and a promise of future employment to an official in financial straits can be value for purposes of the statute. *United States v. Gorman* (6th Cir.1986).

In *United States v. Williams* (2d Cir.1983), Senator Harrison Williams was convicted of charges, including bribery, as a part of Operation Abscam. The Second Circuit found that defendant's acceptance of stock in corporations that he believed had value, was sufficient to support the "anything of value" element and the jury instruction, despite defendant's argument of the stock having no commercial value.

§ 7.04   Bribery—Public Official

The public official element of the bribery statute includes both federal public officials and "persons who have been selected to be public officials." These terms are descriptively defined by the statute. Further, courts have expansively interpreted these definitions.

In *Dixson v. United States* (S.Ct.1984), petitioners were charged with bribery for their acceptance of kickbacks from contractors seeking work on a project arising as part of an urban renewal program.

The City of Peoria, the recipient of two federal block grants from the Department of Housing and Urban Development, designated a social service organization as subgrantee in charge of administering the funds. Petitioners served in a supervisory capacity with this agency with certain fiscal and contracting authority. The issue before the Supreme Court was "whether officers of a private, nonprofit corporation administering and expending federal community development block grants are 'public officials' for purposes of the federal bribery statute."

The Supreme Court affirmed the convictions of the petitioners finding them to be "public officials." The Court was clear, however, to state that the "mere presence of some federal assistance" or being an employee of a local organization responsible for administering a federal grant does not make one a "public official." The Court found that to be a "public official," one "must possess some degree of official responsibility for carrying out a federal program or policy."

Those individuals who may not meet the "public official" element of this statute are not necessarily immune from federal prosecution. In 1984 Congress passed 18 U.S.C. § 666, an act that now extends federal criminality to agents of state and local organizations that receive ten thousand dollars or more in federal funds. Congress stated that the purpose of the act was "to augment the ability of the United States to vindicate significant acts of theft, fraud and bribery involving Federal monies which are disbursed to private organizations or State and local governments pursuant to a Federal program."

When the prosecution of the public official entails a member of the federal Congress, an issue that may arise is the effect of the Constitution's Speech and Debate Clause. Established to protect the independence of the legislature, this constitutional provision provides that "for any Speech or Debate in either House, they [Senators and Representatives] shall not be questioned in any other place."

In *United States v. Brewster* (S.Ct.1972), the Supreme Court rejected the use of the Speech and Debate Clause in a case charging Senator Brewster with bribery under section 201. The Court stated that "a Member of Congress may be prosecuted under a criminal statute provided that the Government's case does not rely on legislative acts or the motivation for legislative acts." The taking of a bribe, the Court stated is not a legislative act and is not "part of or even incidental to the role of a legislator."

§ 7.05 Bribery—Corruptly to Influence Official Acts

When the charge pertains to bribery of a public official, it is incumbent that the government prove that the defendant acted corruptly to influence an official act. The statute defines "official act" as "any decision or action on any question, matter, cause, suit, proceeding or controversy, which may at any time be pending, or which may by law be brought before any public official, in such official's official capacity, or in such official's place of trust or profit." Despite the extensiveness of this definition, courts have not always found a defendant's conduct sufficient to meet this element.

In *United States v. Muntain* (D.C.Cir.1979), the charges against the defendant included illegal gratuities pursuant to section 201. Muntain, employed as the Assistant to the Secretary for Labor Relations at the United States Department of Housing and Urban Development, was convicted after a jury trial based upon evidence of "his involvement in a private scheme to sell group insurance to labor unions as a negotiated benefit in union contracts." Defendant argued on appeal that his actions were not "official acts" in that they did not involve matters that would be brought before him in his official capacity. The District of Columbia Circuit Court of Appeals accepted this argument, finding that the promotion of group automobile insurance was not a matter that would be brought before Muntain in his capacity as the Secretary of Labor Relations at HUD. Thus, although the court found the conduct reprehensible, it did not find it sufficient to meet the element of influencing an official act.

The "official act" language is not limited to future acts. Rather, the legislature's use of the words "at any time" precludes a defendant from escaping "liability for bribe-solicitation by proving that he had successfully hidden the truth of past performance from the bribe-payer." Bribery does not require that the public official actually have the power to perform the act for which the money was received. The crux of the offense is that money is solicited or received on the representation that it is for the purpose of influencing an official act. *United State v. Arroyo* (7th Cir.1978).

Although the bribe must be offered with a corrupt intent to influence any official act, the public official does not need to be aware of the bribe. *United States v. Traitz* (3d Cir.1989). It is, likewise, immaterial to some courts whether the act could or would ever be performed. Thus, a defense of "playacting" would not negate the charge. A public official who gives false promises of assistance to individuals offering money, cannot avoid section 201's criminality claiming that the official's subjective intent was not corrupt. *United States v. Myers* (2d Cir.1982).

Bribery does, however, require proof of an actual or intended quid pro quo. Arguments claiming insufficiency of the quid pro quo mandate are common to cases where the defendant believes that the charge of gratuity, as opposed to bribery, more aptly describes the conduct. Considering the difference in sentencing options for these two offenses, (bribery-15 years, gratuities-2 years) the issue is significant. In distinguishing the bribery offense from the gratuity offense, the Fourth Circuit in *United States v. Muldoon* (4th Cir.1991), stated that "[b]ribery requires proof that the payor acted corruptly with the intent of influencing any official act, influencing a public official to defraud the government, or to do or omit an act in violation of his official duties." In contrast, the court found that proof of a gratuity "need not show that the payor intended to exact action by the recipient, although it must show that the payor gave the gratuity because of the act."

§ 7.06 Overview of Hobbs Act

The Anti–Racketeering Act of 1934 was the predecessor extortion statute of the Hobbs Act. Congress modified this initial act in 1946 in reaction to a United States Supreme Court decision that restrictively applied the 1934 Act to exclude the payment of wages by a bona fide employer to a bona fide employee. *United States v. Local 807* (S.Ct. 1942). Although the predecessor statute criminalized extortion activity, the Supreme Court's ruling in *Local 807* permitted labor unions using coercive extortion to escape liability under the statute if the conduct involved wages paid to a bona fide employee. To correct this deficiency, Congress enacted the Hobbs Act, a new statute that specifically contained a "definition of the term 'extortion' and for the first time proscribed 'extortion' in specific language." *United States v. Mazzei* (3d Cir.1975).

The elements of the present day offense are (1) interference with commerce and (2) robbery or extortion. Extortion is defined within the statute as "the obtaining of property from another, with his consent, induced by wrongful use of actual or threatened force, violence, or fear, or under color of official right." Despite the predecessor statute's emphasis on racketeering activities, 18 U.S.C. § 1951 has no requirement that the government prove racketeering as an element of the offense. *United*

States v. Culbert (S.Ct.1978). The statute permits prosecutions for actual acts of robbery or extortion as well as attempts and conspiracies to rob or extort.

Section 1951 carries a maximum term of imprisonment of not more than twenty years and a fine. The significant prison term afforded by this statute makes its use highly desirable to the government.

§ 7.07 Hobbs Act—Interstate Commerce

It is rare that a court rejects a section 1951 prosecution as not meeting the jurisdictional requirement of interstate commerce. The statute merely requires a showing that one "in any way obstructs, delays, or affects commerce or the movement of any article or commodity in commerce." Interstate commerce has been found where there is criminal activity "affecting commerce" even when the effect is "de minimus." In *United States v. Rabbitt* (8th Cir.1978), the Eighth Circuit stated that, "[i]f the resources of a business which affects interstate commerce are depleted and diminished as a result of extortion, then interstate commerce is affected." An actual or prospective depletion of assets has been found sufficient. Courts are presently reexamining these rulings in light of the Supreme Court's holding in *United States v. Lopez* (see § 1.02).

In *United States v. Pascucci* (9th Cir.1991), Defendant Pascucci was convicted after a jury trial of two offenses, one of which was the Hobbs Act. In support of the charge of attempted extortion, the government presented evidence at trial that included the defendant's threat to deliver an audio tape of the victim's marital infidelity to the victim's employer.

The majority opinion, by the Ninth Circuit, in *Pascucci,* noted the necessity of having a threat transmitted in interstate commerce in order to have a Hobbs Act violation. The court found that "[b]y showing that the defendant made a credible threat to deliver embarrassing materials *directly* to the victim's employer, who was then engaged in interstate commerce, the Government demonstrated that [defendant] introduced a potential impact on interstate commerce." The fact that the defendant's scheme was unsuccessful because he was caught did not dissolve the criminal liability. In addition to the fact that Pascucci was charged with the crime of attempted extortion, it is sufficient if "the scheme, if successful, would have affected commerce."

Circuit Judge Ferguson, dissenting in *Pascucci,* found the nexus with interstate commerce insufficient in this case. The dissent rejected the argument that because the defendant's "victim was employed by a firm engaged in interstate commerce, the jurisdictional nexus is established." Judge Ferguson stated that the "[i]nterstate commerce must be affected by extortion, not by a result of extortion."

United States v. Elders (7th Cir.1978) is an example of the rare instance when the interstate commerce element was not met by the government. The case involved alleged kickbacks to a local public official for contracts on tree removal work. Following a jury conviction, the defendant argued on appeal that his tree removal company (IST) was not involved in interstate commerce. The government, arguing a de minimus effect on commerce, claimed "(1) that the use of equipment purchased or manufactured out-of-state was sufficient to establish jurisdiction; (2) that IST engaged in out-of-state work during the period in question; and (3) that either the extortionate payments depleted the assets of IST and/or the inflated prices paid by Maywood depleted its treasury, thereby impairing the ability of either or both to do business interstate."

Despite the *Elders* court's recognition that the nexus with interstate commerce may be de minimus, the court did require that it exist and that "the connection with/or effect on interstate commerce must have been at least a 'realistic probability' at the time of the extortionate act." In *Elders*, the Seventh Circuit rejected all of the governments' arguments noting first that the out-of-state purchases of equipment were well in advance of the alleged extortions and there was no showing by the government of a "realistic probability" of additional equipment being purchased. The court also rejected the government's claim of IST doing out of state work as a basis for interstate commerce in that the few out of state jobs presented as evidence by the government had no connection with the alleged extortions. Finally, the court rejected the depletion of assets argument noting that not only was this issue not presented at trial but "the affect still must be more than a speculative attenuated 'one step removed' kind of effect."

Some courts require that if the government is proceeding on a depletion of assets theory premised upon the victim's purchase of interstate goods, it is necessary for the purchasing to be continuing in nature. "Where the victim of an extortion scheme *customarily* obtains supplies through interstate commerce, the diminution of the victim's resources impairs his purchasing power and may therefore be found to affect interstate commerce for the purpose of the Hobbs Act." *United States v. Merolla* (2d Cir.1975).

A depletion of assets premised merely upon the receipt of government (FBI) funds as an extortion payment does not establish an actual effect on interstate commerce. This, however, does not mean that the government would be precluded from proceeding on a charge of attempt under the Hobbs Act. *United States v. DiCarlantonio* (6th Cir.1989).

Although a jury decides if the facts presented by the government occurred, the trial judge can determine if the conduct affected commerce. In *United States v. Kuta* (7th Cir.1975), the Seventh Circuit rejected the argument that an instruction given in a trial that charged the defendant with a violation of the Hobbs Act was erroneous because it did not include a definition of commerce. The court stated that "a definition was not necessary, ... because what constitutes interstate commerce and whether it was affected were matters of law that the trial court resolved."

§ 7.08   Hobbs Act—Robbery or Extortion

Section 1951 requires a showing of either robbery or extortion. Robbery is defined by the statute as "the unlawful taking or obtaining of personal property from the person or in the presence of another, against his will, by means of actual or threatened force, or violence, or fear of injury, immediate or future, to his person or property, or property in his custody or possession, or the person or property of a relative or member of his family or of anyone in his company at the time of the taking or obtaining." Despite the specificity of this statute, in the case of *United States v. Nedley* (3d Cir.1958), the Third Circuit applied the common law definition of the term "robbery." Where a defendant argued on appeal that the common law definition of robbery should have been given as a jury instruction, the appellate court found that use of "the Hobbs Act definition of robbery was not plain error." *United States v. Thomas* (11th Cir.1993).

More commonly, the statute is used with acts of extortion. Prior to the 1970s, Hobbs Act extortion prosecutions were premised upon conduct by force, violence, or fear. In recent years there has been a growth and acceptance of prosecutions where the extortion is "under color of official right."

Property extorted from another by "wrongful use of actual or threatened force, violence or fear" is the first of two clauses that a prosecutor can use in alleging extortion. In making a determination as to whether fear exists, one looks at whether "fear was created in the victim's mind, if such fear was a reasonable one, and if the defendants by making use of that fear extorted money or property." *Callanan v. United States* (8th Cir.1955). "Fear" can be met by a showing of the victim being placed in fear of economic loss.

In *United States v. Capo* (2d Cir.1987) the government charged the defendant under the Hobbs Act for conduct involving payments made to the defendant as part of a job selling scheme. The victims were alleged to have paid defendants sums of money for contacting the personnel officer at Eastman Kodak Company for favorable treatment on their job applications. On appeal of the Hobbs Act convictions, the government contended that the charge was premised upon fear of economic loss.

In rejecting the economic fear argument as presented by the government, the Second Circuit in *Capo* stated that "[t]he absence or presence of fear of economic loss must be considered from the perspective of the victim, not the extortionist; the proof need establish that the victim reasonably believed: first, that the defendant had the power to harm the victim, and second, that the defendant would exploit that power to the victim's detriment." Since the evidence in the *Capo* case failed to show any negative influencing on jobs on the part of defendants and failed to show that any victims feared a detriment to them by defendants actions, the requirement of "preclusion or diminished opportunity" had not been satisfied.

The court in *Capo* stressed the necessity of keeping state offenses away from federal prosecutors. The court stated that "[b]ecause these 'victims' faced no increased risk if they did not pay, but rather, stood only to improve their lots by paying defendants, this case is a classic example of bribery."

§ 7.09 Hobbs Act—"Under Color of Official Right"

Extortion "under color of official right" is an alternative basis upon which a prosecutor can claim extortion. It "includes the misuse of one's office to induce payments not due the person or his office. The official need not control the function in question if the extorted party possesses a reasonable belief in the official's powers." *United States v. Rabbitt* (8th Cir.1978). As noted in *Evans v. United States* (S.Ct.1992), there is no need for an affirmative act of inducement. Merely accepting a bribe to misuse one's office is sufficient. The element "under color of official right" has been the subject of two recent Supreme Court cases that involved extortion as related to public officials' campaign contributions.

In *McCormick v. United States* (S.Ct.1991), petitioner McCormick was a member of the West Virginia House of Delegates who sponsored and spoke on behalf of legislation that would exempt foreign medical school graduates with significant work experience from having to take the state licensing examination. McCormick allegedly received cash payments from the doctors both before and after the passage of this legislation. Evidence presented at trial was that he failed to list the funds received as campaign contributions and likewise failed to report it on his income tax return.

Petitioner McCormick was charged with five counts of violating the Hobbs Act and one count of filing a false income tax return. The Supreme Court reversed petitioner's conviction, finding that a quid pro quo is necessary for a conviction that is predicated upon receiving a campaign contribution. The Court stated that "to hold that legislators commit the federal crime of extortion when they act for the benefit of constituents or support legislation furthering the interests of some of their constituents, shortly before or after campaign contributions are solicited and received from those beneficiaries, is an unrealistic assessment of what Congress could have meant by making it a crime to obtain property from another, with his consent, 'under color of official right.' "

The Supreme Court in *McCormick* was clear to note that not all campaign contributions would be outside the scope of the Hobbs Act. "Political contributions are of course vulnerable if induced by the use of force, violence, or fear. The receipt of such contributions is also vulnerable under the Act as having been taken under color of official right, but only if the payments are made in return for an explicit promise or undertaking by the official to perform or not to perform an official act."

This latter form of extortion was the conduct displayed in the case of *Evans v. United States* (S.Ct.1992). Petitioner Evans was a member of the Board of Commissioners of DeKalb County, Georgia. Petitioner was approached by an undercover FBI agent who sought petitioner's assistance on a rezoning. The agent paid petitioner eight thousand dollars, of which petitioner reported a one thousand dollar check as a campaign contribution but failed to include the cash payment in the sum of seven thousand dollars on his state campaign financing disclosure form or his federal income tax return. Evans was charged with a Hobbs Act violation and a tax violation of failure to report income.

The Supreme Court in *Evans* accepted the majority view as expressed by eight circuits that an "affirmative act of inducement by a public official, such as a demand," is not required for extortion "under color of official right." The Court stated, "[w]e hold today that the Government need only show that a public official has obtained a payment to which he was not entitled, knowing that the payment was made in return for official acts." Thus passive acceptance of a benefit by a public official can meet the extortion element of the Hobbs Act when "the official knows that he is being offered the payment in exchange for a specific requested exercise of his official power."

The Supreme Court in this six to three decision also reaffirmed its prior ruling in *McCormick*, finding the instruction given in the *Evans* case sufficient to meet the quid pro quo requirement. The Court stated that "because the offense is completed at the time when the public official receives a payment in return for his agreement to perform specific official acts; fulfillment of the *quid pro quo* is not an element of the offense."

In *United States v. Blandford* (6th Cir.1994), the Sixth Circuit examined the effect of the *Evans* case on *McCormick* in the context of a Hobbs Act charge against the Speaker of Kentucky's House of Representatives. The court in *Blandford* concluded that "[p]ut simply, *Evans* instructed that by 'explicit' *McCormick* did not mean 'express.'"

Courts have also considered the applicability of *McCormick*'s requirement for a *quid pro quo* outside the context of campaign contributions. Some courts have found that a *quid pro quo* was not required or that a "relaxed *quid pro quo* standard" should be used with non-campaign contribution cases. In *Blandford* the court noted that "a strong argument could be advanced for treating campaign contribution cases and non-campaign contribution cases disparately."

§ 7.10 Travel Act

The Travel Act, passed in 1961, was aimed at "organized crime." Then Attorney General Robert Kennedy stated that federal legislation "was needed to aid state and local governments which were no longer able to cope with the increasingly complex and interstate nature of large-scale, multiparty crime." *Perrin v. United States* (S.Ct.1979). The statute used the Commerce Clause of the United States Constitution to reach state and local criminality that had an interstate nexus.

The Travel Act can be seen as a precursor to crimes such as the Racketeer Influenced and Corrupt Organization Act in its use of the commerce power to criminalize what are essentially state offenses. Initially the statute concentrated on unlawful activity in the form of business activities involving gambling, liquor, narcotics, and extortion and bribery that violated state law. The statute was later expanded to include conduct related to controlled substances and arson that violated state law. In 1986 the scope of this offense was again enlarged to encompass the Bank Secrecy Act and the money laundering offenses of sections 1956 and 1957.

18 U.S.C. § 1952, the Travel Act, requires proof of three elements: (1) interstate or foreign travel, or using the mail or any facility in interstate or foreign commerce, (2) intent to promote, direct, or manage illegal business, and (3) an overt act in furtherance of the unlawful activity.

Interstate travel, the jurisdictional element of this offense, mandates that the activity involve at least two states. A state is defined to include "a State of the United States, the District of Columbia, and any commonwealth, territory, or possession of the United States." The required nexus between interstate activity and the criminality is less clear.

In *Rewis v. United States* (S.Ct.1971) the Supreme Court reversed a section 1952 conviction involving a gambling operation that was frequented by out-of-state bettors. The Court, in examining the legislative history of the statute, found that it strongly suggested "that Congress did not intend that the Travel Act should apply to criminal activity solely because that activity is at times patronized by persons from another State."

Eight years later the Supreme Court chose to take a less restrictive approach to the Travel Act when deciding the case of *Perrin v. United States* (S.Ct.1979). Petitioner and co-defendants were charged with a violation of section 1952 for their involvement in a scheme to exploit geological data stolen from a company. The unlawful activity alleged in the indictment was the use of interstate commerce for the purpose of promoting a commercial bribery scheme in violation of state law.

The Supreme Court in *Perrin* rejected petitioner's argument that bribery should be limited to bribery of a public official. The statute, the Court held, would include "bribery of individuals acting in a private capacity." The Court distinguished *Perrin* from *Rewis* finding the interstate nexus that was lacking in *Rewis* sufficient in this case. The Court stated, " ... so long as the requisite interstate nexus is present, the statute reflects a clear and deliberate intent on the part of Congress to alter the federal-state balance in order to reinforce state law enforcement."

Cases have held that requisite to meeting the "business enterprise" element of this offense is a showing of continuity of the activity. Thus, a single action involving the transportation of drugs would not sustain a conviction. *United States v. Bates* (11th Cir.1988). Where there was a showing of three drug deliveries and a drug distribution enterprise, the Fifth Circuit found sufficient continuity to meet the "business enterprise" element. *United States v. Carrion* (5th Cir.1987).

The Travel Act requires that the accused "thereafter performs or attempts to perform" an act as specified in the statute. Although an overt act is required by the statute, the Second Circuit stated in *United States v. Jenkins* (2d Cir.1991) that the government does not have to show that the accused took a substantial step in furtherance of the intended unlawful activity. "Rather, ... to establish a Travel Act violation the government must prove that the defendant used a facility of interstate or foreign commerce to 'make easier or facilitate' the intended unlawful activity, and thereafter did one additional act in furtherance of the unlawful activity."

CHAPTER EIGHT

RACKETEER INFLUENCED AND CORRUPT ORGANIZATIONS (RICO)

§ 8.01 Introduction

The Racketeer Influenced and Corrupt Organizations Act (RICO) is Title IX of the Organized Crime Control Act of 1970. It was enacted by Congress as a tool to combat organized crime. In the initial years after passage, RICO was seldom used by prosecutors. Today, however, it is common for federal prosecutors to bring RICO charges. The addition of RICO as a criminal charge provides the government with federal criminal enforcement in areas that were previously within the state police powers. Its penalty and forfeiture provisions offer the government a strong incentive for using this statute (see § 8.07).

Although some believe that Congress intended RICO to serve as a weapon against organized crime, courts have not required proof to support a RICO charge, of the defendant being a member of organized crime. RICO is "dependent upon behavior and not status." *United States v. Mandel* (D.Md.1976).

The RICO statutes are found in 18 U.S.C. § 1961 through § 1968. Section 1961 of Title 18 serves as a definitions statute for the terms used in the remaining RICO statutes. In defining these terms, it lists nine state and over thirty federal offenses that can serve as predicate acts for a RICO charge. Although it offers basic definitions for most of the elements of the offense, court interpretations have provided language to further assist in this regard.

Section 1962, subsections (a), (b), (c), and (d), provides four separate and distinct types of prohibited conduct. These are: (a) using income from a pattern of racketeering activity to acquire an interest in an enterprise engaged in, or the activities of which affect interstate or foreign commerce; (b) acquiring or maintaining through a pattern of racketeering activity an interest in an enterprise engaged in, or the activities of which affect interstate or foreign commerce; (c) conducting or participating in the conduct, through a pattern of racketeering activity, of such affairs of an enterprise affect interstate or foreign commerce; and (d) conspiring to further any of the activities listed in (a), (b), or (c). Although it is only necessary for there to be one of these four prohibited activities for a RICO offense, some prosecutions use more then one type of prohibited activity in the charging document.

Although most RICO prosecutions involve racketeering activity, this statute can also be used by the government when the criminal activity involves the collection of an unlawful debt. Section 1961 defines the term "unlawful debt" to mean debts relating to either gambling or usurious loans that are incurred in connection with an illegal gambling business or in connection with a business of lending money where the usurious rate is at least twice the enforceable rate.

The essence of a RICO charge is in proving that the defendant, (1) invested the proceeds of a pattern of racketeering in, or acquired or maintained an interest in through a pattern of racketeering, or participated in through a pattern of racketeering, (2) an enterprise, (3) engaged in, or the activities of which affect, commerce. The intricacies of this statute appear, when each of these elements are dissected relative to the four different types of prohibited conduct. One finds that not only do jurisdictions approach these elements differently, but that courts will vary within the same jurisdiction dependent upon the prohibited conduct that has been charged.

Section 1963 provides the penalties available in a RICO prosecution. A maximum term of imprisonment of up to twenty years is provided for by this statute. This term may be increased to life where the violation is based upon racketeering activity that has a maximum penalty of life imprisonment. In addition to imprisonment and fines, RICO also provides for asset forfeiture. RICO not only serves as a criminal statute, but also provides private parties and the government with a civil cause of action. (18 U.S.C. § 1964).

§ 8.02 Enterprise

RICO requires that the defendant have invested in, maintained an interest in, or participated in the affairs of an enterprise. The term "enterprise" is defined in section 1961(4) as including "any individual, partnership, corporation, association, or other legal entity, and any union or group of individuals associated in fact although not a legal entity." The expansiveness of this definition is seen upon examining cases.

In *United States v. Turkette* (S.Ct.1981), the accused successfully argued in the appellate court that RICO was solely intended to protect legitimate businesses and thus criminal participation in an association that performed only illegal acts, and had not infiltrated or attempted to infiltrate a legitimate enterprise, could not form the basis for a RICO charge. The Supreme Court, in reversing the appellate court, conceded that the congressional purpose of RICO was to combat organized crime that infiltrated legitimate businesses. The Court noted, however, that this did not preclude RICO charges where the enterprise was illegal. Since neither the language of the statute nor the structure of RICO limited its application to legitimate enterprises the Court found it proper to follow Congress' intent for RICO to have a broad reading. To hold otherwise, the Court noted, would omit whole areas of organized criminal activity from the reach of the statute. RICO does not, however, require that the enterprise or predicate acts have an economic motive. *National Organization For Women, Inc. v. Scheidler* (S.Ct.1994).

In addition to allowing both legitimate and illegitimate enterprises, courts have permitted the enterprise to be a governmental body. For example, in

United States v. Thompson (6th Cir.1982), defendants entered conditional guilty pleas arguing that it was improper to use the "The Office of Governor" of the State of Tennessee as the enterprise for RICO. The Sixth Circuit in an en banc ruling found that the language and plain meaning of the statute did not exclude governmental offices as RICO enterprises.

Although the court in *Thompson* permitted the use of governmental bodies as RICO enterprises, it noted in dicta its dislike of this practice. The court reflected upon the disruption of comity in federal-state relations and the needless unfair reflection on innocent individuals. The court offered as a better course that prosecutors treat the group of defendants as a group of individuals associated in fact although not a legal entity. Despite this advice, prosecutors have continued to charge RICO with a government entity as the enterprise, and courts have continued to uphold the use of governmental bodies as RICO enterprises.

Courts have disagreed over the necessary structure of an enterprise consisting of a "group of individuals associated in fact although not a legal entity." (§ 1961(4)). They generally agree that attributes of this entity include a common purpose and functioning as a continuing unit. Some courts will even go so far as to require that there be an ascertainable structure. This latter position was taken in *United States v. Bledsoe* (8th Cir.1982).

In *Bledsoe* the Eighth Circuit rejected a position taken by some courts that any confederation of two or more persons, no matter how loose or temporary it may be, can be an association of individuals and thus, an enterprise. The court held that the term "enterprise" is meant to signify an association different from the acts that form the pattern of racketeering activity. In addition to commonality of purpose, an enterprise must "function as a continuing unit," and have an "ascertainable structure." Finding only a loose association without structure, the court in *Bledsoe* reversed the conviction.

The approach taken in *Bledsoe* is rejected by other circuits. Reference is often made to *Turkette* 's holding that the enterprise be separate from the pattern of racketeering. Proof of the enterprise, however, may "coalesce" with the proof of the pattern. *United States v. Perholtz* (D.C.Cir.1988).

Most circuits require that actions brought pursuant to 1962(c) have an enterprise that is separate and distinct from the defendant. In contrast, actions pursuant to section 1962(a) and (b) do not preclude the "person" and "enterprise" being the same party. In *Schofield v. First Commodity Corporation of Boston* (1st Cir.1986), the First Circuit distinguished between provisions (a) and (c) of section 1962. The court noted that 1962(a) does not require a relationship between the person and the enterprise, and thus does not require two separate entities. In contrast 1962(c) requires that the defendant be "employed by or associated with" the enterprise. The court found that since a corporation cannot be employed by or associated with itself, the person must be separate from the enterprise under 1962(c).

The Eleventh Circuit rejects the separate entity-person position, finding that a broad interpretation should be given to the term "enterprise." In *United States v. Hartley* (11th Cir.1982) the Eleventh Circuit reasoned that, "if an individual were named as the enterprise, and a group of persons engaged in a pattern of racketeering with that individual, it would defy reason to suggest that the central figure (the enterprise) could not also be prosecuted under RICO." So too, "no logical or statutory reason" exists for forcing the government through a distinct entity-person position to either relinquish the prosecution of a corporate entity because it is also the enterprise or treat the corporation and its associates as an association-in-fact enterprise.

The person-enterprise rule takes on a new dimension when the issue involves whether a sole proprietor can be an enterprise with which the proprietor can be associated. In *McCullough v. Suter* (7th Cir.1985), the court found that where the enterprise is separable from the individual, section 1962(c) may be employed. Since the defendant, Suter, had several people working for him, as opposed to being "just a one-man band," the person and enterprise were separate and distinct.

§ 8.03 Interstate Commerce

The jurisdiction for the RICO statute is found in its requirement of interstate commerce. In *United*

States v. Robertson (S.Ct.1995), the Supreme Court held that the enterprise's activities could either be "engaged in" or "substantially affect" interstate commerce. The Court found that Robertson had purchased supplies and equipment from out of state, had workers brought in from out of state, and took some of the gold mine's output out of state. The Court found that the activities of the enterprise were engaged in interstate or foreign commerce.

§ 8.04 Pattern of Racketeering Activity

The definitions section of RICO defines a "pattern of racketeering activity" as requiring "at least two acts of racketeering activity, one of which occurred after the effective date of this chapter and the last of which occurred within ten years (excluding any period of imprisonment) after the commission of a prior act of racketeering activity." Courts and the legislature have provided guidance as to what constitutes a pattern and what acts are permissible as racketeering activity.

There are nine state and over thirty federal offenses specifically listed in section 1961 as racketeering activity. The nine state offenses are murder, kidnapping, gambling, arson, robbery, bribery, extortion, dealing in obscene matter, or dealing in narcotics or other dangerous drugs. The statute requires that the state offense be chargeable under state law and punishable by imprisonment for more than one year.

Although it is necessary that the state offense be chargeable under state law, it is unimportant what label is placed on the state statute. In defining the nine state offenses, the legislature intended that a generic definition be used. Thus, violations of the Illinois official misconduct statute can fit a general definition of bribery, and thus form a RICO predicate. *United States v. Garner* (7th Cir.1987).

It is not necessary that the accused actually be charged with the state offense. Further, procedural problems that might preclude the filing of a state charge do not serve as an impediment to the filing of a RICO charge. Courts have held that it is only necessary to show that the offense can be chargeable under state law.

Where the defendant has been charged with the state predicate in state court, the federal courts have still permitted RICO charges to be brought in federal court using the same state act as a RICO predicate offense. This has been allowed even in some instances where the state trial resulted in an acquittal of the state offense. The dual sovereignty rule provides concurrent jurisdiction to both the state and federal governments so collateral estoppel does not apply. The double jeopardy clause also has not barred a subsequent RICO prosecution based upon a federal predicate offense previously used to prosecute the defendant. Since RICO requires proof of a pattern of racketeering, courts have found that it is not the same offense as the predicate act. *United States v. Pungitore* (3d Cir.1990).

Over thirty federal offenses are listed as possible predicate acts for a RICO charge. These offenses are listed in the definitions provision of RICO (18 U.S.C. § 1961), using both the statutory numbers of the offense and descriptions of the conduct. For example, section 201 contains the parenthetical "relating to bribery." Courts have interpreted this language to be merely a description of the statute and not to serve as a limit to the actual statutory provision. Thus, section 201's bribery and gratuities offenses are both included as possible predicate acts.

The expansiveness of RICO is demonstrated by noting the federal offenses included as possible predicate acts. For example, mail fraud, wire fraud, and obstruction of justice are among the list of offenses. Certain drug offenses and currency reporting crimes can also serve as predicate acts of a RICO charge.

Although RICO requires at least two predicate acts within the applicable time period, having merely two acts does not make RICO automatically available. Further, the existence of numerous predicate acts does not conclusively imply satisfaction of the pattern of racketeering element of RICO. The statute requires both the requisite number of acts and a pattern. Courts have provided guidance in defining the term "pattern."

The Supreme Court in the case of *H.J. Inc. v. Northwestern Bell Telephone Co.* (S.Ct.1989), defined "pattern of racketeering" as requiring "continuity plus relationship." The Court stated that " 'continuity' is both a closed-and open-ended concept." Continuity is achieved by proving related acts extending over a substantial period of time or by acts that demonstrate a threat of continued racketeering activity. Predicate acts over a few weeks or months that do not entail a threat of future criminal conduct do not meet the continuity requirement. Where the acts are over a short period of time, but demonstrate a "specific threat of repetition extending indefinitely into the future" or are part of an "ongoing entity's regular way of doing business," they can satisfy continuity.

The Court in *H.J. Inc.* defined the "relationship" requirement by referring to another provision of the Organized Crime Control Act of 1970. (18 U.S.C. § 3575 (e)). "[C]riminal conduct forms a pattern if it embraces criminal acts that have the same or similar purposes, results, participants, victims, or methods of commission, or otherwise are interrelated by distinguishing characteristics and are not isolated events."

Although the Court in *H.J. Inc.* provided a standard for reviewing cases to determine the existence of a pattern of racketeering, it admitted that a precise method of determination could not be fixed in advance. The development of cases applying specific facts to the "continuity plus relationship" test is needed to see the full effect of this definition. Four justices concurring in this opinion, criticized the "continuity plus relationship" test finding it as helpful to the conduct of affairs as saying "life is a fountain." Although these justices invite a future challenge based upon statutory vagueness, certiorari has been denied when the issue has been brought to the Supreme Court.

§ 8.05 Nexus Between Pattern of Racketeering and Enterprise

In the case of 1962(a) and 1962(b) there is no need to reflect upon the nexus requirement in that the statute specifically incorporates the nexus between the racketeering and the enterprise. In 1962(a) a person is using income from a pattern of racketeering activity to acquire an interest in an enterprise and in 1962(b) the accused is acquiring or maintaining through a pattern of racketeering an interest in an enterprise. Thus, in these two provisions the relationship between the racketeering and enterprise is apparent.

Although prosecutions under section 1962(c) also require a nexus between the enterprise and the racketeering activity, the basis of that nexus is less obvious. Section 1962(c) prohibits conducting or participating in conducting, through a pattern of racketeering activity, the affairs of an enterprise affecting interstate commerce. Prior to 1993, a jurisdictional dichotomy existed as to what relationship was required between the enterprise and the racketeering activity or person engaged in the racketeering activity.

In 1993, in the case of *Reves v. Ernst & Young* (S.Ct.1993), the Supreme Court resolved the jurisdictional dichotomy. The Court held that 1962(c) required that one participate in the operation or management of the enterprise. The Court noted,

however, that the "operation or management" test
would not be limited to upper management. "An
enterprise is 'operated' not just by upper management but also by lower-rung participants in the
enterprise who are under the direction of upper
management. An enterprise also might be 'operated' or 'managed' by others 'associated with' the
enterprise who exert control over it as, for example,
by bribery." The Court did not resolve "how far
§ 1962(c) extends down the ladder of operation."

§ 8.06   RICO Conspiracy

Section 1962(d) prohibits a conspiracy to commit
the conduct stated in sections (a), (b), or (c). Unlike
the general conspiracy statute (18 U.S.C. § 371), a
RICO conspiracy is not focused upon the agreement
to commit a specific offense or defraud the government. Rather, the object of a RICO conspiracy is on
the conspiracy to violate a substantive RICO provision. For example, a conspiracy to violate section
1962(c) would have as the object of the offense an
agreement to conduct or participate in the affairs of
an enterprise through a pattern of racketeering. It
would not have as the object of the offense, an
agreement to commit the individual predicate acts
required for a pattern of racketeering. *United States
v. Elliott* (5th Cir.1978).

A jurisdictional dichotomy exists as to whether it
is necessary in order to sustain a RICO conspiracy
that the defendants personally agree to commit two
predicate acts of racketeering. The Supreme Court
recently accepted certiorari to decide whether the

government has to prove that the defendant "personally committed or agreed to commit two RICO predicate acts." *Salinas v. United States* (S.Ct. 1997). Confusion also exists as to whether an overt act is a necessary element for a RICO conspiracy. Most courts examining this latter issue have found that unlike the general conspiracy statute found in section 371, RICO does not require proof that a member of the conspiracy engaged in an overt act in furtherance of the conspiracy.

§ 8.07 Forfeiture

In addition to fines and imprisonment, the RICO statute provides for forfeiture of property. Section 1963(a)(1) provides for forfeiture of "any interest the person has acquired or maintained in violation of section 1962." Additionally, any interest in an enterprise in which the person participated in, that violated section 1962, is subject to forfeiture under § 1963(a)(2). Finally, property from the proceeds of racketeering activity or the unlawful collection of a debt in violation of 1962, is subject to forfeiture under § 1963(a)(3). Property forfeitable under RICO relates back to property owned at the time of the commission of the section 1962 violations. (18 U.S.C. § 1963(c)).

Both tangible and intangible property can be forfeited. Real property, as well as things affixed to it, are subject to forfeiture under § 1963(a)(1). In *Russello v. United States* (S.Ct.1983) the Supreme Court held that profits and income were an "interest" and therefore subject to forfeiture. The Court noted that although the statute did not specifically define the term "interest," the ordinary meaning of the word encompassed profits or proceeds. The *Russello* Court found that Congress, wanted "to remove the profit from organized crime by separating the racketeer from.... dishonest gains." Thus, reading the statute as applying only to interests in an enterprise, would limit its effectiveness and place whole areas of organized criminal activity beyond the reach of the statute. Section 1963(a)(3) codified *Russello* in providing for the forfeiture of the "proceeds" of racketeering activity.

Contract rights are also subject to forfeiture. An example of the forfeiture of a contract right is seen when the court orders an individual to forfeit a union position. The court may not, however, extend this forfeiture to precluding the person from seeking to reattain their office. *United States v. Rubin* (5th Cir.1977).

In *United States v. Caporale* (11th Cir.1986), the Eleventh Circuit found it permissible under the forfeiture provisions of the statute to impose joint and several liability. The government, the court noted, is not required to trace racketeering proceeds to specific assets. All that is necessary is for the government to show the "amount of the proceeds and identify a finite group of people receiving the proceeds."

In personam forfeitures are, however, subject to Eighth Amendment challenges under the Excessive Fines Clause. In *Alexander v. United States* (S.Ct.

1993), the Supreme Court remanded a forfeiture order for the lower court to consider whether the penalty was excessive.

§ 8.08   Civil RICO

In addition to criminal RICO actions, the RICO Act provides a statutory basis for both the government and civil litigants proceeding with a civil cause of action. (18 U.S.C. § 1964). Unlike criminal RICO actions that provide penalties including imprisonment, those premised upon section 1964, the civil RICO statute, have remedies of damages. The government, in pursuing civil RICO actions, can also request equitable relief. The applicability of injunctive relief to private plaintiffs remains an unresolved issue. The statute does provide that "[a]ny person injured in his business or property by reason of a violation of section 1962 ... may sue ... and shall recover threefold the damages he sustains and the cost of the suit, including a reasonable attorney's fee."

Most civil RICO actions do not require that the defendants be convicted of the predicate acts used to form the basis of the pattern of racketeering. *Sedima, S.P.R.L. v. Imrex Co., Inc.* (S.Ct.1985). The right to sue for treble damages under RICO, however, does require a showing of injury to the plaintiff, and that the defendant's actions in violation of the statute were the proximate cause of that injury. Therefore, the plaintiff must show a direct relationship between the conduct alleged and the injury asserted in the complaint. *Holmes v. Securities In-*

vestor Protection Corp. (S.Ct.1992). Recently Congress amended § 1964(c) so that a civil RICO action could not be premised upon "conduct that would have been actionable as fraud in the purchase or sale of securities" unless the individual was criminally convicted in connection with the fraud.

CHAPTER NINE
FALSE STATEMENTS

§ 9.01 Introduction

A myriad of statutes exist today that prohibit the making of false statements. Most of these offenses are specifically tailored to meet explicit prohibited conduct. For example, false statement offenses exist with regard to making false statements under the Federal Trade Commission Act (15 U.S.C. § 50), presenting a false deed, power of attorney or other contract writing that defrauds the United States (18 U.S.C. § 495), presenting a false invoice with the intent to smuggle (18 U.S.C. § 545), making a false statement to obtain a federally backed loan (18 U.S.C. § 1014) and making a false statement with respect to work performed on a highway project (18 U.S.C. § 1020).

Despite the volume of tailored legislation, the most pervasively used provision is the generic false statement statute located in section 1001 of Title 18. Section 1001 has been effectively employed to combat public corruption. The simplicity of proof necessary to obtain a conviction, as well as the substantial penalty provided, has made it a beneficial charge for the government's use.

18 U.S.C. § 1001 emanates from an 1863 Act that made it a criminal offense for a person in the United States armed forces to make a fraudulent claim against the government. In subsequent years the statute was expanded to encompass "every person" and not just those in the military. A 1934 revision modified the language to include fraudulent claims "in any matter within the jurisdiction of any department or agency of the United States." In 1948 the legislature divided the statute designating 18 U.S.C. § 287 as the false claims statute and 18 U.S.C. § 1001 as the prohibition against the making of false statements. As part of the False Statements Accountability Act of 1996, the statute was amended to include "any matter within the jurisdiction of the executive, legislative, or judicial branch" of the United States government.

Section 1001 is divisible into three types of conduct. It can apply to one who "[1] falsifies, conceals or covers up by any trick, scheme or device a material fact, [2] makes any materially false, fictitious, or fraudulent statement or representation, or [3] makes or uses any false writing or document knowing the same to contain any materially false, fictitious, or fraudulent statement or entry."

False statements require proof of the following elements: (1) a statement, (2) falsity, (3) materiality, (4) made knowingly and willfully, (5) within the executive, legislative, or judicial branch of the United States government. Commission of an act prohibited by section 1001 carries a penalty of not more than five years imprisonment and a fine.

§ 9.02   Statements

Section 1001 statements can take a variety of forms. They can be written or oral, sworn or unsworn. False statements that relate to past, present or future activity are covered by the statute. The statement also may be either voluntary or made pursuant to a requirement of law.

If proceeding under the first type of conduct described in the false statement statute ("falsifies, conceals or covers up by trick, scheme or device a material fact"), then an actual statement is not necessary. In this instance it is sufficient to show an affirmative act in which the defendant has used a trick, scheme or device that conceals, covers up or results in a failure to disclose. Thus, a failure to provide information on a government form where there is a duty to disclose the information can serve as the basis for a charge under section 1001. It is "incumbent on the Government to prove that the defendant had the duty to disclose the material facts at the time [the defendant] was alleged to have concealed them." *United States v. Irwin* (10th Cir.1981).

§ 9.03   Exculpatory "No's"

Although the statement element of § 1001 has been interpreted broadly, it is not without exception. The most notable limitation is the "exculpatory no" doctrine that has been accepted in varying degrees by a majority of circuits. One rationale for the adoption of this limitation to section 1001 is premised on a concern for the Fifth Amendment.

The case of *Paternostro v. United States* (5th Cir.1962), is often cited as the source of the "exculpatory no" doctrine. In *Paternostro*, the defendant, while under oath, answered questions propounded to him by an IRS special agent. The Fifth Circuit deciding the case found that the defendant's answers "were mere negative responses to questions propounded to him by an investigating agent during a question and answer conference, not initiated by the appellant." On petition for rehearing, the court issued a per curiam opinion stating that the " 'exculpatory no' answer without any affirmative, aggressive or overt misstatement on the part of the defendant does not come within the scope of the statute."

Not all circuits have endorsed the "exculpatory no" doctrine. For example, the Fifth Circuit has now rejected the "exculpatory no" doctrine. *United States v. Rodriguez–Rios* (5th Cir.1994). The Second Circuit has also rejected use of this doctrine. *United States v. Wiener* (2d Cir.1996). Further, those that have recognized this exception have not proceeded with a consistent philosophy as to when it is applicable. A false response on a customs form may be criminality in one jurisdiction while excluded by the "exculpatory no" doctrine in another.

The variations in interpretation of the "exculpatory no" doctrine have sometimes considered whether the statement was a mere "no" as opposed to a "no" coupled with other explanatory statements. Circuit variations also distinguish the application of the doctrine based upon whether the "no" statement is made outside the context of the defendant making a claim against the government or seeking employment with the government. Some courts concentrate on whether there is a possible conflict with the privilege against self-incrimination. Finally, a distinction has been noted dependent upon whether the fault occurred in an "administrative" rather than an "investigative" setting.

In *United States v. Bedore a/k/a Bedord* (9th Cir.1972), the Ninth Circuit held that a defendant's giving of a false name to an F.B.I. agent, who appeared at his door for the purpose of subpoenaing him for trial, was not within the proscription of the false statement statute. The court stated that "[t]he Statute was not intended to embrace oral, unsworn statements, unrelated to any claim of the declarant to a privilege from the United States or to a claim against the United States, given in response to inquiries initiated by a federal agency or department, except, perhaps, where such a statement will substantially impair the basic functions entrusted by law to that agency."

Despite internal inconsistency in the array of Ninth Circuit court opinions, the circuit has been at the forefront in delineating a test for applying the "exculpatory no" doctrine. Decisions of the Fourth and Eighth circuits have employed the analysis used in the ninth circuit case of *United States v. Medina de Perez* (9th Cir.1986). The criteria used in the *Medina de Perez* test as capsulized in *United States v. Cogdell* (4th Cir.1988) provides that a false statement is not within the purview of section 1001 when: "1) it was made in pursuit of claim to a privilege or a claim against the government; 2) it was made in response to inquiries initiated by a federal agency or department; 3) it did not pervert the basic functions entrusted by law to the agency; 4) it was made in the context of an investigation rather than of a routine exercise of administrative responsibility; 5) it was made in a situation in which a truthful answer would have incriminated the declarant." The Supreme Court recently accepted certiorari to decide whether the "exculpatory no" doctrine should be "embraced by this Court." *Brogan v. United States* (S.Ct.1997).

§ 9.04 Falsity

Falsity can be achieved through either the making of a false statement or by the concealment of a material fact. Where the alleged conduct is premised upon the making of a false statement, it is incumbent upon the government to prove actual falsity. Literally true statements, as well as statements that are merely misleading, have been found insufficient. Although the issue of falsity is a question of fact for a jury to decide, a statement that is subject to more than one interpretation places a burden on the government to refute the meaning attributed by the defendant.

Concealment of a material fact also can provide a basis for the crime of false statements. When proceeding under the concealment aspect of the statute, the government must prove that the defendant's affirmative act in failing to disclose a material fact was by means of trick, scheme or device.

§ 9.05   Knowledge and Intent

Section 1001 requires that the government prove the defendant's knowledge of the falsity of the statement, or that the defendant's action was taken for the purpose of concealing or covering up a material fact. Additionally, proof of willfulness is required.

The level of knowledge required of the defendant can be met by evidence of a reckless disregard of the truth or by a conscious avoidance in learning the truth. Actual knowledge of the statement's falsity is not required. In meeting the knowledge requirement, the government may employ circumstantial evidence.

Willfulness does not mandate proof of an intent to defraud. The false statement statute contains language in the disjunctive: "false, fictitious **or** fraudulent." Thus, willfulness is met with proof that a defendant intended to deceive. Where the government's indictment specifically characterizes the defendant's conduct as fraudulent, as opposed to being false or fictitious, then courts have required that the government prove the allegation.

When proceeding under the concealment provision of the false statement statute, it is also necessary for the government to present sufficient proof of intent to deceive. Additionally, when the indictment is premised upon concealment, it is necessary for the government to substantiate that the defendant knew of the duty to disclose and intentionally failed to comply with that duty.

Although a knowledge and willfulness are required for a violation of section 1001, there is no necessity to show that the defendant had actual knowledge of federal agency jurisdiction. In *United States v. Yermian* (S.Ct.1984), the Supreme Court resolved a then existing jurisdictional dichotomy on whether it was necessary for the government to prove that the defendant actually knew that the matter was before a government agency.

Defendant Yermian was convicted of three counts of making false statements based upon false information supplied to his employer in connection with a Department of Defense security questionnaire. Defendant failed to disclose his mail fraud conviction on the submitted form and additionally listed employment with two companies that had never employed him. The defendant "signed a certification stating that his answers were 'true, complete and correct to the best of [his] knowledge' and that he understood' that any misrepresentation or false statement ... may subject [him] to prosecution under section 1001 of the United States Criminal Code.' "At trial, defendant admitted to the falsity of the statements, but contended that he did not have actual knowledge that the statements would be given to a federal agency.

The Supreme Court, in a 5–4 decision, found no basis for requiring proof of actual knowledge of federal agency jurisdiction. The Court held that the term "knowingly" following the phrase "in any matter within the jurisdiction of any department or agency of the United States," is merely a jurisdictional requirement. The Court found that "[a]ny natural reading of § 1001, therefore, establishes that the terms 'knowingly and willfully' modify only the making of false, 'fictitious or fraudulent statements,' and not the predicate circumstance that the statements be made in a matter within the jurisdiction of a federal agency."

Unresolved by *Yermian* was whether a lesser degree of mens rea would be required with respect to the element of federal agency jurisdiction. In a footnote in the *Yermian* decision, the Supreme Court remarked that the jury had been instructed, without objection from the government, that proof was required that defendant "knew or should have known" that statements were made within the jurisdiction of a federal agency. In this footnote, the Court specifically remarked on the narrowness of the issue being decided. Since the only question before the Court in *Yermian* was whether proof of *actual* knowledge of federal agency jurisdiction was mandated, resolution of the level, if any, of culpable mental state of federal agency jurisdiction remains for future determination. Also left for future interpretation is whether specific inclusion of "executive, legislative, or judicial branch" in the statute alters the required level of knowledge.

In *United States v. Green* (9th Cir.1984), the Ninth Circuit found no abuse of discretion in a trial court's failure to give an instruction on jurisdictional knowledge. The appellate court held that "[n]o culpable mental state must be proved with respect to federal agency jurisdiction in order to establish a violation of section 1001." Other jurisdictions have ruled in accord with this Ninth Circuit decision.

§ 9.06 Materiality

Originally materiality was only listed in the concealment clause of section 1001. ("Falsifies, conceals or covers up by a trick, scheme or device a *material* fact"). The remaining two misrepresentation clauses of the statute omitted the term. ("[2] makes any false, fictitious or fraudulent statements or representations, or [3] makes or uses any false writing or document knowing the same to contain any false, fictitious or fraudulent statement or entry.") Despite the failure to explicitly require materiality in the second and third clauses of the statute, most courts required proof of materiality to sustain a false statement conviction. Materiality was added to sections 2 and 3 of the statute as part of the False Statements Accountability Act of 1996.

In determining whether a false statement or concealment is material, courts examine whether the statement has "a natural tendency to influence, or [be] capable of influencing, the decision of the decisionmaking body to which it is addressed." *Kungys v. United States* (S.Ct.1988). It is not necessary to prove that the government agency was actually influenced or that the statement was relied upon by the government. There is also no requirement that the statement be made directly to a federal official.

In *United States v. Gaudin* (S.Ct.1995), the Supreme Court found that the issue of materiality is a mixed question of law and fact that should properly be submitted to the jury. The defendant in *Gaudin* was accused of making false statements on federal loan documents. The district court ruled as a matter of law that the statements were material. The Ninth Circuit, en banc, reversed finding that the issue of materiality should have been submitted to the jury. In affirming the Ninth Circuit, Justice Scalia wrote that "[t]he Constitution gives a criminal defendant the right to have a jury determine, beyond a reasonable doubt, his guilt or every element of the crime with which he is charged."

In *Gaudin*, the parties had "agreed that materiality was an element of 18 U.S.C. § 1001, but disputed whether materiality was a question for the judge or jury." Recently in *United States v. Wells* (S.Ct. 1997), the Supreme Court found that 18 U.S.C. § 1014, a statute pertaining to false statements to a federally insured financial institution, did not require the government to prove materiality.

§ 9.07 Matters Within the Jurisdiction of the Executive, Legislative, or Judicial Branch

It is first necessary to consider the scope of the term "jurisdiction." In *United States v. Rodgers* (S.Ct.1984), the United States Supreme Court held that "jurisdiction," although undefined in the statute, does not suggest support for a narrow construction. Section 1001 "expressly embraces false statements made 'in *any* matter within the jurisdiction of *any* department or agency of the United States.' "Thus, a man who lied to the F.B.I. by telling them his wife had been kidnapped and lied to the Secret Service in telling them his wife was involved in a plot to kill the President, was not entitled to a dismissal of a false statement charge as not within the bounds of the term, "jurisdiction," as used in section 1001. Since the F.B.I. is authorized to investigate crimes, including kidnapping, and the Secret Service is charged with protecting the President, statements to these agencies were within their statutory bases. The Court noted that reading section 1001 broadly furthered the "valid legislative interest in protecting the integrity of [such] official inquiries."

For many years courts struggled with the limits of the term "department or agency." In *United States v. Bramblett* (S.Ct.1955), the Supreme Court found that the Disbursement Office of the House of Representatives was, in fact, a "department or agency of the United States." Defendant Bramblett, a former member of Congress, was charged with falsely representing to the Disbursement Office that an individual was entitled to compensation for being his official clerk. The Court, providing guidance on how to interpret the term "department," stated that "as used in this context, [it] was meant to describe the executive, legislative and judicial branches of the government." *Bramblett* permitted the term "department" to include numerous government agencies, sub-agencies, and boards. In *Hubbard v. United States* (S.Ct.1995), however, the Supreme Court overruled *Bramblett* finding that a court was not an agency or department for purposes of § 1001.

The False Statements Accountability Act of 1996 modifies the statute to explicitly provide "the jurisdiction of the executive, legislative, or judicial branch" of the United States government. The section, however, specifically excludes "statements, representations, writings or documents submitted by" a party or counsel in a judicial proceeding. The new provision also limits the scope of matters of the legislative branch by stating that it applies only to administrative matters or certain Congressional investigations or reviews.

§ 9.08   Other Crimes

In examining the recent surge of cases relating to government procurement fraud, it is evident that a myriad of criminal statutes may be used in prosecuting the criminal conduct. False statements pursuant to section 1001 has traditionally been a major offense used in procurement fraud cases. In 1988 Congress passed the Major Fraud Act (18 U.S.C. § 1031) that created the specific offense of procurement fraud for government contract fraud involving one million dollars or more.

Also used when proceeding against procurement fraud is the false claims statute located in 18 U.S.C. § 287. This offense, originally combined with the false statements statute, was separated by Congress in 1948. The false claims statute is more restrictive in its application than section 1001 in that it applies only to false claims to the government. False claims actions can be presented by private individuals acting on behalf of the United States. Section 3730 of Title 31 permits qui tam plaintiffs the right to bring civil actions on behalf of themselves and the government for violations of the False Claims Act.

When false statements under section 1001 are charged in conjunction with another criminal offense, courts are left to decide the propriety of the prosecutor's selection of multiple charges. In *United States v. Woodward* (S.Ct.1985), the Supreme Court considered the acceptability of indictments under 18 U.S.C. § 1001 and 31 U.S.C. § 1058, 1011 for willfully failing to report the carrying of cash in excess of five thousand dollars. The charges arose from the defendant's response of "no" on a customs form followed by a search and finding of monies in excess of five thousand dollars on the defendant and his wife. The Supreme Court found substantiation of Congress' intent to punish under both 18 U.S.C. § 1001 and 31 U.S.C. §§ 1058, 1101 "by the fact that the statute's 'are directed to separate evils.'"

A court has, however, refused to permit a conviction and sentence to stand when the same conduct was being punished under two different false statement statutes. In *United States v. Avelino* (2d Cir. 1992), the Second Circuit held that it was a violation of the double jeopardy clause to convict and sentence a defendant for both false statements pursuant to section 1001 and making false statements to Customs officials pursuant to 18 U.S.C. § 542. The court noted that "every element needed to prove a crime under Section 1001 is an element of a Section 542 offense and that there is no clear indication of a congressional intent to provide for cumulative punishments for Sections 1001 and 542."

CHAPTER TEN
PERJURY AND FALSE DECLARATIONS

§ 10.01 Introduction

Perjury statutes exist throughout the United States Code. They are evident in Title 18, as well as in sections of the Code that are not focused predominantly upon crimes. For example, in Title 26 one observes a tax offense that is predicated upon the filing of a perjurious tax return (26 U.S.C. § 7206). In some instances the statute will authorize an individual to give an oath and refer violations of the oath to the perjury provisions found in Title 18. For example, Title 8 contains a statute pertaining to false evidence or swearing before the Immigration and Naturalization Service (8 U.S.C. § 1357) and authorizes prosecution pursuant to the criminal perjury statute. (18 U.S.C. § 1621).

Key statutes related to false and perjurious testimony are located at 18 U.S.C. § 1621 (perjury) and 18 U.S.C. § 1623 (false declarations). Today's perjury statute (§ 1621) dates back to statutes enacted by Congress for the purpose of criminalizing all false swearing. *United States v. Smull* (S.Ct.1915). The false declarations statute (§ 1623) was added by Congress in 1970 as part of the Organized Crime

164

Control Act of 1970 to "facilitate perjury prosecutions and thereby enhance reliability of testimony before federal courts and grand juries." *Dunn v. United States* (S.Ct.1979). Although this new statute eased the evidentiary requirements in prosecuting perjury, it's scope was limited to proceedings before or ancillary to federal courts or grand juries.

Perjury (18 U.S.C. § 1621) requires the government prove that the defendant: (1) under oath, by one authorized to administer the oath; (2) before a competent tribunal, officer, or person; (3) made a false; (4) material statement; (5) willfully and with knowledge of its falsity. Perjury carries a penalty of not more than five years imprisonment and a fine.

False declarations (18 U.S.C. § 1623) requires the government prove that the defendant: (1) under oath; (2) before or ancillary to any court or grand jury of the United States; (3) made a false; (4) material statement; (5) with knowledge of its falsity. False declarations carries a penalty of not more than five years imprisonment and a fine.

Perjury and false declarations permit prosecutions of statements that are made both inside or outside the United States. Further, these statutes incorporate 28 U.S.C. § 1746, thereby permitting certain unsworn statements to be subject to prosecution.

The key distinctions between these two offenses are noted in examining the scope, defenses, and evidentiary rules surrounding the two statutes. Most notable is the fact that perjury includes a broader range of proceedings than false declarations. Where perjury applies to false statements before any "competent tribunal, officer, or person," false declarations is limited to statements "before or ancillary to any court or grand jury of the United States."

An additional distinction between these two statutes is noted in the fact that unlike the perjury statute, the false declarations statute does not require two witnesses. Also, the false declarations statute permits the use of inconsistent statements to prove falsity, without specification as to which statement is false. Finally, the false declarations statute provides for a recantation defense in certain circumstances.

When sections 1621 and 1623 both apply to the applicable criminal conduct, prosecutors have discretion to choose under which offense to proceed. Defense attorneys have unsuccessfully contested the use of the perjury statute when the statement was before a court or grand jury, and therefore subject to a false declarations charge. Arguments that the government has deprived the defendant of the recantation defense, by proceeding with a perjury charge, have failed to merit reversals. In one case, however, the Ninth Circuit treated a charge pursuant to section 1621 as if it had been filed under section 1623. *United States v. Clizer* (9th Cir.1972).

Immunization of a witness does not preclude a perjury or false declarations charge against that witness. The federal immunity statute, 18 U.S.C.

§ 6002, specifically excepts "a prosecution for perjury, giving a false statement, or otherwise failing to comply with the order." Both the truthful and untruthful immunized testimony may be used in a subsequent false swearing prosecution for making false statements in the immunized testimony. *United States v. Apfelbaum* (S.Ct.1980) (see § 19.12).

§ 10.02   Oath

Both perjury (18 U.S.C. § 1621) and false declarations (18 U.S.C. § 1623) require proof that the defendant's statement was under oath. In most circumstances this oath will be a sworn declaration. It is possible, however, to prosecute for perjury or false declarations, absent an oath, when the criteria encompassed in 28 U.S.C. § 1746 have been met.

Congress passed section 1746 of Title 28 in 1976. That same year the legislature amended sections 1621 and 1623 to incorporate this alternative to the sworn oath requirements of the perjury and false declarations statute. Section 1746 provides that where a law, "rule, regulation, order, or requirement made pursuant to law" permits or requires an oath, then an unsworn declaration can suffice. The unsworn declaration must, however, be in substantially the same form as specifically set forth in the text of section 1746. The form provided includes a declaration, under penalties of perjury, that the statement is true and correct. The statute offers alternative forms for the unsworn declaration dependent on whether it is executed inside or outside the United States.

Although sections 1621 and 1623 of Title 18 require an oath, there is no necessity that the indictment allege the name of the person administering the oath. In *United States v. Debrow* (S.Ct.1953), the Supreme Court reversed a district court's dismissal of a perjury indictment that failed to state the name and authority of the individual administering the oath. The Court found that the oath requirement could be met by the indictment's allegations "that the defendant had 'duly taken an oath.' "The term "duly taken" was interpreted by the Court to mean "an oath taken according to a law which authorizes such oath."

Although the indictment does not have to name the person who administered the oath, a court has required that it be proven in a section 1621 prosecution. In *Smith v. United States* (5th Cir.1966), the Fifth Circuit found insufficient evidence of the oath requirement where the government's case consisted of a court clerk identifying a certified copy of the transcript containing the alleged perjury. The clerk in *Smith* failed to state that he was present at the hearing or that he observed the administration of an oath to the defendant. The court found that "the bare statement in the transcript, unsupported by testimony, that the defendant had been duly sworn was insufficient evidence to support a conviction of perjury."

In contrast, one court held that the false declarations statute (18 U.S.C. § 1623) does not make the identity of the one who administered the oath an essential element of the offense. In *United States v.*

Molinares (11th Cir.1983), the Eleventh Circuit discussed the distinction in proof required for 1621 and 1623. The court found that section 1621 required greater proof of the oath in that the statute used the language "taken an oath before a competent tribunal, officer, or person ...". In contrast, section 1623, the false declarations statute, merely required "the government prove that the maker of a knowingly false declaration before a court be under oath at the time of the statement." The court in *Molinares* found direct evidence by two witnesses of the administration of the oath, coupled with a transcript of the proceedings indicating the defendant being duly sworn prior to testifying, sufficient evidence for sustaining a prosecution pursuant to section 1623.

Although courts require that the oath be taken before an individual authorized to administer the oath, the person may be a de facto officer. A prosecution involving a violation of 18 U.S.C. § 1623 was predicated upon false testimony given under an oath administered by an "assistant" deputy foreperson of a grand jury. The court had designated an assistant deputy foreperson due to the absence of the foreperson. In response to the defendant's challenge of this oath, the Eastern District of Virginia found the use of the word "assistant" to be mere surplusage. The court stated that "generally it is considered immaterial whether the person administering the oath is an officer de jure or de facto, if his act takes place in the presence of the Court or one authorized to administer the oath, and with its apparent sanction." *United States v. Allen* (E.D.Va. 1975).

§ 10.03 Within Tribunals and Proceedings

Section 1621 requires that the statement be made before "a competent tribunal, officer, or person, in any case in which a law of the United States authorizes an oath to be administered." In contrast, section 1623 is more limited in that the statement has to be "in any proceeding before or ancillary to any court or grand jury of the United States."

The competency of the person administering the oath has been challenged in several section 1621 cases. Courts have found district court judges, deputy clerks, Senate subcommittees, an internal revenue agent, and public notaries as competent tribunals, officers, or persons authorized to administer an oath.

Even a court proceeding that is later found to be premised upon a defective indictment can serve as a competent tribunal for purposes of section 1621. All that is required is court power to proceed to a determination on the merits. Thus, a later showing of a statute being unconstitutional or a holding of insufficient evidence to prove the crime will not bar a prosecution of false testimony presented at the trial. *United States v. Williams* (S.Ct.1951). A false declaration indictment, however, was found to be improper when based upon a declaration made two days after the grand jury term had expired. *United States v. Fein* (2d Cir.1974).

The scope of proceedings is more restrictive in section 1623 than in section 1621. In *Dunn v. United States* (S.Ct.1979), the Supreme Court found that a sworn statement taken at an interview in a private attorney's office did not constitute a proceeding ancillary to a court or grand jury. The Court in *Dunn* examined the legislative history surrounding section 1623 and also noted a comment of the Department of Justice on the proposed legislation "that the scope of the inconsistent declarations provision was 'not as inclusive' as the perjury statute." Despite this comment, the government argued that since pre-trial depositions were covered in a letter sent by Senator McClellan to the Assistant Attorney General, it could also be interpreted that affidavits and certificates were meant to be included. The Court in *Dunn* agreed with the Court of Appeal's conclusion that the interview in this case "lacked the degree of formality required by § 1623." Implied throughout this decision, however, is that depositions, taken pursuant to Rule 15 of the Federal Rules of Criminal Procedure and 18 U.S.C. § 3503 can be ancillary proceedings for the purposes of a section 1623 prosecution.

§ 10.04 Falsity

Prosecutions of both perjury and false declarations require a false statement. Actual falsity has been demanded by the courts. Thus, literally true but misleading statements will not constitute falsity. Likewise, ambiguous questions that call for varying interpretations cannot be used as the basis for obtaining a perjury or false declarations conviction.

Bronston v. United States (S.Ct.1973), is the Supreme Court's seminal decision holding that literally true statements cannot be the basis of a perjury conviction. In *Bronston*, the defendant was being questioned in a bankruptcy hearing by a lawyer representing a creditor. The questions sought to elicit whether the defendant, sole owner of Bronston Productions, had any Swiss bank accounts. The attorney first asked defendant if he had any Swiss bank accounts. To this question the defendant answered "no." The attorney for the creditor then asked defendant Bronston, "[h]ave you ever?" The defendant responded that "[t]he company had an account there for about six months, in Zurich." The defendant failed, however, to mention that although he presently had no bank accounts in Switzerland, he had held such an account for the past five years. Thus, although defendant's answers were literally true, in that he did not presently have an account and the company did at one point have one, he had failed to respond specifically to whether he had a Swiss bank account in the past.

In rejecting the government's use of this second question as the basis for a perjury conviction, the Court stated that it is the responsibility of the "questioner to pin the witness down to the specific object of the questioner's inquiry." Even though the witness may be deliberately avoiding the question, "it is the lawyer's responsibility to recognize the evasion and to bring the witness back to the mark, to flush out the whole truth with the tools of adversary examination." Literally true, but unresponsive answers should not be the subject of a federal perjury prosecution.

Falsity is a question to be determined by the jury. In making this determination, the jury should examine the answer to the question objectively. "The jury should determine whether the question—as the declarant must have understood it, giving it a reasonable reading—was falsely answered." *United States v. Lighte* (2d Cir.1986). Questions and answers are examined in the context in which they are set, as opposed to being viewed in a vacuum.

Falsity cannot exist when the question itself is "fundamentally ambiguous." A test for determining if a question is "fundamentally ambiguous" is set forth in the case of *United States v. Lattimore* (D.D.C.1955), where the District Court for the District of Columbia found vagueness in a phrase that "is not a phrase with a meaning about which ordinary men of ordinary intelligence could agree, nor one which could be used with mutual understanding by a questioner and answerer unless it were defined at the time it were sought and offered as testimony."

To determine if a statement is "fundamentally ambiguous" it is necessary to examine the statement in its context. The asking of some ambiguous questions does not preclude a perjury conviction. *United States v. Lighte* (2d Cir.1986). Further, a question in not "fundamentally ambiguous" just because some of the words used in the question may have different meanings.

The false declarations statute (18 U.S.C. § 1623) specifically provides that in certain circumstances a defendant who knowingly makes "two or more declarations, which are inconsistent to the degree that one of them is necessarily false, [the indictment] need not specify which declaration is false ..." The statute specifies that each declaration must be material to the point in question, and the declarations must be made within the applicable statute of limitations for the offense being charged. It is a defense if the accused believed the declaration to be true at the time it was made.

§ 10.05 Materiality

Materiality is an element of both perjury and false declarations. Although required, the element is met with minimal evidence. "The test of materiality is whether the false testimony was capable of influencing the tribunal on the issue, or whether the false testimony would have the natural effect or tendency to influence, impede, or dissuade the Grand Jury from pursuing its investigation." *United States v. Gremillion* (5th Cir.1972). The statement does not have to actually influence the tribunal or impede the investigation. It suffices when it is capable of this result.

The government bears the burden of proving materiality. *United States v. Bednar* (8th Cir.1984). It need only be proven as of the time the statements were given. Materiality does not require that the statement relate to a main issue in the case. Statements relating to subsidiary matters have been found to be material.

§ 10.06   Knowledge and Willfulness

It is incumbent in a perjury or false declarations prosecution that the defendant have acted with knowledge of the statement's falsity. Although the statutes differ in this mens rea terminology, (perjury uses "not believe to be true," false declarations uses "knowingly"), courts have been consistent in finding that both provisions require that the defendant must have believed when delivering the testimony that it was untrue. *United States v. Reveron Martinez* (1st Cir.1988).

Whether the accused acted with knowledge of the statement's falsity is a question for the jury to resolve. Oftentimes circumstantial evidence is presented to satisfy the knowledge requirement. "The trier of fact may infer this element of knowledge from the surrounding circumstances." *United States v. Larranaga* (10th Cir.1986).

Willfulness is an element of a section 1621 offense. It is not, however, used in the statutory language found in section 1623. Refusal of a defendant's willfulness instruction in a section 1623 prosecution has been upheld by an appellate court, since willfulness is not an element of a section 1623 offense. *United States v. Fornaro* (2d Cir.1990).

§ 10.07   Two Witness Rule

Perjury prosecutions are subject to a two-witness rule. *Hammer v. United States* (S.Ct.1926). This evidentiary rule bars a conviction for perjury that is based solely upon one witness. *Weiler v. United States* (S.Ct.1945). The rule requires "that the falsity of the defendant's statements must be proved by the testimony of two witnesses or the testimony of one witness, plus corroborating evidence." *United States v. Davis* (9th Cir.1977).

The two-witness rule is not applicable to charges brought pursuant to section 1623, the false declarations statute. Congress specifically stated in the false declarations statute that although proof beyond a reasonable doubt would be sufficient for a conviction, it would not be necessary that such proof include a particular number of witnesses or evidence.

The policy rationale offered for adoption of a two-witness rule in perjury prosecutions is that it prevents a perjury conviction resting solely on one person's oath against another. Further, the rule encourages witnesses to come forward in that it prevents witnesses from being harassed or subjecting themselves to a possible false perjury prosecution.

Although called the two-witness rule, in actuality it does not require two separate witnesses. The rule can be satisfied either with two witnesses, or alternatively, one witness and sufficient corroborative evidence. Jurisdictions have differed over the precise level of sufficiency required for corroboration.

Generally, the corroborating evidence does not have to be sufficient for a conviction. It cannot, however, consist of merely peripheral testimony not tending to show the falsity of the accused's statements while under oath. *United States v. Diggs* (7th Cir.1977). Most courts require that the corroborative evidence "be inconsistent with the innocence of the accused and must tend to show the perjury independently of the testimony which it is intended to corroborate." *United States v. Forrest* (5th Cir. 1981). Independent evidence has been defined as "evidence coming from a source other than that of the direct testimony." *United States v. Diggs* (7th Cir.1977).

Some jurisdictions, however, have not mandated that the corroborative evidence, taken by itself, be inconsistent with the innocence of the accused. These courts find it sufficient if the corroborative evidence, taken in conjunction with the direct testimony, is inconsistent with the innocence of the accused.

Courts have accepted circumstantial evidence as corroboration. The evidence must, however, be trustworthy. Some jurisdictions have permitted the defendant's own statements and conduct to serve as the corroboration. The jury decides the weight to be accorded to the corroborative evidence.

§ 10.08 Recantation

The false declarations statute, section 1623, permits a limited defense of recantation. The statute provides one with the opportunity to admit false testimony and avoid a false declarations prosecution. The statute requires that the admission be made in the same continuous court or grand jury proceeding of the original declaration. The statute, however, is only applicable in certain circumstances.

Congress offered this recantation defense in an effort to "encourage truthful testimony by witnesses appearing before courts and grand juries." *United States v. Moore* (D.C.Cir.1979). The House Committee on the Judiciary reported that recantation "serves as an inducement to the witness to give truthful testimony by permitting him voluntarily to correct a false statement without incurring the risk [of] prosecution by doing so."

Recantation does not apply to perjury prosecutions under section 1621. Defendants have unsuccessfully raised the issue that the government has deprived them of their right of recantation by charging perjury when the conduct could have been charged pursuant to the false declarations statute. In *United States v. Kahn* (2d Cir.1973), the Second Circuit expressed concern with the prospect of prosecutors using section 1621 when a recantation existed and section 1623 when it did not. In *Kahn* the court found it unnecessary to reach the merits of this argument in that even if the defendant had been charged pursuant to the false declarations statute, he would not have been entitled to a recantation defense.

Eligibility for a recantation defense is statutorily limited in that "at the time the admission is made, the declaration has not substantially affected the proceeding, or it has not become manifest that such falsity has been or will be exposed." Despite the disjunctive wording of this provision, most courts hold that "and" should be substituted for the "or" in section 1623(d). Thus, a defendant desiring a recantation defense must avail themselves of the opportunity before it substantially affects the proceeding and prior to it being exposed. The Eighth Circuit, however, found that "or" should be given "its ordinary meaning, reading the statute as setting forth two alternative conditions, satisfaction of either of which will allow a declarant to employ the recantation defense to bar prosecution for perjury." *United States v. Smith* (8th Cir.1994).

The rationale as to why most courts require both conditions for a recantation defense is seen in examining the statute's aim of truthtelling in judicial proceedings. To permit a defendant the right to recant upon realization of a possible prosecution, would encourage a witness to initially lie. Only when threatened with exposure or prosecution would the witness come forward to recant. *United States v. Fornaro* (2d Cir.1990).

In *United States v. Moore* (D.C.Cir.1979), the defendant initially testified before a grand jury investigating police corruption. Learning of a tape recording that contradicted his testimony, he attempted to recant his prior grand jury statements. The government, however, stopped a rehearsal of this recantation claiming his new version to be lacking credibility. The district court dismissed defendant's indictment when the government refused to permit defendant Moore the opportunity to reappear before the grand jury to recant his prior statements.

On appeal, the District of Columbia Circuit Court reversed and remanded, finding that the defendant was not entitled to a recantation defense when the government was already aware that Moore had lied to the grand jury. The court recognized that the recantation defense was premised upon a New York statute that used a conjunctive interpretation. It permitted a recantation defense only when the falsity had not substantially affected the proceeding and when it had not become manifest that such falsity had been or would be exposed.

In addition to these two conditions, courts have precluded a recantation defense when a defendant is using this avenue to attempt to explain prior inconsistent testimony. Outright retraction and repudiation of the prior statement has been required. *United States v. Tobias* (9th Cir.1988). Implicit recantation, such as claiming memory loss, has been held not to suffice.

A recantation defense must be raised by the defendant prior to trial. Courts differ, however, on which party bears the burden of proving recantation. Some find that once the defendant raises the issue, then the prosecution has the burden of proving the inapplicability of the recantation defense beyond a reasonable doubt. Other courts place the burden on the defendant to prove proper recantation pursuant to section 1623(d). It is, however, clear that recantation is a question of law for the court.

CHAPTER ELEVEN

TAX CRIMES

§ 11.01 Introduction

White collar crime prosecutions commonly include tax charges. Title 26 of the United States Code provides an array of available offenses. Additionally, tax offenses can sometimes be prosecuted through general criminal statutes found in Title 18.

Charges are often premised on attempts to evade or defeat tax. (26 U.S.C. § 7201). Also noteworthy to criminal tax prosecutions are charges of failure to file a return or pay a tax (26 U.S.C. § 7203), and the filing or aiding and assisting in the filing of a false tax return. (26 U.S.C. § 7206). On occasion the prosecution also will include a charge of delivering a fraudulent return. (26 U.S.C. § 7207).

Fewer prosecutions have been premised on other tax offenses, such as a willful failure to collect or truthfully account for and pay over any tax (26 U.S.C. § 7202), a willful furnishing of a fraudulent statement or failing to furnish a statement to employees as required by section 6051 of the Internal Revenue Code (26 U.S.C. § 7204), and a willful failure to supply withholding information or the supplying of false withholding information to an employer (26 U.S.C. § 7205).

181

Section 7212 criminalizes two types of behavior. Under section 7212(a) one who corruptly or by force or threats of force endeavors to interfere with the administration of the internal revenue laws is subject to prosecution. Section 7212(b) criminalizes forcible rescue of property seized under the Internal Revenue Code. A tax offense also exists specifically to combat offenses such as extortion and obstruction by officers and employees "of the United States acting in connection with any revenue law of the United States." (26 U.S.C. § 7214).

There are also statutes for specific criminal conduct that arises in the context of tax issues. For example, false statements to purchasers or lessees relating to tax (26 U.S.C. § 7211), failure to obey a summons pursuant to certain sections of the Internal Revenue Code (26 U.S.C. § 7210), and disclosure or use of information by preparers of returns can in certain circumstances result in misdemeanor penalties (26 U.S.C. § 7216).

Criminal statutes located in the crimes section of the United States Code also provide a basis for the prosecution of tax charges. For example, a conspiracy (18 U.S.C. § 371) charge can be used where the accused conspires with another to commit an offense defined in other federal statutes or conspires to defraud the United States. *United States v. Helmsley* (2d Cir.1991). As previously noted, conspiracy under this general conspiracy statute requires an overt act in furtherance of the conspiracy. (see chap. 3).

False statements (18 U.S.C. § 1001), false claims (18 U.S.C. § 287), perjury (18 U.S.C. § 1621), and mail fraud (18 U.S.C. § 1341) have also been used when the conduct involves tax violations. Recently the Department of Justice restrained prosecutorial discretion by internally limiting the application of mail fraud charges to tax offenses. Authorization is now required to prosecute tax violations as mail fraud. Further, the Department of Justice Guideline states that this authorization will only be given in "exceptional circumstance[s]." This restriction not only serves to limit the prosecution of tax violations through mail fraud charges, but also limits tax violations that might be prosecuted under the Racketeer Influenced and Corrupt Organization Act (RICO). Because mail fraud serves as one of the possible predicate acts for a RICO offense, but tax violations do not, the restriction has the effect of precluding most tax violations from being used in RICO prosecutions. This guideline, however, is not enforceable as a matter of law in that it is merely an internal guideline of the Department of Justice.

§ 11.02   Willfulness

An element common to the tax fraud offenses (§§ 7201–7207) is the mens rea element of willfulness. Although willfulness is not defined in these sections, the Supreme Court has ruled that it has the same meaning in each section. Thus, irrespective of whether the offense is a misdemeanor or a felony, the level of willfulness required remains the same. *United States v. Bishop* (S.Ct.1973). Although the willfulness element remains consistent in all tax fraud prosecutions, it "is a word of many meanings, its construction often being influenced by its context." *Spies v. United States* (S.Ct.1943).

Historically courts interpreted willfulness to mean acts done with "bad purpose or evil intent," *United States v. Murdock* (S.Ct.1933), "evil motive and want of justification in view of all the financial circumstances of the taxpayer," *Spies v. United States* (S.Ct.1943), or "willful in the sense that he knew that he should have reported more income than he did." *Sansone v. United States* (S.Ct.1965). This historical view is outlined in the Supreme Court's decision in *United States v. Bishop* (S.Ct. 1973).

Bishop, a lawyer convicted of three counts of the felony of filing a false return (26 U.S.C. § 7206(1)), contested the failure of the trial court to give his requested instruction on the misdemeanor offense of delivering a fraudulent return (26 U.S.C. § 7207). He argued that section 7207 was a lesser included offense of the felony and that "willfully" as found in the misdemeanor statute should be construed to require less scienter than the term would require in the felony offense.

In rejecting defendant's argument, the Supreme Court in *Bishop* stated that " 'willfully' has the same meaning in § 7207 that it has in § 7206(1)." While adhering to the historical standard of willfulness, the Supreme Court in *Bishop* also stated that willfully "connotes a voluntary, intentional violation of a known legal duty."

In *United States v. Pomponio* (S.Ct.1976), the Supreme Court elucidated upon its holding in *Bishop*. Petitioners in *Pomponio* were convicted of willfully filing false income tax returns (26 U.S.C. § 7206(1)). The Supreme Court reversed the appellate court's ruling that the jury had been improperly instructed concerning willfulness. The instruction given by the trial court had not required a finding of bad purpose or evil motive. The Court in *Pomponio* stated that *Bishop* did not require "proof of any motive other than an intentional violation of a known legal duty." Thus, the trial court did not err in failing to instruct the jury on bad purpose or evil motive.

Although courts continue to refer to bad purpose and evil motive, it is clear that the government is not required to present such proof in establishing the element of willfulness. It is, however, incumbent upon the government to prove beyond a reasonable doubt that the accused intentionally and voluntarily violated a known legal duty.

Whether the accused acted with the requisite intent is a question of fact subject to jury determination. Often the prosecution offers circumstantial evidence as proof of this mens rea. A jury may infer willfulness from the facts presented. In practice, juries are often provided with evidence of the accused engaging in fraudulent type conduct ("badges of fraud").

Negating the element of willfulness can be a crucial aspect of the defense. In the landmark case of *Cheek v. United States* (S.Ct.1991), the Supreme Court resolved the standard to be used by a jury in deciding whether a defendant had a good faith misunderstanding of the law that negated willfulness.

Petitioner Cheek, a commercial airline pilot, was convicted by a jury of six charges of failing to file federal income tax returns (26 U.S.C. § 7203) and for alleged tax evasions (26 U.S.C. § 7201). Petitioner, acting pro se at trial, argued that he acted without willfulness in that he believed his actions were lawful and further that he believed that the tax laws were being unconstitutionally enforced.

The district court instructed the jury on three occasions regarding aspects of willfulness. The latter two occasions were as a result of questions submitted to the court by the jury. On appeal Cheek argued that the trial court erred in instructing the jury "that only an objectively reasonable misunderstanding of the law negates the statutory willfulness requirement." The Seventh Circuit rejected Cheek's argument and affirmed his convictions.

The Supreme Court granted certiorari and thereafter vacated the judgment of the Court of Appeals and remanded the case for further proceedings consistent with its opinion. Justice White, writing the majority opinion, commenced by noting that the term "willfully" as used in federal criminal tax offenses served to "carv[e] out an exception to the traditional rule" that ignorance of the law or mistake of law is no defense to criminal prosecution. The Court further reaffirmed that the standard for willfulness is the "voluntary, intentional violation of a known legal duty."

In resolving the issues presented in this case, the Court concentrated on the "knowledge" requirement of willfulness. The government must prove that the defendant is "aware of the duty at issue, which cannot be true if the jury credits a good-faith misunderstanding and belief submission, whether or not the claimed belief or misunderstanding is objectively reasonable." To characterize a belief as not objectively reasonable transforms the question to a legal issue and precludes the jury from properly resolving this factual question. It was, therefore, improper for the trial court to instruct the jury in such a way that they were precluded from considering petitioner's asserted beliefs that wages were not income and that he was not a taxpayer within the meaning of the Internal Revenue Code. The Court determined that these are rightfully issues to be decided by a jury in considering whether Cheek had acted willfully.

The Court in *Cheek*, however, rejected the defendant's claim that he had a good-faith belief that the income tax laws were unconstitutional as applied to him. Claims of unconstitutionality reveal that the accused's conduct is not arising from innocent mistakes. Rather, it provides a showing of full knowledge of the law. A defendant's view of the law is irrelevant to the issue of willfulness. It was, therefore, not error in this case for the trial court to instruct the jury to disregard defendant's claims that the tax laws were unconstitutional.

In his concurring opinion, Justice Scalia voiced his dissatisfaction with the Court's test for willfulness. He argued that willfulness should not be interpreted so "that belief in the nonexistence of a textual prohibition excuses liability, but belief in the invalidity (*i.e.*, the legal nonexistence) of a textual prohibition does not."

A dissent authored by Justice Blackmun, and joined by Justice Marshall, criticized the Court for exceeding the limits of common sense. The dissent expressed the view that a person of defendant's intelligence should not be permitted to assert, as a defense to willfulness, that the wages he receives for labor is not income.

On retrial, defendant Cheek argued a good faith belief premised upon his reliance on the advice of counsel. The trial court, however, refused defendant's request for an instruction on advice of counsel. The Seventh Circuit affirmed, finding insufficient evidence to warrant the giving of the instruction. *United States v. Cheek* (7th Cir.1993).

Willfulness also can be negated when there is uncertainty in the tax law. *James v. United States* (S.Ct.1961). In *United States v. Garber* (5th Cir. 1979), the Fifth Circuit in an en banc rehearing examined the defendant's conviction for tax fraud that stemmed from her alleged failure to report income from the sale of her blood. The court reversed and remanded this section 7201 conviction finding that the district court had acted improperly in failing to permit experts from testifying on the question of whether the income was taxable. The court also found it improper for the trial court to have refused to instruct the jury that a reasonable misconception of tax law would negate defendant's intent. Because of the novel and unsettled nature of the law, the defendant should have been afforded the opportunity to present this position.

Some jurisdictions adhere to the position taken in *Garber*, finding uncertainty in the law as a proper defense to a tax charge. Subsequent Fifth Circuit cases, however, have limited *Garber* to the facts of that case. *United States v. Burton* (5th Cir.1984). Additionally, not all jurisdictions accept the position expressed in *Garber*. For example, in *United States v. Curtis* (6th Cir.1986), the Sixth Circuit rejected this view in part because it placed in the hands of the jury a legal question that should be resolved by the court. In *Curtis* the court expressed the view that a jury should not be asked "to read and interpret statutes to determine whether or not the governing law is uncertain or debatable."

§ 11.03 Tax Evasion

Tax evasion is considered the "capstone" of the tax offenses. Its purpose is to "induce prompt and forthright fulfillment of every duty under the income tax law and to provide a penalty suitable to every degree of delinquency." *Spies v. United States* (S.Ct.1943). The elements of a charge pursuant to

26 U.S.C. § 7201 are: (1) the existence of a tax deficiency, (2) an affirmative act of evasion or attempted evasion of tax, and (3) willfulness. The felony of tax evasion carries a penalty of not more than five years imprisonment and a fine. When the evasion is by a corporation, the fine can be increased.

The government is required to prove beyond a reasonable doubt the existence of a tax deficiency. Courts often require that the deficiency be "substantial." In *United States v. Marashi* (9th Cir. 1990), however, the Ninth Circuit rejected defendant's *de minimis* argument. The court stated that "[t]he language of section 7201 does not contain a substantiality requirement. It simply states that willful attempts to evade 'any tax' under the Tax Code is a felony." In reality, the Justice Department seldom prosecutes a tax evasion case absent a showing of a sufficient level of tax due and owing.

A mere tax deficiency, however, will not suffice to sustain an evasion conviction. It is also essential that the government show an affirmative act of evasion and willfulness. The evidence supporting these latter two elements often coalesces.

In *Spies v. United States* (S.Ct.1943), the Supreme Court examined the predecessor evasion statute as it relates to the misdemeanor of willful failure to pay a tax. According to the Court, the factor that distinguishes these two offenses is the "affirmative action implied from the term 'attempt,' as used in the felony subsection." While the misdemeanor can be a willful omission, the felony of evasion requires a positive attempt to evade tax.

The willful attempt to defeat or evade tax can be accomplished "in any manner." In *Spies* the Court offered illustrations of conduct (so-called "badges of fraud") from which a willful attempt could be inferred. The examples provided were "keeping a double set of books, making false entries or alterations, or false invoices or documents, destruction of books or records, concealment of assets or covering up sources of income, handling of one's affairs to avoid making the records usual in transactions of the kind, and any conduct, the likely effect of which would be to mislead or conceal." The filing of a false tax return has been found to be a sufficient affirmative commission to satisfy this element. *Sansone v. United States* (S.Ct.1965).

§ 11.04   Methods of Proof

It is necessary for the government to prove a tax deficiency for a prosecution under section 7201. One way this can be accomplished is through the direct or specific item method. Alternatively, the government can use indirect methods of proof. The indirect methods include the net worth method, the expenditures method, and bank deposit method.

The direct or specific item method is considered the simplest method of proving a tax deficiency. It employs specific items to prove the underpayment. For example, a defendant's records could be used to prove that a specific deduction listed on the return was improper.

Indirect methods of proving a tax deficiency use circumstantial evidence to establish this element. One such method is the net worth method that examines the defendant's net worth at the beginning of a year in contrast to the net worth at the end of the year.

In *Holland v. United States* (S.Ct.1954), the Supreme Court examined the use of the net worth method. The Court noted the flaws inherent in this method, but upheld its legality cautioning that it be subject to the "exercise of great care and restraint." It is essential that the government establish the net worth at the beginning of the year with "reasonable certainty." Because the net worth method rests solely on circumstantial evidence, courts require the government to investigate all reasonable explanations offered by the defendant that are inconsistent with guilt.

Using the cash expenditures method, a variant of the net worth method, the government shows that the defendant's expenditures exceeded the reported income. Presumably the source of funds for these expenditures must be taxable income.

Finally, the government can use the bank deposit method for proving the tax deficiency. The government examines the bank deposits of the defendant, excluding deposits that are not taxable income. These deposits are then compared to the reported income of the accused. The excess in the amount deposited over the reported income represents the unreported income.

The government also may use a combination of methods. In *United States v. Scott* (7th Cir.1981), the defendant William J. Scott, former Attorney General for the State of Illinois, was convicted of one count of violating section 7206(1). The government used the net worth, cash expenditures, and specific items methods to prove that Scott had falsely reported his adjusted gross income for 1972.

§ 11.05   Failure to File a Return or Pay a Tax

Section 7203 criminalizes the willful failure to pay any tax, make any return, keep any records, or supply any information as required by law or regulations. The government must prove beyond a reasonable doubt that the accused, (1) willfully, (2) failed to make a return, to pay a tax, to keep records or supply information, (3) having a legal duty to do so, (4) at the time required by law. This misdemeanor offense carries a penalty of up to one year imprisonment and a fine. In the case of a corporation, this fine can be increased. If, however, the failure to pay involves an estimated tax, the section is inapplicable if there is no addition to tax under section 6654 or 6655. The statute becomes a felony offense where the willful violation involves section 6050I of the Code. (see § 12.06). In this circumstance the offense carries a penalty of up to five years imprisonment.

This section is commonly employed to prosecute tax protesters who fail to file a return or who file incomplete returns. It is rare that the government proceeds with a section 7203 case absent a certain threshold of unpaid tax. Failure to file can be proven by testimony of an individual from the Internal Revenue Service stating that a search was made of the government's records and no return was found. As with other tax offenses, the government is required to prove that the accused acted willfully.

§ 11.06 False Returns

Section 7206 is divided into two separate offenses. Subsection one is a perjury tax offense in that it prohibits one from willfully making and subscribing a return, statement, or other document under penalties of perjury which the person did not believe to be true and correct as to every material matter. Subsection two criminalizes the conduct of one who aids or assists in the preparation of a false return.

In order to sustain a conviction under section 7206(1), the government must prove that the accused: (1) willfully, (2) signed a return, statement, or other document, (3) under penalties of perjury, (4) that the return, statement, or document was materially false, and (5) that the accused did not believe it to be true and correct. Section 7206(2) requires the government to prove that the accused: (1) willfully, (2) aided or assisted in, or procured, counseled or advised the preparation or presentation of any document in connection with any matter arising under the internal revenue laws, (3) which document is materially false.

Both subsections to this statute are felony offenses. They carry penalties of up to three years imprisonment and a fine. In the case of a corporation, the fine can be increased.

Unlike the tax evasion statute, there is no requirement for the government to prove a tax deficiency. It is only necessary to show that the return is materially false.

In *United States v. DiVarco* (7th Cir.1973), defendants' convictions included violations of section 7206(1). Defendants argued on appeal that the government's failure to show that they understated their income precluded the use of this statutory provision. The Seventh Circuit noted that although most cases involving misstatement of source of income also involve an understatement of taxable income, "the purpose behind the statute is to prosecute those who intentionally falsify their tax returns regardless of the precise ultimate effect that falsification may have." In *DiVarco*, the court found that misstatement of the source of one's income could be a material matter.

In *United States v. Greenberg* (2d Cir.1984), the Second Circuit rejected defendant's argument that the misstatements were not material in that "they resulted in, at most, minimal underpayments of taxes." The court found that materiality referred to the impact the statement may have on the ability of the agency to perform its assigned functions. "The question is not what effect the statement actually had, ... rather whether the statement had the potential for an obstructive or inhibitive effect." The court in *Greenberg* found the false statements of income material, even though they resulted in the minimal underpayment of taxes.

Courts have not ruled consistently on whether materiality under § 7206 is a question of law to be decided by the court, or a question of fact to be decided by the jury. In *United States v. Gaudin* (see § 9.06), the Supreme Court held that issues of materiality of alleged false statements were questions for the jury to decide. In *United States v. Klausner* (2d Cir.1996), the Second Circuit distinguished *Gaudin* finding that the "determination of materiality in the present case under § 7206(2) was purely a legal question." Other courts, however, have followed *Gaudin*, finding "no obvious of substantive distinction between the 'materiality' element of 18 U.S.C. § 1001 and the 'materiality' element of 26 U.S.C. § 7206(1)." *United States v. DiRico* (1st Cir.1996).

A tax preparer can be charged under either subsection of this statute. In *United States v. Shortt Accountancy Corp.* (9th Cir.1986), the defendant corporation was convicted of seven counts of violating section 7206(1). The corporation, through its chief operating officer, improperly structured certain investments to appear as if they occurred before a change in law. This permitted clients to receive an undeserved tax benefit.

The corporation argued on appeal that a tax preparer could not be charged under subsection one of this statute, but rather 7206(2) was the applicable offense. The accounting corporation also maintained that the actual subscriber of the return was unaware of the fraud involved and therefore did not have the requisite intent of willfully making and subscribing a false return.

The Ninth Circuit, in *Shortt*, rejected defendant's arguments, finding that section 7206(1) was not limited to taxpayers. Being a perjury statute, the court found that anyone who makes a false return could be prosecuted pursuant to this provision. The court also held that the corporation could be convicted of section 7206(1) even though the particular employee subscribing the return had no knowledge of the fraudulent scheme. To hold otherwise would permit a tax preparer to escape liability "by arranging for an innocent employee to complete the proscribed act of subscribing a false return."

CHAPTER TWELVE

CURRENCY REPORTING CRIMES

§ 12.01 Introduction

Currency reporting crimes emanate from statutes that are of recent vintage. In an effort to monitor financial transactions, Congress enacted legislation concentrating on reporting and recordkeeping by banks. This initial act, commonly referred to as the Bank Secrecy Act, includes a requirement that financial institutions report to the government certain cash transactions.

A second major effort to use currency transaction reporting as a method to combat criminality is seen in 26 U.S.C. § 6050I. Unlike the Bank Secrecy Act, which is limited to financial institutions, section 6050I requires the reporting of certain monetary transactions by those engaged in a "trade or business." The Bank Secrecy Act and section 6050I both, however, require that parties who meet the defined class, as specified in each of these statutes, report the transaction irrespective of any criminal conduct being involved.

The Bank Secrecy Act and section 6050I include provisions prohibiting the structuring of a transaction to evade the reporting requirements. Addition-

198

ally, Congress enacted sections 1956 and 1957 of Title 18 to combat money laundering. These latter two provisions fill a gap that became apparent in initial prosecutions under the Bank Secrecy Act.

Sections 1956 and 1957 emanate from the Anti–Drug Abuse Act of 1986. Specifically 18 U.S.C. § 1956 concentrates on financial transactions involving proceeds of unlawful activity. It does, however, criminalize transactions involving proceeds of unlawful activity "knowing that the transaction is designed in whole or in part ... to avoid a transaction reporting requirement under State or Federal Law ...". Section 1957 pertains to those who knowingly engage or attempt to engage in monetary transactions involving "criminally derived property that is of a value greater than ten thousand dollars and is derived from specified unlawful activity."

Both sections 1956 and 1957 focus on transactions involving tainted funds. Often drug related activity is prosecuted through the use of these money laundering offenses. In recent years, white collar criminality has also produced charges under sections 1956 and 1957. This is perhaps in part a result of the simplicity in proving a section 1956 and 1957 offense and the severe penalty accompanying these charges.

§ 12.02 Bank Secrecy Act

Congress passed the Bank Secrecy Act in 1970. The Act was "designed to obtain financial information having 'a high degree of usefulness in criminal, tax, or regulatory investigations or proceedings.' *"California Bankers Association v. Shultz* (S.Ct.1974). Title I of the Act, presently codified in Title 12 of the United States Code, pertains to the requirements of financial institutions to keep records, including the maintaining of records of customer identity and the microfilming of checks. Title II of the Bank Secrecy Act, presently codified in Title 31 of the United States Code, requires the reporting to the federal government of certain foreign and domestic transactions. The Act authorizes the Secretary of the Treasury to prescribe via regulation the specified bank recordkeeping and reporting requirements.

Pursuant to 31 U.S.C. § 5313 and its accompanying regulations, it is incumbent that financial institutions file reports on certain domestic transactions. Statutes also exist regarding the recordkeeping and reporting on foreign financial agency transactions (31 U.S.C. § 5314), reports on foreign currency transactions (31 U.S.C. § 5315), and reports on exporting and importing monetary instruments (31 U.S.C. § 5316).

One who causes or attempts to cause a financial institution to fail to file a report required by section 5313(a), or causes or attempts to cause a financial institution to file a report that contains a material omission or misstatement of fact, can find themselves subject to the penalties imposed under this Act. The Bank Secrecy Act also prohibits the structuring of a transaction to evade the currency reporting requirements of section 5313(a). (31 U.S.C. § 5324).

Approximately two years after the passage of the Bank Secrecy Act, an action was brought in the District Court for the Northern District of California contesting the constitutionality of the Act. Although this action's principle focus was a claimed violation of the Fourth Amendment's guarantee against unreasonable searches and seizures, plaintiffs also claimed a violation of the First, Fifth, Ninth, Tenth and Fourteenth Amendments of the Constitution. The Supreme Court, in its eventual ruling in *California Bankers Association v. Shultz* (S.Ct.1974), found that the recordkeeping requirements imposed by the regulations of the Secretary of the Treasury did not deprive the plaintiff bank of due process of law and did not invade the Fourth Amendment's guarantee against unreasonable searches and seizures.

In rejecting this constitutional challenge to the Act, the Court in *California Bankers Association* noted that the recordkeeping requirements, as imposed by the Secretary of the Treasury, did not place an unreasonable burden on banks. The Supreme Court further found that a requirement of maintenance of records did not constitute a seizure. The Court found the application of the reporting requirements to both foreign and domestic transactions to be reasonable and that the bank depositors lacked standing to challenge the Act under the Fourth and Fifth Amendment.

In the later case of *United States v. Miller* (S.Ct. 1976), the Supreme Court held that a bank depositor had no interest protected by the Fourth Amendment in records maintained by a bank pursuant to the Bank Secrecy Act, despite the allegation that these records were obtained by the government through defective subpoenas. The Court found that defendants had no legitimate expectation of privacy in business records of the bank. The Court stated that "[t]he depositor takes the risk, in revealing his affairs to another, that the information will be conveyed by that person to the Government."

In its initial years, the Bank Secrecy Act was seldom employed by the government as a prosecutorial tool. In recent years, however, the Act has significantly influenced the banking industry and has served as a source for the prosecution of financial institutions.

The Bank Secrecy Act and its accompanying regulations impose civil and criminal penalties for noncompliance with many of the reporting requirements. Willful violations of most of the provisions found in Title 31 carry criminal penalties of up to five years imprisonment and a fine. This penalty can be enhanced up to ten years with a fine when there is a willful violation that occurs while violating another law of the United States or engaging in conduct that is part of a pattern of illegal activity involving transactions exceeding $100,000 in a twelve month period. (31 U.S.C. § 5322). The penalty for structuring transactions to evade reporting requirements also carries imprisonment of up to five years, with an additional five years possible in certain aggravated cases. (31 U.S.C. § 5324).

Willful violations of a regulation under the recordkeeping statutes found in Title 12 can result in imprisonment of up to one year and a fine. (12 U.S.C. § 1956). This can be increased up to five years imprisonment with a fine where the violation is committed in furtherance of the commission of any violation of federal law punishable by imprisonment for more than one year. (12 U.S.C. § 1957).

§ 12.03   Domestic Financial Institutions

Section 5313 concerns reports required to be filed by domestic financial institutions. A financial institution is defined in 31 U.S.C. § 5312 and in the regulations of the Secretary of the Treasury. The breadth of this term is apparent in the inclusion of businesses well beyond the typical banking association. For example, financial institutions include "a dealer in precious metals, stones, or jewels," "a pawnbroker," "a travel agency," "a telegraph company," "a business engaged in vehicle sales, including automobile, airplane, and boat sales," and "persons involved in real estate closings and settlements."

In *United States v. Gollott* (5th Cir.1991), defendants challenged their status as a financial institution. In upholding defendants' convictions, the Fifth Circuit examined the definition of financial institution as stated in the amended regulations. The court stated that, "[t]his language is broader than and perhaps counterintuitive to everyday understanding of what a financial institution is, but it is not vague as applied to appellants' dealings." The court decided that the jury had rationally found defendants to be a financial institution as defined by applicable regulations.

In *United States v. Bucey* (7th Cir.1989), the Seventh Circuit reversed a defendant's convictions premised on 31 U.S.C. §§ 5313 and 5322(b). The court found defendant Bucey, acting in his individual capacity, not to be a financial institution, where the definition of the term included the language "agency, branch, or office." The court in *Bucey* did, however, note that the term financial institution was amended in 1987 after the time of defendant's alleged violations. The amended regulation added the word "agent" prior to "agency, branch, or office."

Most circuits find that an individual may be a financial institution. In *United States v. Goldberg* (2d Cir.1985), the Second Circuit noted that "[t]he regulations define a financial institution in part as 'a person.' There is no indication in the statute or the regulations that a natural person cannot be considered a financial institution, and it seems strained to assume that the term 'person' was intended to exclude natural persons."

A financial institution has been defined to encompass a bank, including each of its branches. Thus, if there are multiple cash transactions at different branches of the same financial institution that meet the reporting requirements, then the bank must file a currency transaction report. *United States v. Giancola* (11th Cir.1986).

The terms "domestic financial agency" and "domestic financial institution" are defined in section 5312 as to "apply to an action in the United States of a financial agency or institution." In a case under a somewhat differently worded predecessor statute, the Eleventh Circuit held that even though transactions were negotiated and completed in Columbia, the defendants were a domestic financial institution where their currency exchange business deposited money in a United States bank and the bank relayed information concerning each transaction from the United States to Columbia. *United States v. Eisenstein* (11th Cir.1984).

§ 12.04 Recordkeeping and Reporting Requirements

The Bank Secrecy Act and its accompanying regulations specify both recordkeeping and reporting requirements. Certain records by financial institutions involving extensions of credit, transfers of currency or monetary instruments, or intents to transfer currency or monetary instruments, are subject to be retained in original, microfilm, or other form of reproduction. The threshold monetary value for this retention requirement is ten thousand dollars.

Regulations also specify records that are to be retained by brokers and dealers in securities, records to be made and retained by casinos, and those that are to be made and retained by currency dealers or exchangers. Financial institutions may not issue or sell a bank check or draft, cashier's check, money order or traveler's check for three thousand dollars or more unless it maintains a log with certain information as specified by regulation. (31 C.F.R. § 103.29).

The Bank Secrecy Act through its regulations also require the filing of three types of reports. Domestic financial institutions are required to file a report for transactions that exceed ten thousand dollars. (31 C.F.R. § 103.22). This report (CTR) is submitted to the Internal Revenue Service. Each person who transports or causes one to transport in excess of ten thousand dollars in currency and other monetary instruments into or outside the United States needs to file a report (CMIR). (31 C.F.R. § 103.23). Finally, a report is mandated for each person subject to United States jurisdiction who has interests in foreign financial accounts. (31 C.F.R. § 103.24). All three of these reports have to be filed irrespective of the involvement of any criminal conduct. The regulations accompanying the Bank Secrecy Act give the Secretary of the Treasury authority in certain instances to institute additional recordkeeping and reporting requirements.

Treasury Form 4789 is the applicable form for the reporting of a currency transaction of ten thousand dollars or more. The financial institution needs to file this report within fifteen days following the day on which the reportable transaction occurred. Additionally, the financial institution is required to maintain a copy of the report for five years. The financial institution is required by regulation to verify the identity of the individual presenting the transaction. (31 C.F.R. § 103.28).

Form 4789 is incorporated into the regulations through the requirement that "[a]ll information called for in [the CTR] forms shall be furnished." (31 C.F.R. § 103.27). Financial institutions have an obligation pursuant to the reporting requirements to disclose on the form a real party in interest to reportable currency transactions. *United States v. Belcher* (11th Cir.1991).

The regulations list certain parties that are exempt from filing reports of currency transactions. Included within the exempt category are transactions with Federal Reserve Banks or Federal Home Loan Banks, transactions between domestic banks, and a nonbank's financial institutions transactions with a commercial bank. A commercial bank must, however, report transactions with a nonbank financial institution.

Banks are also authorized to exempt certain specified parties from this reporting requirement. For example, a bank may exempt "[d]eposits or withdrawals of currency from an existing account by an established depositor who is a United States resident and operates a retail type of business in the United States." (31 C.F.R. § 103.22). The regulations, however, do contain restrictions for the applicability of these exemptions. Further, a bank must prepare a specified written statement detailing the reasons why the exemption applies. A bank, may request additional exemptions from the Commissioner of Internal Revenue.

Reports on exporting and importing monetary instruments are the subject of 31 U.S.C. § 5316. Certain monetary instruments transported from the United States to a place outside this country or from outside the United States to within this country are subject to the reporting requirements. Additionally, monetary instruments received from outside the United States may be subject to these reporting requirements. In 1986 this section of the Bank Secrecy Act was amended to increase the reportable amount from five thousand dollars to ten thousand dollars.

The regulations provided by the Secretary of the Treasury pursuant to this statutory provision on reports of transportation of currency or monetary instruments contain an array of exemptions from this filing requirement. (31 C.F.R. § 103.23). For example, a federal reserve bank is not subject to this reporting requirement. Regulations also provide the procedure, including time limitations for the filing of reports. (31 C.F.R. § 103.27).

§ 12.05 Knowledge and Willfulness

Criminal prosecutions under the Bank Secrecy Act often require willfulness. Recent legislation removed the willfulness requirement when a structuring offense is involved.

In *Ratzlaf v. United States* (S.Ct.1994), the Supreme Court examined willfulness in the context of an alleged structuring offense under 31 U.S.C.

§ 5324. In reversing defendant's conviction, the Court held that to willfully violate "the antistructuring law, the Government must prove that the defendant acted with knowledge that his conduct was unlawful." The Court in *Ratzlaf* stated that they were "unpersuaded ... that structuring is 'so obviously "evil" or inherently "bad" that the "willfulness" requirement is satisfied irrespective of the defendant's knowledge of the illegality of structuring.'"

In response to the *Ratzlaf* decision, Congress modified § 5324 as part of the Riegle Community Development and Regulatory Improvement Act of 1994. The modified statute omits the term willfully. By placing penalty provisions directly in § 5324, the mens rea for the structuring statute is now met when the government shows that the defendant intended to evade the reporting requirement.

In *United States v. Bank of New England, N.A.* (1st Cir.1987), the First Circuit found that a trial court's collective knowledge instruction was proper where a bank had a structure similar to that of a large corporation. The court stated that "[c]orporations compartmentalize knowledge, subdividing the elements of specific duties and operations into smaller components. The aggregate of those components constitutes the corporation's knowledge of a potential operation." (see chap. 2).

§ 12.06   Section 6050I

Section 6050I of the Internal Revenue Code (Title 26) was modeled after the Bank Secrecy Act. A shortcoming of the Bank Secrecy Act, as being limited to financial institutions, was met by the adoption of a statute that extended currency transaction reporting to individuals engaged in a trade or business. Section 6050I, as passed in 1984, was intended to encourage the reporting of cash income in order to reduce the deficit. In reality, this section has become a tool for monitoring criminal activity.

26 U.S.C. § 6050I is applicable to trades or businesses that receive in excess of ten thousand dollars in cash. It requires the reporting of these transactions to the Internal Revenue Service. The section excludes transactions that would be reported pursuant to the Bank Secrecy Act. A provision of section 6050I prohibits the evading or assisting in the structuring of a transaction to avoid the reporting requirement. The Internal Revenue Service's form for complying with section 6050I is found in Form 8300.

Section 6050I and Form 8300 have proved controversial in the legal community. Because the statute applies to all trades or businesses, the question has arisen as to the section's applicability to payments received by attorneys.

In *United States v. Goldberger & Dubin, P.C.* (2d Cir.1991), the Second Circuit found that section 6050I did not conflict with the United States Constitution. Analogizing to cases reported under the Bank Secrecy Act, the court found no Fourth or Fifth Amendment violation. The court noted that the reporting requirements targeted transactions without regard to the underlying purpose and irrespective of any criminality involved in the transaction.

The *Goldberger* court also dismissed defense arguments that section 6050I was a deprivation of the right to counsel under the Sixth Amendment. The court found the section less intrusive than the recent Supreme Court decisions that permitted forfeiture of attorney fees. The Second Circuit stated that section 6050I did not preclude clients from their choice of counsel, "they need only pay counsel in some other manner than with cash."

Equally unpersuasive to the *Goldberger* court was appellant's contention that section 6050I conflicted with the attorney-client privilege. "Absent special circumstances," the court found that client identity and fee information were not privileged matters. (see § 22.01). Since the practice of law is considered a "trade or business" for purposes of the income tax laws and the Sherman Act, *Goldberger* found that absent a specific congressional intent to exclude attorneys, section 6050I applied to lawyers.

In *United States v. Sindel* (8th Cir.1995), the Eighth Circuit examined when the attorney-client privilege would protect client identity and fee information. "Special circumstances" exceptions were found to include "the legal advice exception," "the last link exception," and the "confidential communications exception." "After examining Sindel's *in camera* testimony about client's special circumstances," the court found the release of information with respect to one client, could not be accomplished without revealing "confidential communication." According to the court, "special circumstances," however, did not exist with respect to a second client.

It is necessary for the government to use the procedural process correctly when seeking to obtain information from an attorney about their client. In *United States v. Gertner* (1st Cir.1995), the First Circuit did not address the applicability of § 6050I to attorneys, finding that summons enforcement should be denied in that the government failed to adhere to the proper procedure for the service of John Doe summonses (see § 17.04).

CHAPTER THIRTEEN
BANKRUPTCY CRIMES

§ 13.01　Introduction

Statutes pertaining to bankruptcy crimes are, for the most part, found in sections 151 through 157 of Title 18. General criminal statutes also have been employed in the prosecution of criminal conduct related to bankruptcies.

Historically 18 U.S.C. § 152 served as the key bankruptcy crime statute for the prosecution of bankruptcy fraud. This statute concentrates on the concealment of assets, false oaths, and bribery and extortion conduct occurring in connection with a bankruptcy.

Section 153 pertains to embezzlement by a trustee, officer, or their agent. A penalty of up to five years imprisonment and fine can be imposed against a trustee, custodian, marshal, or other officer who "knowingly and fraudulently appropriates" to their "own use, embezzles, spends, or transfers any property or secrets or destroys a document" in their charge that is from the debtor's estate.

A custodian, trustee, marshal, or other officer of the court, who "knowingly purchases, directly or indirectly, any property of the estate of which he is such an officer in a case under Title 11" is subject to a fine and a forfeiture of the office held by the individual. Section 154 not only contains this adverse interest statute, but also imposes the same penalty when an officer refuses a court direction permitting parties in interest a reasonable opportunity to inspect documents or refuses a United States Trustee a reasonable opportunity to inspect documents.

Section 155 prohibits a party in interest from knowingly and fraudulently agreeing with another party in interest to the fixing of a fee or other compensation from the assets of the estate. A violation of this latter provision can result in imprisonment of up to one year and a fine.

Section 156, a new bankruptcy fraud provision, penalizes a bankruptcy petition preparer "if a bankruptcy case or related proceeding is dismissed because of a knowing attempt" by the preparer to disregard the bankruptcy statutes and rules. The bankruptcy petition preparer, defined as "a person, other than the debtor's attorney or an employee of such attorney, who prepares for compensation a document for filing" faces up to one year imprisonment and a fine for the knowing disregard of a bankruptcy law or rule.

Section 157, also a new bankruptcy fraud provision, is modeled after the mail fraud statute. Like mail fraud, it authorizes a penalty of up to five years imprisonment and a fine against individuals who devise or intend to devise a scheme or artifice to defraud. The execution of the scheme can be through filing a bankruptcy petition, bankruptcy document, or the making of a "false or fraudulent representation, claim, or promise concerning or in relation" to a bankruptcy proceeding. The extent to which section 157 will displace section 152 in bankruptcy fraud prosecutions remains to be seen.

Despite the existence of specific bankruptcy crime statutes, prosecutors have on occasion bypassed these statutes and proceeded with actions under general criminal statutes. Most often, bankruptcy crimes are charged in conjunction with charges using general criminal offenses found in Title 18. For example, agreements by two or more individuals to commit a bankruptcy offense have been prosecuted under both section 152 and the general conspiracy statute. (18 U.S.C. § 371). When there is a scheme to defraud coupled with a mailing in furtherance of the scheme, mail fraud has been included by prosecutors. (18 U.S.C. § 1341). Prosecutors have also included charges of wire fraud, tax evasion, and perjury in bankruptcy fraud cases.

In addition to these general criminal provisions, when there is a pattern of racketeering involving fraud connected with a case under Title 11, the offense may be the subject of a RICO prosecution. To proceed with a RICO charge it is, of course, necessary for the government to prove all the elements of this offense (see chap. 8). As a predicate act of RICO, bankruptcy fraud can be pursued in both criminal and civil RICO actions.

§ 13.02   Bankruptcy Fraud

Historically prosecutors used section 152 of Title 18 to prosecute bankruptcy fraud. The essence of this statute is to provide criminality when the debtor or others associated with the bankruptcy attempt to avoid the required distribution of non-exempt assets to creditors as provided for by the Bankruptcy Code.

The statute contains a variety of fraudulent acts upon which a criminal prosecution can be premised. Most notable among the listing is the general concealment provision. Under this aspect of the statute, criminality is imposed when one "knowingly and fraudulently conceals from the custodian, trustee, marshal, or other officer of the court charged with the control or custody of property, or from creditors in any case under Title 11, any property belonging to the estate of a debtor."

In addition to this general prohibition against concealment, section 152 specifically prohibits the knowing and fraudulent (2) making of a false oath or account, (3) making of a false declaration, (4) presenting of a false proof of claim, (5) receiving any material amount of property from a debtor, after the filing of a case under Title 11, (6) giving, offering, receiving, or attempts to obtain any money, property, or advantage for acting or forbearing to act in a bankruptcy case, (7) transferring or concealing of property in contemplation of a Title 11 case, (8) concealing, destroying, or falsifying documents relating to property or financial affairs of a debtor after or in contemplation of the filing of a Title 11 case, and (9) withholding recorded information relating to the property or financial affairs of the debtor, from an officer, after the filing of a Title 11 case. Thus, this act provides criminality to acts of concealment, false oaths, and bribery that occur in relation to a bankruptcy.

To sustain a conviction under the general concealment clause of section 152, the government must prove beyond a reasonable doubt that the accused (1) knowingly and fraudulently, (2) concealed from an officer or the creditors, (3) in a Title 11 case, (4) property belonging to the estate of the debtor. To sustain a conviction under the false oath clause of section 152, the government must prove beyond a reasonable doubt that the accused (1) knowingly and fraudulently, (2) made a false oath or account, (3) that was material, (4) in relation to a Title 11 case. A violation of section 152 is a felony and can result in a penalty of up to five years imprisonment and a fine.

§ 13.03 Concealment and False Oath

Concealment, in a variety of ways, can form the basis of a prosecution under section 152. Secreting, falsifying, and mutilating of property or information have been found to be evidence of concealment. Mere omission of an asset on a bankruptcy schedule does not, however, indicate conclusively the existence of concealment.

In *Coghlan v. United States* (8th Cir.1945), the Eighth Circuit discussed the circumstances of when a failure to schedule property would constitute a concealment. The court noted that although omission of assets from a schedule indicates concealment, taken alone this is inconclusive. "The conduct of the bankrupt, the relative extent of the omission, the character of the asset itself, and the reasons given for the difference between financial statements of the business and the bankruptcy schedules are the other circumstances in every case." When these circumstances explain the omission, the element of concealment is lacking. The court in *Coghlan* noted, however, that facts supporting a continued concealment consummate the offense.

The knowing and fraudulent filing of a false account or schedule of assets under oath, also can form the basis of a prosecution under the false oath provision of section 152. *Goetz v. United States* (7th Cir.1932). Actions premised upon the false oath provision of section 152 have been held as not requiring all of the elements of a perjury charge. *United States v. Lynch* (7th Cir.1950).

Some courts, however, examine the false oath in the context of perjury law. Thus, literally true, but unresponsive answers to questions cannot form a perjury charge when the examiner is put on notice to ask additional questions to clarify the answers provided. *Bronston v. United States* (S.Ct.1973) (see § 10.04). Perjury, however, is established if in the context in which the statement is made, it is materially untrue. Thus, a false oath prosecution can be upheld despite the existence of statements that are literally true in isolation. *United States v. Schafrick* (2d Cir.1989).

Actions involving false oaths and accounts require the government to prove materiality. Materiality has been defined as referring "not only to the main fact which is the subject of inquiry, but also to any fact or circumstance which tends to corroborate or strengthen the proof adduced to establish the main fact." *Metheany v. United States* (9th Cir.1966). Materiality does not require the government to prove that creditors were harmed by the false statement.

Matters "pertinent to the extent and nature of [a] bankrupt's assets, including the history of a bankrupt's financial transactions," have been found material. Statements designed to secure adjudication by a particular bankruptcy court have been found to be material. *United States v. O'Donnell* (9th Cir. 1976). Failing to disclose prior bankruptcies has been found to be material in that this information can "impede an investigation into a debtor's financial affairs." *United States v. Lindholm* (9th Cir. 1994). Additionally, statements aimed at obtaining a particular status before a court, such as *in forma pauperis*, have been held to be material. *United States v. Yagow* (8th Cir.1992).

In *United States v. Phillips* (9th Cir.1979), the Ninth Circuit found misstatements in a bankruptcy petition material, and as included in the indictment, these false statements were properly read to the jury. The statements were a false social security number, false prior addresses, and failure to give past names by which the accused had been known. The court stated that the false social security number and fabrication of prior addresses may have misled creditors as to the petitioner's identity and financial background. The failure to provide prior names can obstruct attempts to acquire a full credit history and hinder the determination of assessing one's eligibility for bankruptcy.

Crucial to a bankruptcy fraud prosecution is a bankruptcy proceeding. Provisions within section 152 permit prosecutions to be premised upon concealment in contemplation of a bankruptcy case. A defendant's belief in the invalidity of a bankruptcy proceeding does not negate the bankruptcy fraud. *United States v. Beery* (10th Cir.1982).

It is necessary that the actions of concealment or false oath relate to the bankruptcy. In an action premised upon the false statement provision within section 152, the Eighth Circuit held that the "in relation to" requirement should be interpreted broadly. The court found that statements made in cases arising from a central bankruptcy proceeding would be "in or in relation to any case under Title 11." *United States v. Yagow* (8th Cir.1992).

§ 13.04 Knowingly and Fraudulently

Section 152 requires that the defendant act knowingly and fraudulently. This intent requirement mandates proof by the government that the accused acted willfully as opposed to through mistake, excusable neglect, or inadvertence. A defendant who acts with willful blindness can be found to have acted knowingly and fraudulently. Most often this element is proved through circumstantial evidence. A jury may infer intent from the evidence presented.

In *United States v. Goodstein* (7th Cir.1989), the Seventh Circuit upheld convictions, including a violation of section 152, against an attorney with experience in bankruptcy matters who practiced for over forty years. The court found that the jury could have concluded that the defendant fraudulently intended to evade the requirements of the bankruptcy laws. In assessing this jury determination, the appellate tribunal noted that the defendant was a "knowledgeable businessman and lawyer." The court found that this "extensive legal background and integral role in" these bankruptcy affairs indicated that a failure to notify the bankruptcy court and creditors of a transfer was not something done inadvertently.

Where the accused, in a bankruptcy fraud action alleging concealment, lacked knowledge of the bankruptcy order for relief or the appointment of a receiver, a court reversed the defendant's convictions. The defendant in *United States v. Guiliano* (2d Cir.1981), was neither the owner or an officer of the debtor. As a salesperson, the court found that he was not required to be familiar with the financial condition of the company. Although it was possible to speculate that when the business closed the accused should have realized that a bankruptcy would follow, mere conjecture was insufficient to meet the knowledge requirement.

With respect to one count, the Second Circuit in *Guiliano* was satisfied that there was evidence to support a jury inference of the defendant's knowledge of the bankruptcy order for relief or the appointment of a trustee. This count accused the defendant of fraudulently concealing certain equipment from the bankruptcy trustee. According to the court, there was evidence that the defendant had been requested to remove this equipment and sell it for as much cash as possible. Upon removal of these items, the defendant knew of the company's financial crisis. The court noted that the defendant also worked closely with another individual after the bankruptcy order for relief and appointment of a trustee. Although the *Guiliano* court found evidence inferring knowledge, this count was reversed and remanded for a retrial in that there was a risk that the jury was influenced in its disposition of this count by improper evidence and by allegations of a reversed RICO count.

CHAPTER FOURTEEN
ENVIRONMENTAL CRIMES

§ 14.01 Introduction

Like so many of the white collar crime areas, the environmental sector also demonstrates an overlap between civil and criminal law. A person violating a federal environmental statute is often subject to civil proceedings, criminal prosecution, or dual civil and criminal actions (see chap. 18).

There exists a wealth of environmental statutes throughout the United States Code. Many of the environmental related Acts contain provisions that criminalize conduct for noncompliance. There is, however, no single comprehensive set of environmental crimes found within the United States Code.

In recent years there has been an increasing number of federal prosecutions for environmental offenses. Typically environmental violations are investigated by the Environmental Protection Agency (EPA). Most often federal criminal prosecutions arise when the EPA refers the matter to the Department of Justice. In 1982, the Department of Justice established a separate environmental crimes unit for the prosecution of these offenses.

The prosecution of environmental crimes is not limited to the indictment of individuals for alleged violations. A significant number of prosecutions have concentrated on the corporate entity. Principles of corporate criminal liability, as well as personal criminal liability in the corporate setting, play a factor in the environmental arena. Prosecutions under the Occupational Health and Safety Act (OSHA) and the Federal Food, Drug, and Cosmetic Act (FDA) have examined principles of corporate criminal liability (see § 2.06).

Water, air, and energy are among the array of environmental areas that have incorporated criminal provisions for enforcement of specific Acts. With respect to water, one observes criminal penalties for noncompliance in Acts such as the Rivers and Harbors Appropriations Act (33 U.S.C. § 401 et seq.), Safe Drinking Water Act (42 U.S.C. § 300f et seq.), and the Water Pollution Control Act (Clean Water Act) (33 U.S.C. § 1251 et seq.). Criminal penalties are provided for in the Clean Air Act (42 U.S.C. § 7401 et seq.), the Resource Conservation and Recovery Act of 1976 (Solid Waste Disposal Act) (RCRA) (42 U.S.C. § 6901 et seq.), the Toxic Substances Control Act (TSCA) (15 U.S.C. § 2601 et seq.), the Federal Insecticide, Fungicide, and Rodenticide Act (FIFRA) (7 U.S.C. § 136 et seq.), the Atomic Energy Act (42 U.S.C. § 2011 et seq.), and the Comprehensive Environmental Response, Compensation, and Liability Act of 1980 (CERCLA) (42 U.S.C. § 9601 et seq.). These are, however, by no means an exhaustive list of the federal environmental Acts that contain criminal enforcement provisions. Scattered throughout federal law are environmental statutes that use criminal sanctions for the purposes of enforcement. Many states have also incorporated environmental crimes statutes as part of their laws.

Federal prosecutions related to environmental crimes have not always been limited to the specific provisions found within an environmental Act. On occasion the government will prosecute under general criminal provisions or add general criminal provisions as additional counts against a defendant. For example, prosecutors have included conspiracy charges, pursuant to 18 U.S.C. § 371, when there are two or more offenders who agree to commit a specific offense and an overt act is performed in furtherance of the conspiracy. (see chap. 3). A false reporting of a material fact to a government agency can result in a prosecution under the false statements statute. (18 U.S.C. § 1001). (see chap. 9). Environmental crime prosecutions have also added charges of mail fraud when there is a scheme to defraud and a mailing in furtherance of that scheme. (18 U.S.C. § 1341) (see chap. 4).

§ 14.02   Mens Rea

Most environmental offenses emanate from a violation of regulatory statutes. It is common for defendants to concentrate their defense on arguing the level of intent necessary for proving a violation of the applicable statute.

Courts have not always ruled consistently when examining the issue of intent as it pertains to an environmental statute. For example, the Sixth Circuit in *United States v. Wulff* (6th Cir.1985), found that a felony provision of the Migratory Bird Treaty Act (MBTA), that did not require proof of scienter, violated due process. The court found that because the felony was a "crime unknown to the common law" which carried a substantial penalty, the government was required to prove that the defendant acted with some degree of scienter. In contrast, the Third Circuit in *United States v. Engler* (3d Cir. 1986), found that the absence of a scienter requirement, in the strict liability provisions of a felony under the MBTA, did "not offend the requirements of due process."

Most environmental crimes require proof of the defendant acting knowingly. Courts usually permit knowledge to be inferred from the surrounding circumstances. In *United States v. International Minerals & Chemical Corp.* (S.Ct.1971), the Supreme Court held that "[w]here ... dangerous or deleterious devices or products or obnoxious waste materials are involved, the probability of regulation is so great that anyone who is aware that he is in possession of them or dealing with them must be presumed to be aware of the regulation."

Knowledge also can be found when there is a deliberate avoidance to learn all the facts. A willful blindness instruction, however, is only proper when the defendant claims a lack of guilty knowledge and the evidence at trial supports an inference of deliberate ignorance. *United States v. Pacific Hide & Fur Depot, Inc.* (9th Cir.1985).

Most courts interpreting the term knowledge in the context of environmental statutes have held that there is no requirement that a defendant know the specific law being violated. For example, in examining knowledge in the context of the Comprehensive Environmental Response, Compensation, and Liability Act (CERCLA), a Sixth Circuit Court held that " ... knowledge as used in such regulatory statutes means knowledge that one is doing the statutorily prescribed acts, not knowledge that the statutes or potential health hazards exist." *United States v. Buckley* (6th Cir.1991).

§ 14.03 Refuse Act

The Rivers and Harbors Appropriations Act of 1899, (33 U.S.C. § 401 et seq.), has been one source of prosecution of environmental crimes. The Act, a codification of prior statutes, includes section 13 which forbids "the deposit" of all kinds of "refuse matter" into navigable rivers "other than that flowing from streets and sewers and passing therefrom in a liquid state." (33 U.S.C. § 407).

This Refuse Act provides criminal penalties for the improper discharge into navigable or tributary waters of the United States. The government can charge each separate act of discharging or depositing refuse as a separate count. The number of acts chargeable "cannot be deduced from the mere size or length of time of a discharge without more, unless discontinuity of the flow or change in composition or other evidence indicates that certain action necessarily were taken to further the discharging or depositing of refuse." *United States v. Allied Chemical Corporation* (E.D.Va.1976).

Refuse has been defined as "all foreign substances and pollutants apart from those 'flowing from streets and sewers and passing therefrom in a liquid state' into the watercourse." *United States v. Standard Oil Company* (S.Ct.1966). In *United States v. Standard Oil Company,* the Supreme Court held that commercially valuable gasoline discharged into a navigable river could come within the definition of "refuse" under the Rivers and Harbors Act.

Most courts find this Act to be a strict liability statute. *United States v. White Fuel Corporation* (1st Cir.1974). One court noted that depositing refuse in navigable waters is malum prohibitum, within the category of public welfare offenses, and therefore a statute of strict liability. "The public is injured just as much by unintentional pollution as it is by deliberate pollution, and it would have been entirely reasonable for Congress to attack both." *United States v. U.S. Steel Corporation* (N.D.Ind. 1970). The Supreme Court reserved for future determination, the question of what scienter requirement is imposed by this Act. *United States v. Standard Oil Company* (S.Ct.1966).

§ 14.04 Water Pollution Control Act

The Federal Water Pollution Control Act, commonly referred to as the Clean Water Act, (33 U.S.C. § 1251 et seq.), objective "is to restore and maintain the chemical, physical, and biological integrity of the Nation's waters." The Act prohibits the discharge of pollutants into navigable waters unless authorized. The Act provides for the adoption of effluent limitations for the control of pollution and permits selected point source discharges. (33 U.S.C. § 1311).

Criminal penalties exist for negligent violations of these discharge limits, with increased penalties provided for knowing violations. Repeat offenses also carry increased penalties. When the actions place another individual in "imminent danger of death or serious bodily injury" there is a possible penalty of imprisonment of up to fifteen years and fine. The fine may be increased when the knowing endangerment is by a corporation. (33 U.S.C. § 1319(c)). In *United States v. Borowski* (1st Cir. 1992), the First Circuit held that a knowingly endangerment prosecution could not "be premised upon danger that occurs before the pollutant reaches a publicly-owned sewer or treatment works."

Although most prosecutions are for violations of specific discharge limits, defendants who had failed to apply for a permit, were held to be criminally liable despite the fact that effluent standards were not promulgated against them. The Third Circuit noted that it was necessary to provide flexibility to the government for industries not yet considered threats to the environment. To hold otherwise, the court stated, would permit these industries to escape liability merely because the government had not established effluent limitations. The absence of effluent limitations does not nullify the basic prohibition against the discharge of pollutants. It merely places the burden on those discharging pollutants to apply for and to obtain a permit. *United States v. Frezzo Brothers, Inc.* (E.D.Pa.1978).

In *United States v. Ahmad* (5th Cir.1996), the defendant was indicted under the Clean Water Act. Defendant argued that "his discharge of the gasoline was not 'knowing' because he believed he was discharging water." The government argued that the term "knowingly violates" required it to "prove only that Ahmad knew the nature of his acts and that he performed them intentionally." At issue was whether the term "knowingly" applied to the element of the discharge's being a pollutant. In reversing the convictions because of inadequate jury instructions, the Fifth Circuit held that "[w]ith the exception of purely jurisdictional elements, the mens rea of knowledge applies to each element of the crimes."

Responsible corporate officers are statutorily included as "persons" that are subject to criminal penalties under this Act. (33 U.S.C. § 1319 (c)(6)). This inclusion, however, does not serve to limit the prosecution of individuals who violate the act. *United States v. Brittain* (10th Cir.1991).

Applicable discharges must be reported by "any person in charge." Corporations are included as a "person" under the Act. 33 U.S.C. § 1321(a)(7). "Further, the knowledge of the employees is the knowledge of the corporation."*Apex Oil Co. v. United States* (8th Cir.1976).

§ 14.05 Resource Conservation and Recovery Act (RCRA)

Congress enacted the Resource Conservation and Recovery Act (RCRA) to provide a national system for the safe management of hazardous waste and to promote a system that conserved valuable material and energy resources. This statute authorizes the EPA, through its adoption of regulations, to place controls on solid and hazardous wastes. The Act is divisible into two sections, one pertaining to non-hazardous solid waste management, and another regarding hazardous waste management. *United States v. White* (E.D.Wash.1991).

The RCRA enacted in 1976 has been termed a " 'cradle to grave' regulatory scheme for toxic materials, providing 'nationwide protection against the dangers of improper hazardous waste disposal.' "*United States v. Johnson & Towers, Inc.* (3d Cir.1984). Although originally the statute authorized misdemeanor penalties for the disposal of waste without a permit, later amendments increased the penalties for noncompliance to felonies. The amendments also expanded coverage to include not only the disposal of waste, but also the improper treatment and storage of waste.

The Act's criminal provisions have been found applicable to "any person" that stores, treats, or disposes of hazardous wastes. "Any person" is defined in 42 U.S.C. § 6903(15) as meaning "an individual, trust, firm, joint stock company, corporation (including a government corporation), partnership, association, State, municipality, commission, political subdivision of a State, or an interstate body and shall include each department, agency, and instrumentality of the United States." Courts have not limited the provisions of the RCRA only to those who are owners or operators of facilities. *United States v. Johnson & Towers, Inc.* (3d Cir.1984). Further, federal employees working at a federal facility have not been precluded from prosecution under this statute. In *United States v. Dee* (4th Cir.1990), the Fourth Circuit found that sovereign immunity did not immunize federal employees from prosecution for criminal acts that violated the RCRA.

Criminality under the RCRA is found in section 6928(d) and (e) of Title 42. Where subsection (d) provides for penalties when one "knowingly," commits certain acts specified by the statute, subsection (e) increases the penalty for a knowing endangerment in committing a violation. The terms "knowing" and "knowingly," as used throughout this statute, have been the focal point of many appellate decisions. Only recently has the government proceeded with prosecution under the knowing endangerment aspect of this statute. The Tenth Circuit found the "serious bodily injury" provision of this statute not to be unconstitutionally vague when it was applied to a corporate defendant whose employees were alleged to have suffered "psychoorganic syndrome," which may cause impairment to mental facilities. *United States v. Protex Industries, Inc.* (10th Cir.1989).

Despite the requirement for a "knowing" violation, courts do not require that the government prove that a defendant know they are violating specific provisions of the RCRA. Being a public welfare offense, "it is completely fair and reasonable to charge those who operate in such areas with knowledge of the regulatory provisions." *United States v. Hayes International Corp.* (11th Cir.1986). Courts have, therefore, rejected a defense premised upon ignorance of the law. This position is consistent with the knowing requirement of most other environmental crime statutes. For example, although knowledge is an element for a violation of the Clean Air Act, the "statute requires knowledge only of the emissions themselves, not knowledge of the statute or of the hazards that emissions pose." *United States v. Buckley* (6th Cir.1991).

Courts, however, have not ruled consistently on whether knowledge of a permit is required. One court found that although the term "knowingly" is omitted in subsection (2)(A) of the statute, its inclusion in subsection (2)(B) implies that there must be knowledge of the requirement of a permit. In *United States v. Johnson & Towers* (3d Cir.1984), the Third Circuit held that, "[i]t is unlikely that Congress could have intended to subject to criminal prosecution those persons who acted when no permit had been obtained irrespective of their knowledge (under subsection (A)), but not those persons who acted in violation of the terms of a permit unless that action was knowing (subsection (B))." The court in *Johnson & Towers, Inc.* concluded that either the word "knowingly" was inadvertently omitted from subsection (A), or that "knowingly" as introducing subsection (2) applies to (B).

Many courts, however, have rejected the view taken in *United States v. Johnson & Towers,* (3d Cir.1984), finding that there is no requirement of knowledge of a lack of a permit for conviction under subsection (A) of this statute. As noted by the Ninth Circuit, "[t]he statute makes a clear distinction between non-permit holders and permit holders, requiring in subsection (B) that the latter knowingly violate a material condition or requirement of the permit. To read the word 'knowingly' at the beginning of section (2) into subsection (A) would be to eviscerate this distinction." *United States v. Hoflin* (9th Cir.1989). In rejecting the view taken by the court in *Johnson & Towers, Inc.*, the Sixth Circuit noted that "[t]he 'knowingly' which begins section 6928(d)(2) cannot be read as extending to the subsections without rendering nugatory the word 'knowing' contained in subsections 6928(d)(2)(B) and (C)." *United States v. Dean* (6th Cir.1992).

Although the extent to which "knowingly" modifies terms within the statute remains to be resolved by the United States Supreme Court, there is a clear consensus among the circuits that knowledge of the statutory provision is not mandated. The government must, however, prove that the defendant knew the general hazardous character of the waste material being handled. *United States v. Dee* (4th Cir.1990).

One appellate court has specifically refused to apply a responsible corporate officer doctrine to establish knowledge. In *United States v. MacDonald & Watson Waste Oil Company* (1st Cir.1991), the First Circuit held that proof of a defendant being a responsible corporate officer would be insufficient to show the required knowledge for conviction under the RCRA. The court stated that "[s]imply because a responsible corporate officer believed that on a prior occasion illegal transportation occurred, he did not necessarily possess knowledge of the violation charged. In a crime having knowledge as an express element, a mere showing of official responsibility under *Dotterweich* and *Park* is not an adequate substitute for direct or circumstantial proof of knowledge."

CHAPTER FIFTEEN
COMPUTER CRIMES

§ 15.01 Overview

Although computer offenses have not been extensively prosecuted by the federal government, one can predict an increase in prosecutions with the development and use of technology. Prior to 1984, computer criminal offenses were subject to prosecution under existing statutes that had no computer emphasis. For example, computer improprieties were on occasion prosecuted pursuant to the federal wire fraud statute. (18 U.S.C. § 1343) (see § 4.08). Today there exists specific legislation to criminalize illegal computer activities.

In 1984, Congress enacted a criminal statute (the Counterfeit Access Device and Computer Fraud and Abuse Act of 1984) that exclusively focused on computer offenses. This statute, 18 U.S.C. § 1030, concentrated on improper computer access as opposed to other improprieties, such as, computer use. This statute was amended in 1986 (the Computer Fraud and Abuse Act of 1986) to cure some of the deficiencies evident in the initial legislation. More recent amendments have also modified the language of the statute. The statute is no longer restricted to crimes related to computer access. Despite the existence of section 1030 in the federal criminal code, computer crimes are still facing prosecution under other statutory offenses. For example, prosecutions may be predicated upon charges of copyright infringement (17 U.S.C. § 506), conspiracy (18 U.S.C. § 371), wire fraud (18 U.S.C. § 1343), illegal transportation of stolen property (18 U.S.C. § 2314), illegal interception devices and equipment (18 U.S.C. § 2512), and unlawful access to stored communications (18 U.S.C. § 2701).

§ 15.02   Section 1030

Section 1030 contains seven variants of conduct that are subject to prosecution. As opposed to a consistent mens rea and jurisdictional predicate, each of the seven subsections specifies its own requisite jurisdiction and mens rea. Likewise, the penalties for some of these varying forms of improper computer conduct differ. In addition to imprisonment, the statute also provides for imposition of a fine.

Subsection (a)(1) basically criminalizes the conduct of one who "having knowingly accessed a computer without authorization or exceeding authorization," thereby obtained confidential national security information "with reason to believe that such information so obtained could be used to the injury of the United States, or to the advantage of any foreign nation willfully" attempts to or communicates it to someone "not entitled to receive it, or willfully" "fails to communicate it to a United States officer or employee entitled to receive it."

This electronic espionage provision carries the greatest penalty specified by this statute in permitting imprisonment of up to ten years. Additionally, a repeat offender is subjected to imprisonment of up to twenty years.

Subsection (a)(2) pertains to one who "intentionally accesses a computer, without authorization or exceeds authorized access, and thereby obtains" financial information of a financial institution or a card issuer, "information from a department or agency of the United States," or "information from a protected computer if the conduct involved an interstate or foreign communication." This conduct is punishable by imprisonment of up to one year. The statute provides for an increase to five years if the offense is committed for private or commercial gain, "in furtherance of a criminal or tortious act in violation of the Constitution" or federal or state laws, or "the value of the information exceeds five thousand dollars." The statute also provides for an increase to ten years for the repeat offender.

Subsection (a)(3) of this statute pertains to browsing in a government computer. It applies to those who access "intentionally, without authorization to access a nonpublic computer" of a federal department or agency, said computer being exclusively for government use or the conduct "affects" the government's use of the computer. The penalty for commission of this offense is one year, but may be increased to ten years for the repeat offender.

Subsection (a)(4) concentrates on theft from protected computers. It applies to one who "knowingly and with intent to defraud, accesses a protected computer without authorization or exceeds authorized access," furthering the fraud and obtaining anything of value. An exception is provided when the object of the fraud is the computer and the value of such use does not exceed five thousand dollars in any one year period. The statute, in subsection (e), explicitly defines a "protected computer." In addition to computers used by the government and financial institutions, the term "protected computer" also includes computers "used in interstate or foreign commerce or communication." This offense is punishable with up to five years of imprisonment, with an additional five years possible for the repeat offender.

Subsection (a)(5) is divided into three parts. Subsection A pertains to one who "knowingly causes a transmission of a program, information, code or command, and as a result of such conduct intentionally causes damage without authorization to a protected computer." Subsection B criminalizes the intentional access of "a protected computer without authorization, and as a result of such conduct recklessly causes damage." Finally, Subsection C criminalizes those who "intentionally" access a "protected computer without authorization, and as a result of such conduct, causes damage." Subsections A and B carry a penalty of up to five years imprisonment with an additional five years possible for the repeat offender. Subsection C provides for imprisonment of up to one year, with an additional ten years possible for repeat offenders.

Subsection (a)(6) of this statute criminalizes interstate trafficking of passwords. The government must show that the defendant "knowingly and with intent to defraud trafficks" "in any password or similar information." The trafficking must affect "interstate commerce or foreign commerce," or the computer must be used by or for the federal government. This provision carries imprisonment of not more than one year with the possibility of ten years imposed for the repeat offender.

The final subsection (a)(7), added as part of the National Information Infrastructure Protection Act of 1996 (Economic Espionage Act of 1996, Title II), criminalizes the conduct of one who "with intent to extort from any person, firm, association, educational institution, financial institution, government entity, or other legal entity, any money or other thing of value, transmits in interstate or foreign commerce any communication containing any threat to cause damage to a protected computer." This provision carries imprisonment of up to five years, with repeat offenders facing the possibility of ten years.

Often conduct relating to accessing a computer may qualify under more than one provision of the statute. Additionally, the statute provides for punishment by those who attempt to commit the offense. The statute also provides for civil actions by those who are damaged as a result of a violation of the statute.

Aspects of a prior version of section 1030 were the subject of appellate review in the case of *United States v. Morris* (2d Cir.1991). The Second Circuit was faced with the issue of whether the intent requirement in subsection (a)(5) applied only to accessing information or also to preventing the authorized use of the computer's information and thereby causing loss. Defendant Robert Morris, a graduate student at Cornell University had transmitted a "worm into INTERNET, which is a group of national networks that connect university, governmental, and military computers around the country." In transmitting this worm, Morris had underestimated the damaging effect.

The court in *Morris* found that "[d]espite some isolated language in the legislative history that arguably suggests a scienter component for the 'damages' phrase of section 1030(a)(5)(A), the wording, structure, and purpose of the subsection, examined in comparison with its predecessor provision persuade us that the 'intentionally' standard applies only to the 'accesses' phrase of section 1030(a)(5)(A), and not to its 'damages' phrase." The court also rejected defendant's argument that the statute only covered those who lacked access to any federal interest computer. The court noted that "Congress did not intend an individual's authorized access to one federal interest computer to protect him from prosecution, no matter what other federal interest computers he accesses."

In *United States v. Sablan* (9th Cir.1996), the Ninth Circuit found that it was constitutional to omit a mens rea for the damages element of the offense in that the defendant "must have had a wrongful intent in accessing the computer in order to be convicted under the statute." Recent amendments to the statute now provide a mens rea for the damages clause in the amended (a)(5)(A) and (B). There is no mens rea, however, for the damages clause in (a)(5)(C).

PART THREE

PROCEDURAL AND EVIDENTIARY ISSUES

CHAPTER SIXTEEN

GRAND JURY INVESTIGATIONS

§ 16.01 Investigative Advantages

Federal investigations of white collar crime commonly involve use of the powers of the grand jury in addition to (or often, in lieu of) traditional police investigative authority. The grand jury offers various advantages over police investigations as a result of six structural elements of the grand jury process: (1) use of the court's subpoena authority, (2) lay participation, (3) closed proceedings, (4) immunity grants, (5) grand jury secrecy, and (6) the role of the prosecutor in leading the investigation. The sixth feature—the role of the prosecutor—is the prerequisite that leads the government to take advantage of the others. The prosecutor serves as the primary legal advisor to the grand jury, deciding initially which witnesses will be called before the grand jury (although the grand jury can request the issuance of additional subpoenas), questioning those witnesses (although the grand jurors can pose additional questions), and exercising absolute dominion over the granting of immunity.

The grand jury process allows the prosecution to accomplish several investigative objectives that cannot be achieved through an investigation by federal law enforcement officers. These include: (1) compelling witnesses and suspects to provide information (subject to their exercise of evidentiary privileges) through the use of the court's subpoena authority, which is backed up by contempt sanctions for failure to comply with the subpoena's directive; (2) requiring these persons (who generally could not be arrested and subjected to custodial interrogation by law enforcement officers) to respond to the questions posed by the prosecutor in a setting in which the only other persons present are the grand jurors and grand jury personnel (the witness' counsel, in particular, not being present); (3) requiring those persons to testify under oath, thereby making them subject to the penalties of perjury for falsehoods; (4) providing witnesses assurance through grand jury secrecy requirements that their testimony will not be divulged to the subject of the investigation (or others) except under limited conditions (e.g. with court approval); (5) compelling the production of documents without revealing with any specificity the possible criminal activity under investigation and without any showing of probability as to the relationship of the documents to criminal activity (in contrast to the search warrant process which law enforcement officers ordinarily would need to use to obtain documents); (6) precluding witness reliance upon the self-incrimination privilege to refuse to provide testimony or documents by supplanting that privilege with a grant of immunity (a grant that can be used only as to persons subject to a legal obligation to testify and which therefore is not available to law enforcement officers to compel responses to their questions); (7) providing the prosecutor with a protective cloak of grand jury secrecy in refusing to respond to media inquiries regarding ongoing investigations; and (8) providing the prosecutor with the symbolic shield of grand juror participation in responding to claims that its investigations are motivated by partisan influences or are designed to harass.

The value of these "advantages" varies with the activities and persons being investigated. In some instances they may be superfluous and in others, a particular "advantage" (e.g. grand jury secrecy) may actually be a hindrance. The grand jury investigative process also tends to be expensive, time consuming, and logistically cumbersome as compared to police investigations. Hence the process is useful primarily where investigators will face one or more of the following tasks: unraveling a complex criminal structure; obtaining information from witnesses reluctant to cooperate (or reluctant to appear to be cooperating voluntarily); gaining information from lower level participants where the prosecutor is willing to relinquish their prosecution in return for their cooperation; obtaining information buried in extensive business records; controlling the information revealed about the investigation while the investigation is ongoing; and countering the likely claims of the target that the investigation is being used for the purpose of harassment or political manipulation.

§ 16.02   Rule 17   Subpoenas

Federal grand jury subpoenas are issued pursuant to Fed.R.Crim.P. 17, which governs subpoenas to compel testimony (the subpoena ad testificandum) and to compel the production of documents and other physical items (the subpoena duces tecum) issued in connection with any type of proceeding governed by the Federal Rules of Criminal Procedure. Rule 17 provides that the subpoena will be "given in blank to a party requesting it," and in the grand jury proceeding, that "party" is the prosecutor (the legal advisor to the grand jury) acting on its behalf. The prosecutor fills in the name of the witness, who is commanded to "attend and give testimony" before the grand jury at a time and place designated by the prosecutor. Pursuant to USAM § 9–11.150 (discussed at § 19.05), an "Advice of Rights Form" is attached to the subpoena. It includes a brief, very general description of the subject matter of the grand jury's investigation, usually by reference either to the generic character of the offenses under investigation (e.g., "tax offenses") or the general character of the transactions under investigation (e.g., "zoning in Baltimore County").

Where the prosecutor also seeks documents from the witness, the subpoena, as provided in Rule 17(c), will "command the person * * * to produce the books, papers, [and] documents, * * * designated therein." Ordinarily, the documents demanded will be described in an attachment to the subpoena. Documents may be described by type (e.g., all "invoices"), by general subject matter (e.g., all "records of purchases"), or by relationship to a specific activity (e.g., all documents that "relate to the setting of prices" for a particular item). The description usually will refer to a specific time period (e.g., "invoices for 1996–97"), unless the characterization is by reference to an event that implicitly limits the time frame. The subpoena will direct that the documents be produced before the grand jury, but prosecutors often give the party the option of simply delivering the documents to the prosecutor. This tends to be more convenient as the documents will be screened initially by the prosecutor's staff, and often only a summary will be presented to the grand jury.

§ 16.03 The Fourth Amendment's Overbreadth Prohibition

In *Boyd v. United States* (S.Ct.1886), the Supreme Court concluded that a court order to produce a document constituted a search under the Fourth Amendment. The order in question directed an importer to either produce the invoice for an item the

government alleged to have been illegally imported
or be bound by the government's allegation of what
would be shown by the invoice. While the order was
not a subpoena duces tecum, as the subpoenaed
party was not subject to contempt for failure to
produce the document, the consequences of failing
to produce were severe and the Supreme Court
treated the order as the equivalent of a subpoena
duces tecum. The Court acknowledged that a court
order directing the recipient to produce a document
"lacked certain aggravating incidents of actual
search and seizure, such as forcible entry into a
man's house and searching among his papers," but
stressed that it nonetheless "accomplish[ed] the
substantial object of those acts in forcing from a
party evidence against himself." Accordingly, a
"compulsory production of a man's private papers"
would be treated as "within the scope of the Fourth
Amendment to the constitution, in all cases in
which a search and seizure would be." Moreover,
this particular "search and seizure, or what is
equivalent thereto," was unreasonable within the
meaning of that Amendment because the court order was seeking to compel the defendants to give
what was, in effect, self-incriminatory testimony
(see § 20.01).

Only twenty years after *Boyd* was decided, in
Hale v. Henkel (S.Ct.1906), the Supreme Court dra-
matically modified *Boyd*'s Fourth Amendment analysis. *Hale* basically rejected *Boyd*'s interpretation of
that Amendment's reasonableness requirement, although it reaffirmed the applicability of the Fourth

Amendment to a "compulsory production of a man's private papers." The *Hale* majority initially held that *Boyd* had erred in reading together the Fourth and Fifth Amendment protections. The Fifth Amendment provided a completely separate source of protection against compelled production of documents (see § 20.01), which did not apply in *Hale* since the challenged grand jury subpoena was directed to corporate documents and corporations do not have the benefit of the self-incrimination privilege (see § 20.07). However, the Court continued, the corporation was entitled to the protection of the Fourth Amendment, and "an order for the production of books and papers" could still constitute "an unreasonable search and seizure." In defining what constitutes unreasonableness in this context, *Hale* utilized a standard that would have sustained the *Boyd* order for a single, obviously relevant document as a "reasonable search." The key issue, the Court noted, was whether the subpoena duces tecum was "far too sweeping in its terms to be regarded as reasonable." The subpoena in *Hale* failed in this regard as it required production of virtually "all the books, papers, and documents found in the offices" of the subpoenaed corporation. Such a broad request, the Court noted, was capable of preventing the corporation from carrying on its business. While the government might have need for many of these documents, it would have to make some showing of that need before it could "justify an order for the production of such a mass of papers."

In the area of police searches, the Fourth Amendment generally requires that the search be based on probable cause. *Hale* imposed no such requirement, insisting only that the search not be overbroad. The Supreme Court did not explain in *Hale* why overbreadth is the only concern of Fourth Amendment reasonableness in the context of a subpoena duces tecum. One possibility is that the subpoena does not require a probability showing because it is a less invasive form of "search." The *Hale* Court acknowledged that the execution of a subpoena did not present the usual physical attributes of the search. The service of the subpoena involved "no element of trespass or force," nor was it "secret and intrusive." The subpoena could not be "finally enforced except after challenge, and a judgment of the court upon the challenge." These qualities led Justice McKenna in dissent to conclude that the Fourth Amendment simply was not implicated. The majority arguably reasoned that there was a "search" for Fourth Amendment purposes, but its less invasive character meant that it did not have to meet the requirements commonly associated with the "warrant clause" of the Fourth Amendment (i.e., the clause providing that "no warrants shall issue but upon probable cause supported by oath and affirmation and particularly describing the place to be searched and the persons or things to be seized"). Rather, under the Fourth Amendment's first clause (guaranteeing the "right of the people to be secure in their persons, houses, papers, and effects against unreasonable searches"), it was sufficient that the subpoena not be overbroad in its reach.

Support for the above analysis is found in *Oklahoma Press Publishing Co. v. Walling* (S.Ct.1946), involving subpoenas duces tecum issued by an administrative agency. The Court there noted that "these cases present no question of actual search and seizure," as they involved no attempt by government officials "to enter petitioners' premises against their will, to search them or to seize or examine their books." To avoid "misconceptions," a distinction must be drawn between the "so called 'figurative' or 'constructive' searches" of subpoenas and "cases of actual search and seizure." As to the former, the Fourth Amendment "if applicable," did no more than "guard against abuse only by way of too much indefiniteness or breadth" in the subpoena. The interests to be protected were "not identical with those protected against invasion by actual search and seizure" but arose out of the right of persons to be free from "officious examination [that] can be expensive, so much so that it eats up men's substance," and thereby "become[s] persecution when carried beyond reason."

§ 16.04 Applying the Overbreadth Prohibition

Post-*Hale* cases applying the constitutional prohibition against overly broad subpoenas duces tecum frequently start out by noting that the stated standard proscribing breadth "far too sweeping * * * to be regarded as reasonable" necessarily requires a fact-specific judgment, with each ruling tied to the circumstances of the individual case. At the same time, the courts have sought, with limited success, to develop some general criteria to guide that judgment. Initially, the subpoena poses difficulties only if it has sufficient breadth to suggest either that compliance will be burdensome or that the subpoena's scope may not have been shaped to the purposes of the inquiry. If it has that breadth, the court then will turn to the three "components" of reasonableness developed by the lower federal courts: "(1) the subpoena may command only the production of things relevant to the investigation being pursued; (2) specification of things to be produced must be made with reasonable particularity; and (3) production of records covering only a reasonable period of time may be required." *United States v. Gurule* (10th Cir.1970). The second component in the above formulation is commonly described as having "two prongs": first, "particularity of description" so that the subpoenaed party "know[s] what he is being asked to produce' " and second, "particularity of breadth" so that the subpoenaed party "is not harassed or oppressed to the point that he experiences an unreasonable business detriment."

While many courts have treated the elements of relevancy, particularity of description, particularity as to breadth, and limited time period as separate requirements of reasonableness, with a deficiency as to any one invalidating the subpoena, it is clear that these elements are interrelated. Greater particularity as to breadth, by narrowing the range of documents to be produced, will extend the time period into which the subpoena may reach. On the other hand, as a subpoena reaches farther into the past, a court is more likely to require a stronger showing of relevancy. So too, the significance of the burden of production will be weighed against the strength of the showing as to relevancy and the reasonableness of the time period.

While the subpoenaed party bears the ultimate burden of establishing that a challenged subpoena is unreasonable, many courts insist that the government make an initial showing of relevancy since it alone knows the precise nature of the grand jury inquiry. Ordinarily, this showing requires no more than a general description of the relationship of the material sought to the subject matter of the investigation. Moreover, the government generally is thought to be entitled to considerable leeway on the issue of relevancy. Courts recognize that "some exploration or fishing necessarily is inherent" since the grand jury will not ordinarily have a "catalog of what books and papers exist" nor "any basis for knowing what their character or contents immediately are." *Schwimmer v. United States* (8th. Cir. 1956).

§ 16.05 Other Fourth Amendment Objections

Where a subpoena is not "too sweeping," are there other Fourth Amendment grounds for challenging the subpoena? In the companion cases of *United States v. Dionisio* (S.Ct.1973), and *United*

States v. Mara (S.Ct.1973), the Supreme Court rejected one such possibility, which rested on treating the subpoena directing a person to appear before the grand jury as the equivalent of a "seizure" of the person. Both cases involved grand jury subpoenas directing witnesses to produce identification evidence (voice and handwriting exemplars). The lower court, looking to the analogy of a court order allowing police to take persons into custody to obtain such exemplars, concluded that the Fourth Amendment required the government to show (1) some reasonable suspicion justifying the selection of these persons to provide the exemplars, and (2) that the request for the exemplars was relevant to the subject of the grand jury's inquiry and was not excessive in light of that inquiry. The Supreme Court held that the Fourth Amendment did not apply and neither showing should be required.

The *Dionisio* majority concluded that the lower court's analogy to police-detention cases was flawed because "a subpoena to appear before a grand jury is not a 'seizure' in the Fourth Amendment sense." There was a dramatic difference between the "compulsion exerted" by a subpoena and an "arrest or even an investigative stop." The "latter is abrupt, is effected with force of the threat of it and often in demeaning circumstances, * * * [while the] subpoena is served in the same manner as other legal process; it involves no stigma whatever * * * and it remains at all times under the control and supervision of a court." Admittedly, appearing before a grand jury could be both "inconvenient" and "burdensome," but these were simply "personal sacrifices" inherent in the "historically grounded obligation of every person to appear and give evidence before the grand jury." The subpoena's directive to give identification evidence did not alter the nature of that burden because the taking of voice and handwriting exemplars did not itself involve a search, as both related to physical characteristics "constantly exposed to the public" and were to be distinguished, for example, from the taking of a blood sample.

Having found that the Fourth Amendment had no application to either the summons to appear or the directive to provide identification exemplars, the Court concluded that there was "no justification for requiring the grand jury to satisfy even the minimal requirement of 'reasonableness' imposed by the [lower court]." The grand jury "could exercise its 'broad investigative powers' on the basis of 'tips, rumors, evidence offered by the prosecutor, or [the jurors'] own personal knowledge,' " and it should not be required to explain the basis for each of its subpoenas. To "saddle a grand jury with minitrials and preliminary showings would assuredly impede its investigation and frustrate the public's interest in the fair and expeditious administration of the criminal laws."

Looking to the distinction drawn in *Dionisio* between a subpoena and an investigative stop, lower courts have suggested that a subpoena calling for "forthwith" compliance (i.e., the immediate production of evidence for presentation to the grand jury or the immediate appearance before the grand jury) should be treated as a Fourth Amendment seizure if the individual is forced to comply by the agents serving the subpoena without being given the opportunity to first challenge the subpoena. The Department of Justice's guidelines authorize employment of forthwith subpoenas only where justified by necessity (e.g., where there is a risk of flight or of destruction of evidence), USAM § 9–11.240, but neither those guidelines nor the courts insist that the process servers inform the subpoenaed party of his right to first challenge the subpoena in court (although that certainly makes it easier for the government to show that compliance without objection was voluntary).

United States v. Calandra (S.Ct.1974), rejects still another possible Fourth Amendment objection. Under *Calandra*, a grand jury witness cannot successfully challenge being subpoenaed to testify, or being asked particular questions, because the government was led to the witness or to its questions by a search that violated the Fourth Amendment. The Supreme Court in *Calandra* refused to extend the Fourth Amendment's exclusionary rule to prohibit the use before the grand jury of the fruits of an illegal search. The Court reasoned that sufficient deterrence against unconstitutional searches was provided by the prohibition against use of the fruits of such a search at trial. Due to a special provision in Title III of the Omnibus Crime Control and Safe Streets Act of 1968, 18 U.S.C. § 2515, the fruits of illegal electronic surveillance are treated differently.

That Act prohibits the government from using conversations intercepted by illegal electronic surveillance, or information derived from those conversations, in a grand jury proceeding. Accordingly, a
grand jury witness can object to government questioning based upon information obtained from an
illegal wiretap. *Gelbard v. United States* (S.Ct.1972).

§ 16.06   Rule 17(c) Objections

Rule 17(c), governing the subpoena duces tecum,
provides that the court "may quash or modify the
subpoena if compliance would be unreasonable or
oppressive." *United States v. R. Enterprises* (S.Ct.
1991), provides the leading interpretation of that
provision as applied to a grand jury subpoena. The
Supreme Court there rejected the contention that a
grand jury subpoena was not "reasonable" under
17(c) unless it met the same standards applied to a
subpoena duces tecum directing production of documents for use at trial. In the trial context, the
moving party must show that the document subpoenaed is relevant, admissible, and adequately specified. There was no challenge as to the need for
adequate specification in *R. Enterprise*, but the government there insisted, and the Court agreed, that
there was no need for a showing as to relevancy and
admissibility. The requirement of evidentiary admissibility made no sense as to the grand jury, as it
had long been held that the grand jury's "operation
generally is unrestrained by the technical procedural and evidentiary rules governing the conduct of
criminal trials." Requiring a preliminary showing

as to relevancy, "would invite procedural delays and detours while courts evaluate the relevancy * * * of [the] documents sought," exactly the kind of disruptive "minitrial" warned against in *Dionisio* (see § 16.05). So too, a mandated preliminary showing, by requiring the government to "explain in too much detail the particular reasons underlying a subpoena," could very well "compromise 'the indispensable secrecy of grand jury proceedings'" and "afford the targets of the investigation far more information abut the grand jury's internal workings * * * than the Federal Rules of Criminal Procedure appear to contemplate."

Turning to the fashioning of an appropriate Rule 17(c) standard for the unique setting of the grand jury, the Court noted that several considerations had to be balanced. Initially, it had to be recognized that "the investigatory powers of the grand jury are * * * not unlimited," that the grand jury cannot, for example, "engage in arbitrary fishing expeditions" or "select targets of investigation out of malice or an intent to harass." Fashioning a procedure to enforce such limits, however, required consideration of conflicting elements in the grand jury process. On the one hand, the decision as to the appropriate charge "is routinely not made until after the grand jury has concluded its investigation," and "one simply cannot know in advance whether information sought during the investigation will be relevant and admissible in the prosecution for a particular offense." On the other hand, the party to whom the subpoena is directed "faces a

difficult situation" in challenging the improper use
of a subpoena. Grand juries ordinarily "do not
announce publicly the subjects of their investigations," and the subpoenaed party therefore "may
have no conception of the Government's purpose in
seeking production of the requested information."
Thus, what was needed was a Rule 17(c) standard
of reasonableness that "gives due weight to the
difficult position of subpoena recipients but does
not impair the strong governmental interests in
affording grand juries wide latitude, avoiding minitrials on peripheral matters, and preserving a necessary level of secrecy."

Several general guidelines, the Court noted, gave
substance to such a standard. Initially "the law
presumes, absent a strong showing to the contrary,
that a grand jury acts within the legitimate scope of
its authority." Consequently, "a grand jury subpoena issued through normal channels is presumed to
be reasonable, and the burden of showing unreasonableness must be on the recipient who seeks to
avoid compliance." In this case, that party "did not
challenge the subpoena as being too indefinite, nor
did [it] claim that compliance would be overly burdensome." The challenge was strictly on relevancy
grounds and for such a challenge, the presumption
of regularity produced the following standard:
"[T]he motion to quash must be denied unless the
district court determines that there is no reasonable
possibility that the category of materials the Government seeks will produce information relevant to

the general subject of the grand jury's investigation."

Recognizing that the above standard imposed an "unenviable task" upon the party raising a relevancy objection, the Court noted that the district court had authority to ease that task through appropriate procedures. Because a subpoenaed party who does not even know the general subject matter of the grand jury's investigation is "unlikely" to make the necessary showing "no matter how valid that party's claim," a district court "may be justified in a case where unreasonableness is alleged in requiring the Government to reveal the general subject of the grand jury's investigation before requiring the challenging party to carry its burden of persuasion." The district court, however, in fashioning appropriate procedures for this purpose would also have to take account of "the strong governmental interests in maintaining secrecy, preserving investigatory flexibility, and avoiding procedural delays." One possibility, the Court noted, was to require the government simply to "reveal the subject of the investigation to the trial court *in camera*, so the court may determine whether the motion to quash has a reasonable prospect for success before it discloses the subject matter to the challenging party."

A three-justice concurrence in *R. Enterprise* maintained that the subpoenaed party might succeed on a showing less demanding than the Court's "no-reasonable-possibility" standard where that party also could show that either (1) responding to the subpoena would be particularly burdensome due to the volume and location of the subpoenaed documents, (2) the "subpoena would intrude significantly on * * * privacy interests or call for the disclosure of trade secrets or other confidential matter," or (3) that "compliance would have First Amendment implications." So far, however, only the third situation has resulted in a reshaping of standards by the lower courts (see § 16.07).

§ 16.07 "Chilling Effect" Objections

Grand jury witnesses have argued in various contexts that even though the testimony or documents demanded of them clearly would be relevant, the grand jury should be required to show a compelling need for that information where the impact of its inquiry is to chill the exercise of a constitutionality protected right. The Supreme Court's ruling in *Branzburg v. Hayes* (S.Ct.1972) often is viewed as standing against such a requirement, at least with respect to a chilling impact upon First Amendment rights. *Branzburg* rejected the contention that newspaper reporters could not be compelled to reveal to state grand juries the identity of their confidential sources (who were apparent participants in drug offenses) unless the prosecution first established a compelling need for obtaining that information from the reporters. The Court majority questioned the potential adverse impact of such disclosures upon a reporter's ability to obtain confidential sources, and concluded that any resulting impact upon the capacity of the press to gather and report news was more than offset by the interest of the public in criminal investigation, as reflected in the traditional investigative authority of the grand jury.

How far *Branzburg* should be taken is unclear. Noting that *Branzburg* was concerned with the press function of news gathering, which has never been placed at the core of First Amendment rights, several courts have held that the government should bear a special burden of justification where the disclosure required by a subpoena bears upon the direct exercise of a First Amendment right. These courts typically speak of requiring the government to show that the information sought by the subpoena is "substantially related" to a "compelling government interest." *Branzburg*, however, is viewed as having established that the government interest in investigating crime is per se a "compelling interest," so that standard is automatically met by a government showing of a substantial relationship to a grand jury's investigation, absent factors strongly suggesting that the grand jury investigation was initiated in bad faith. *National Commodity and Barter Association v. United States* (10th Cir. 1991). To establish that the information sought is "substantially related" to the grand jury's investigation, the prosecution ordinarily must offer an explanation as to how the information sought relates to the subject of the investigation. This explanation must establish a linkage somewhat more substantial than the *R. Enterprises* standard of a "reasonable possibility" of relevancy, but it may fall far short of establishing a critical need for the information.

Other courts have rejected entirely the contention that the government must ordinarily make a special showing to sustain a subpoena that has the potential for chilling the exercise of First Amendment rights. The Fourth Circuit adopted that position upon remand in the *R. Enterprises* case, considering there a First Amendment claim (not presented to the Supreme Court) that compliance with the challenged subpoena would chill the petitioner's continued operations in the distribution of sexually explicit magazines. *In re Grand Jury 87–3 Subpoena Duces Tecum* (4th Cir.1992). It reasoned that *Branzburg,* in recognizing the sufficiency of the district court's capacity to respond to a "bad faith exercise of grand jury powers," rejected the need to impose any special burden on the government. Consistent with this reading of *Branzburg*, First Amendment interests are adequately protected by the district court applying, "with special sensitivity where values of expression are potentially implicated," the standards of *R. Enterprises*, keeping in mind the "traditional rule," as set forth in *R. Enterprises*, that "grand juries are not licensed to engage in arbitrary fishing expeditions, nor may they select targets out of malice or an intent to harass."

A "chilling effect" argument also has been raised where the grand jury requires the testimony of an attorney, asking questions concerning client identity or the source of fee payments (matters generally not within the attorney-client privilege, see § 22.02). Finding that the attorney-client privilege provides adequate protection of the lawyer-client relationship, the lower courts generally have refused to require a special governmental showing of need to compel the attorney to testify as to matters not within the privilege. Indeed, the Second Circuit has held that no such showing was needed even where the attorney was currently representing the target of the grand jury investigation on a related criminal charge and the act of testifying before the grand jury could conceivably lead to his disqualification at trial on that charge. *In re Grand Jury Subpoena Served Upon Doe* (2d Cir.1986) (en banc). The First Circuit has noted, however, that the district court has sufficient discretionary authority to quash such a subpoena where it concludes that compliance could have an overly chilling impact upon the defendant's right to counsel on the pending criminal charge. *In re Grand Jury Matters* (1st Cir.1984).

§ 16.08 Misuse Objections

Blair v. United States (S.Ct.1919) generally is viewed as barring a subpoenaed party from challenging the authority of the grand jury to indict for (and therefore investigate) the activities that are the subject of its inquiry. In *Blair*, the witness claimed that the transaction under investigation was beyond the grand jury's investigative authority because the applicable federal criminal statute was unconstitutional. The Supreme Court initially noted

that consideration of the constitutionality of the
statute at this point, prior to any indictment, would
be contrary to the long-established practice of "refrain[ing] from passing upon the constitutionality of
an act of Congress unless obliged to do so." It then
proceeded, however, to speak in quite general terms
of a witness' lack of capacity to challenge the "authority * * * of the grand jury," provided the jury
had "de facto existence and organization." The
Court treated the position of the grand jury witness
as analogous to that of the trial witness. Neither
could raise objections of incompetency or irrelevan-
cy, for those matters were of "no concern" to a
witness, as opposed to a party. For the same reasons, witnesses also should not be allowed "to take
exception to the jurisdiction of the grand jury or the
court over the particular subject matter that is
under investigation." The grand jury operates as a
"grand inquest," which requires broad investigative
powers. It must have authority, in particular, "to
investigate the facts in order to determine the question of whether the facts show a case within [its]
jurisdiction." The witness could not be allowed "to
set limits to the investigation that the grand jury
may conduct."

A long line of cases, in contrast to *Blair*, recognize the right of the subpoenaed party to challenge
prosecutorial misuse of the grand jury's subpoena
authority. Such instances of misuse include: (1)
employment of the grand jury subpoena primarily
to elicit evidence for use in a pending or future civil
action; (2) employment of the grand jury subpoena

"for the sole or dominating purpose of preparing an already pending indictment for trial;" (3) employment of the grand jury process to further independent investigations by police or prosecutor rather than to produce evidence for grand jury use; and (4) calling a witness for the purpose of "harassment," with "harassment" described as encompassing various objectives other than producing relevant evidence, such as burdening the witness with repeated appearances or seeking to punish the witness by forcing the witness into a situation where s/he will refuse to answer (or lie) and be held for contempt (or perjury). Where the target of the misuse is a person other than the subpoenaed individual (e.g., where the grand jury, is seeking to obtain from the witness information to be used against the witness' employer in a civil case), lower courts have also recognized the standing of the target to quash the subpoena. *In re Grand Jury Proceedings (Diamante)* (1st Cir.1987).

A common thread running through the judicial treatment of misuse objections is that "a presumption of regularity" attaches to the grand jury proceeding and the objecting party bears a substantial burden in seeking to overcome that presumption. It clearly is not sufficient simply to show that the use of the grand jury process has (or will) benefit the government with respect to civil discovery, criminal discovery on a pending indictment, or some other alleged improper purpose. Courts have stressed that misuse exists only if the "primary" prosecutorial purpose is improper, and that the prosecutor will not be enjoined from carrying forward a legitimate grand jury investigation simply because one byproduct may be the production of evidence useful in other proceedings in which the government has some interest. To gain an evidentiary hearing on a claim of alleged misuse, the objecting party ordinarily must at least point to surrounding circumstances "highly suggestive" of improper purpose.

Even where the surrounding circumstances strongly suggest improper use to obtain civil discovery or discovery on a pending criminal indictment, courts have expressed a reluctance to judge the dominant purpose of the investigation while it is still ongoing. The objecting party, it is noted, should not be allowed to "break up the play before it was started and then claim the government was offsides." *United States v. Doe (Ellsberg)* (1st Cir. 1972). A preferable remedy, they note, is to allow the investigation to continue to its completion and then judge its purpose if the government should attempt to utilize the fruits of its alleged misuse in another proceeding. Where the alleged improper purpose is the development of evidence for a civil proceeding, the Rule 6(e) motion needed to disclose the grand jury material to civil attorneys ordinarily will provide the objecting party with an opportunity to challenge the purpose of the investigation after it has been completed (see § 18.06). Where the alleged improper purpose is gaining additional information for use in a trial on a pending indictment, the judge presiding at that trial can determine whether to require an inquiry into the dominant purpose of the post-indictment grand jury investigation when (and if) the government makes use in its prosecution of the fruits of that allegedly tainted investigation.

§ 16.09   Challenging Secrecy Violations

Rule 6(e)(2) the Federal Rules of Criminal Procedure sets forth the general secrecy requirements of federal grand jury proceedings. It provides that the grand jurors, grand jury personnel, government attorneys, and personnel assisting government attorneys (see § 18.05) may not disclose "matters occurring before the grand jury." Rule 6(e)(2) further provides that no obligation of secrecy may be imposed on any person "except in accordance with this Rule." Rule 6(e)(3) recognizes five "exceptions" to the general rule of secrecy imposed by Rule 6(e)(2)(see § 18.06). Individuals or entities who have furnished information to the grand jury, or whose activities are the subject of the grand jury investigation, often seek to challenge a disclosure by government personnel that the government acknowledges but justifies as consistent with Rules 6(e)(2) and 6(e)(3). As discussed in § 18.06, such persons may challenge proposed court orders that would authorize disclosure to third persons or other governmental units under Rule 6(e)(3)(C)(i) (disclosure "preliminary to or in connection with a judicial proceeding"). So too, as noted in § 18.05, subjects of an investigation may seek relief with respect to disclosures that government personnel have made without a court order—i.e., where the government claims that the disclosures either were not covered by Rule 6(e)(2) because they did not include "matters occurring before the grand jury" or were authorized without a court order under Rule 6(e)(3). In both of the above situations, no question exists as to who disclosed (or intends to disclose) what information to whom, and the primary issue is whether the disclosure meets the standards of Rule 6(e)(3) or is outside the coverage of Rule 6(e)(2). A quite different type of challenge is presented where the individual or entity claims that there have been "leaks" of grand jury matter to the media. Here, the issue ordinarily is not whether the alleged disclosures to the media by persons clearly subject to the Rule 6(e)(2) secrecy requirements (in particular, government attorneys and assisting personnel) would fall within the exceptions recognized in Rule 6(e)(3), or otherwise would be justified under Rule 6(e)(2) (they clearly would not), but whether those persons actually did leak grand jury matter, and, if so, what is an appropriate remedy.

Courts rarely have had to rule definitively on the issue of remedy because of the almost insurmountable hurdle of establishing that there was a leak. Initially, to establish the grounding even for an evidentiary hearing, the complaining party must make a prima facie showing that there has been an unauthorized disclosure. This requires showing both that the information disclosed probably was within the protection of grand jury secrecy (i.e., was "grand jury matter," see § 18.05, rather than, for example, information acquired by government agents through their own investigative efforts) and that the disclosure was likely to have come from government personnel, the grand jurors, or grand jury personnel, rather than from a person not sworn to secrecy under Rule 6(e)(2) (in particular, a witness). Thus, newspaper articles that refer only to the general character of the investigation (rather than grand jury testimony or grand jury actions) ordinarily will be insufficient, and even articles that refer specifically to grand jury matter (e.g., a witness having refused to testify on self-incrimination grounds) may be insufficient because it may reflect speculation by the journalists or information furnished by the witness or someone with whom the witness shared that information. *In re Grand Jury Investigation (Lance)* (5th Cir.1980).

Should a prima facie case be established, the government will be required to respond at an evidentiary hearing. The leading appellate opinions provide little guidance as to the scope of that hearing. Typically, the government will seek to rely on affidavits stating that all relevant government personnel deny any disclosure on their part. Courts may be wary of requiring the government even to disclose on the record the names of all such personnel on the ground that it would provide the subject of the investigation with discovery of internal grand jury operations. *United States v. Eisenberg* (5th Cir.1983). Although journalists can be called as witnesses and questioned as to their source, they are most unlikely to respond even though that information will not be privileged under federal law. *Branzburg v. Hayes* (see § 16.07).

Rule 6(e)(2) provides that "a knowing violation of Rule 6 may be punished as a contempt of court." A few lower court opinions suggest that this provision refers only to criminal (and not civil) contempt, and therefore creates no right in anyone except the court to insist upon sanctions for a secrecy violation. Under this view, neither the witness whose testimony is leaked, nor the person who is the subject of the information leaked, has a cause of action for which relief can be demanded, as the initiation of criminal contempt lies solely in the discretion of the court. Such individuals or entities may notify the court of the alleged violation and urge it to hold an evidentiary hearing for the purpose of determining whether imposition of a criminal contempt is appropriate, but the court has discretion to pursue the alternative route of referring the matter to the Department of Justice's Office of Professional Responsibility for internal investigation and the possible imposition of internal sanctions. *Matter of Grand Jury Investigation* (90–30–2) (E.D.Mich.1990).

Other courts have stated that Rule 6(e)(2) also authorizes civil contempt, and a witness or subject of the investigation victimized by the leak has a right to proceed against the violator upon showing a knowing violation. *Barry v. United States* (D.C.Cir. 1989). A few courts also have suggested that the contempt sanction specified in Rule 6(e)(2) might not be exclusive. Thus, if leaks persist and their source cannot be identified, a court could quash a subpoena on behalf of a witness who would suffer prejudice if his testimony were leaked. Since courts have agreed that whatever relief is available should not "unnecessarily interfere with the grand jury process," such relief would be rare, and arguably a court should never be compelled to go so far as to dismiss the grand jury and terminate the investigation because of continued leaks. *Barry v. United States*.

Although claims of secrecy violations usually are directed at disclosures, persons who are the subject of an investigation have also raised objections to prosecutorial efforts to preclude witnesses from discussing their testimony with those persons. Since Rule 6(e)(2) does not include the witness in the list of persons sworn to secrecy, and further provides that "no obligation of secrecy may be imposed on any person except in accordance with this Rule," many lower courts have concluded that the Rule prohibits the imposition of a requirement of secrecy upon a witness. The one exception, under this view, would be the financial institution subject to the Right to Financial Privacy Act (RFPA). The RFPA prohibits a financial institution from notifying a customer of a grand jury subpoena for the customer's records under limited circumstances, and allows for issuance of a court order to prohibit such disclosure for a 90 day period in a broader range of circumstances (e.g., upon a showing of a "reason to believe" that the disclosure would "seriously jeopardize" the investigation). 12 U.S.C. §§ 3409, 3420.

Other federal courts have concluded that their "inherent authority to maintain the integrity of grand jury proceedings" would allow them to impose an obligation of secrecy upon a witness, even in a case that is not within the RFPA, where disclosure by the witness would substantially impede the grand jury's capacity to investigate. They read Rule 6(e)(2) as only prohibiting the extension to witnesses of the obligation of secrecy imposed by that Rule. Of course, even under this view, the prosecution has no authority to silence witnesses on its own initiative, and the question therefore arises as to what distinguishes a permissible prosecutorial request that witnesses not inform others of their subpoena or their testimony from a prohibited prosecutorial directive not to do so. *In re Grand Jury Subpoena (Diamante)* (1st Cir.1987) (government could not characterize as mere request a letter that could lead a reasonable person to believe s/he was "legally obligated" not to disclose).

§ 16.10   Challenges to the Indictment

Challenges to an indictment based on alleged prosecutorial misconduct during the course of the grand jury proceedings must overcome four major hurdles. First, there is the practical problem of establishing that the misconduct occurred. The best source for determining what happened before the grand jury usually is the transcript of the grand jury proceedings, but under Rule (6)(e)(3)(C)(ii), that transcript can be obtained by the defendant only "when permitted by the court * * * upon a showing that grounds may exist for a motion to dismiss the indictment because of matters occurring before the grand jury." Federal courts generally hold that disclosure will not be permitted under this provision unless the defense first makes a preliminary showing, from the sources available to it, of specific likely misconduct that might justify dismissal.

Second, the range of "misconduct" that can provide a grounding for challenging an indictment is quite narrow. In *United States v. Williams* (S.Ct. 1992), the Supreme Court concluded that "as a general matter at least," federal courts lack the authority to independently prescribe standards of appropriate prosecutorial conduct before the grand jury and then dismiss indictments because of the prosecutor's failure to abide by those standards. Federal courts can utilize their supervisory authority to dismiss indictments "as a means of enforcing or vindicating legally compelled standards of prosecutorial conduct before the grand jury," but those standards must be found basically in statutes, the Federal Rules of Criminal Procedure, or constitutional prohibitions. Accordingly, *Williams* held, a federal court cannot dismiss an indictment because the prosecutor failed to present before the grand jury known exculpatory evidence, as there is no statute, court rule, or constitutional provision that requires the prosecutor to present such evidence to the grand jury.

The *Williams* court cited examples of "those few, clear rules which were carefully drafted and approved by the Court and Congress to ensure the integrity of the grand jury" and therefore could be enforced by a dismissal of an indictment. They consisted largely of the provisions of Rule 6 and a series of limited statutory prohibitions (such as the prohibition against presenting unlawful wiretap evidence before the grand jury and the prohibition against subornation of perjury). Those provisions do not encompass much of what would be viewed as prosecutorial misconduct in many states (e.g. inflammatory remarks about the witness or target, expressions of personal opinions as to the target's guilt, and misstatements of the law). As for constitutional violations, the Supreme Court has not yet identified any action by the prosecutor that would constitute a violation of due process or the defendant's Fifth Amendment right to be prosecuted by indictment.

Third, should defendant establish prosecutorial misconduct violating the constitution, a statute, or Federal Rule 6, dismissal of the indictment still may not be obtained if that violation constituted a "harmless error." In *Bank of Nova Scotia v. United States* (S.Ct.1988), the Supreme Court held that "dismissal of the indictment is appropriate only if it established that the violation substantially influenced the grand jury's decision to indict or if there is 'grave doubt' that the decision to indict was free from the substantial influence of such violations." Since the *Bank of Nova Scotia* Court noted that that case did not present any constitutional error, arguably the harmless error standard applicable to prosecutorial constitutional trial error would also apply to such prosecutorial misconduct as might constitute constitutional error in the grand jury setting. If so, dismissal for constitutional error would be required unless the court is convinced "beyond a reasonable" doubt that the constitutional error "did not contribute" to the grand jury's decision to indict. *Chapman v. California* (S.Ct.1967). Of course, as *Bank of Nova Scotia* noted, prosecutorial misconduct that does not relate to the presentation of the prosecution's case before the grand jury almost always constitutes harmless error under either standard, because only in the most unusual circumstances will it have contributed to the grand jury's decision to indict. Thus, the Court noted that the Rule (6)(e) secrecy violations raised there (disclosing grand jury matter to third parties and imposing secrecy obligations upon witnesses), clearly constituted harmless error because they simply "could not have affected the charging decision."

Finally, even should the defense establish a prosecutorial violation of a court rule or statute that seems likely to have affected the grand jury's decision, *United States v. Mechanik* (S.Ct.1986) suggests that no relief is available if the challenge is being considered after the defendant was convicted at trial. In *Mechanik*, the defense learned of a Rule 6(d) violation (the presence of unauthorized persons—here multiple witness—before the grand jury) during the middle of the trial, and the trial court postponed consideration of defense's subsequent challenge to the indictment until the trial ended. The Supreme Court in *Mechanik* held that at that point, with the defendant already convicted, the misconduct before the grand jury had become a moot issue. Even if the Rule 6(d) violation might have influence the grand jury on its finding of probable cause necessary to indict, the "petit jury's subsequent guilty verdict" rendered that irrelevant because it "not only means that there was probable cause to believe that the defendants were guilty as charged, but that they are in fact guilty as charged beyond a reasonable doubt." Thus, the "petit jury's verdict rendered harmless any conceivable error in the charging decision that might have flowed from the [Rule 6(d)] violation".

Federal lower courts have disagreed as to how broadly *Mechanik* should be read. Reasoning that *Mechanik* was "carefully crafted along very narrow lines" and involved misconduct that "at worst, was [a] technical [violation]," the Tenth Circuit holds postconviction review available for allegations of misconduct suggesting the prosecutor "attempted to unfairly sway the grand jury or to otherwise affect the accusatory process" and misconduct that "transgressed the defendant's right to fundamental fairness." *United States v. Taylor* (10th Cir.1986). Other circuits have rejected such a narrow reading. They acknowledge that *Mechanik* does not extend to misconduct which denies fundamental fairness and thereby presents a constitutional claim, but see it as extending to the broad range of nonconstitutional improprieties that might justify dismissal if considered prior to conviction.

§ 16.11 Assistance of Counsel

The Supreme Court has twice indicated that a grand jury witness does not have a constitutional right to the assistance of counsel while testifying before a grand jury. In *In re Groban* (S.Ct.1957), a case holding that a witness in a fire marshall's investigative proceeding did not have a constitutional right to the assistance of counsel, the Court drew an analogy to grand jury proceedings and stated: "A witness before a grand jury cannot insist, as a matter of constitutional right, in being represented by counsel." In *United States v. Mandujano*, discussed in § 19.05, the plurality opinion rejected the defendant's contention that, as a putative defendant called before the grand jury, he should have been told not simply that "he could have a lawyer outside the room with whom he could consult", but that counsel would be appointed to assist him if he was indigent. The plurality reasoned that, since "no criminal proceedings had been instituted," the "Sixth Amendment right to counsel had not come into play." That Amendment, which provides the usual constitutional grounding for requiring appointed counsel for the indigent, describes that right as one of the "accused", and the Court had previously held that a person does not become an "accused" until subjected to "adversary judicial proceedings", which does not include grand jury proceedings. *Miranda v. Arizona* recognized a Fifth Amendment right of the indigent arrestee (also not an "accused") to insist upon receiving the advice of an appointed counsel when subjected to custodial interrogation, but the *Mandujano* plurality, for reasons set forth in § 19.05, concluded that *Miranda* did not extend to the grand jury setting.

While the government has no constitutional obligation to provide counsel for persons subpoenaed to appear before the grand jury, it does not necessarily follow that it constitutionally could preclude those persons from consulting with retained counsel prior to complying with the subpoena. The longstanding federal practice has been to facilitate consultation even at the point where the witness appears before the grand jury. Federal Rule 6(d) operates to preclude counsel's presence within the grand jury room as it allows for the presence only of the witness, the jurors, the prosecutor, and needed grand jury personnel. However, the federal practice, is to allow the witness to interrupt her/his testimony and consult with retained counsel located in the anteroom. Indeed, the notification of rights attached to the subpoena (see § 19.05) states: "If you have retained counsel, the grand jury will permit you a reasonable opportunity to step outside the grand jury to consult with counsel if you desire."

When counsel represents more than one witness in a grand jury proceeding, more than one target or subject of the investigation, or a combination of witnesses and non-witness targets or subjects, the government may move to bar such representation as presenting an actual or potential conflict of interest. The Supreme Court has recognized the authority of a trial court to preclude joint representation of criminal defendants, in the interest of both protecting the defendant's right to effective assistance of counsel and preserving the "appearance of fairness" in legal proceedings, even where the defendants are willing to "waive" their right to conflict-free counsel. *Wheat v. United States* (S.Ct.1988). Lower courts have assumed that the same authority exists with respect to the grand jury setting—especially since the participants here cannot rely on any Sixth Amendment right to counsel of choice, but must rely, at best, on an due process right not to have the government arbitrarily interfere in the participant's efforts to obtain legal advice.

Wheat recognized the right of the trial judge to preclude multiple representation not only where an actual conflict existed (i.e. where the clients' current positions make action favoring one harmful to the other), but also where there exists a "serious potential for conflict." The latter situation encompasses many of the settings in which the government has challenged multiple representation, such as the representation of a target and witnesses who might testify against the target, the representation of targets who had minor and major roles in the activities under investigation, and the representation of the corporate employer and the employee whose actions can give rise to the corporation's liability. The government has also challenged multiple representation of same-level targets or subjects who adopt a "united front" position of all refusing to testify on self-incrimination grounds. It occasionally has been argued that disqualification should be ordered in such cases because the united front threatens the effectiveness of the grand jury's investigation. The few federal courts considering such an argument have found this contention unpersuasive, but disqualification in such cases commonly can be reached under the *Wheat* standard (particularly where the government might well grant concessions to one person willing to testify against the others, and the joint representation thereby keeps each client from obtaining conflict-free advice as to whether s/he should be that person).

CHAPTER SEVENTEEN
ADMINISTRATIVE AGENCY INVESTIGATIONS

§ 17.01   Administrative Subpoenas

Most federal administrative agencies have been authorized by Congress to issue administrative subpoenas (also called "summonses") to compel testimony and the production of documents. While that authority has been given to the agencies only to facilitate their investigation of activities that may violate the various regulatory statutes that are within their enforcement domain, its use for that purpose can readily have a direct bearing on criminal prosecutions, particularly as to white collar crime. Violations of those regulatory statutes may constitute crimes as well as civil wrongs, and even when that is not the case, the circumstances surrounding a violation may suggest that a non-regulatory crime has been committed. Of course, the agency may not itself initiate criminal enforcement, but it may deliver the evidence it has collected to the appropriate prosecuting official, along with the agency recommendation for prosecution (see § 18.02). Should further investigation be desired, the prosecutor may utilize the expertise of the agency investigators already familiar with the case (see § 18.06). Should a prosecution eventually be brought, the evidence collected by the agency may be used in the criminal trial.

Unlike grand jury subpoenas, an administrative subpoena is not process of the district court. To enforce it, the agency must bring an independent civil action as authorized in the statute granting it subpoena authority. One consequence of this distinction is that a court order enforcing the subpoena is a final judgment and may be appealed in the same manner as a civil judgment (in contrast to the enforcement of the grand jury subpoena, where the party directed to comply ordinarily can gain review only by being held in contempt and then appealing that order).

The administrative subpoena, like the grand jury subpoena, is subject to the subpoenaed party's testimonial privileges. The individual may rely on the self-incrimination privilege, the lawyer-client privilege, and other privileges recognized in federal courts to refuse to provide particular documents or to answer specific questions put to the witness while testifying before an agency examiner. The subpoenaed party also may raise in the enforcement proceeding several other challenges, the most significant of which are discussed below.

§ 17.02   Fourth Amendment Overbreadth

In its initial response to broad administrative subpoenas duces tecum, the Supreme Court warned against administrative "fishing expeditions" and suggested that Fourth Amendment principles limited the agency to compelling production only where it had "some ground * * * for supposing" the documents subpoenaed contained information relevant to a violation of the statute the agency was charged with enforcing. *FTC v. American Tobacco Co.* (S.Ct. 1924). That view was flatly rejected, however, in *Oklahoma Press Publishing Co., v. Walling* (S.Ct. 1946), and *United States v. Morton Salt Co.* (S.Ct. 1950). *Oklahoma Press* distinguished subpoenas duces tecum from traditional searches (see § 16.03), and concluded that "the Fourth [Amendment], if applicable, at the most guards against abuse only by way of too much indefiniteness or breadth in the things required to be 'particularly described', if also the inquiry is one the demanding agency is authorized by law to make and the materials specified are relevant." That was the "gist" the Court noted, of the Fourth Amendment requirement of "reasonableness." In *Morton Salt*, the Court specifically acknowledged that the *Oklahoma Press* standard allowed for some "fishing expeditions." The administrative agency, the Court noted, had been given by Congress "the power of inquisition". This was a power "more analogous to the grand jury" than to that of a court which issues a subpoena in a specific "case or controversy", and it therefore allowed the agency to "investigate merely on suspicion that the law is being violated, or even just because it wants assurance that it is not."

The standard set forth in *Oklahoma Press*, as explained in *Morton Salt*, is very much like the overbreadth doctrine applied to grand jury subpoenas duces tecum (see § 16.03). *Oklahoma Press* did cite as separate elements the requirements that the investigation be within the scope of the agency authority as granted by Congress and that the documents requested be "relevant" to the investigation. The former requirement basically insists that the subject matter be within the agency's jurisdiction. Its practical significance is limited by the well established standard of review that gives to the agency the opportunity to explore the potential coverage of its mandate, and therefore allows it to investigate for the very purpose of deciding whether or not the particular activity falls within its bailiwick. *Endicott Johnson Corp. v. Perkins* (S.Ct.1943). As for relevancy, that is a factor considered in any event in applying the overbreadth standard (see § 16.04).

§ 17.03   The *Powell* Prerequisites

In *United States v. Powell* (S.Ct.1964), the Supreme Court set forth four prerequisites for district court enforcement of an Internal Revenue Service summons. The statutory provision on enforcement noted simply that the district court was given "jurisdiction by appropriate process" to enforce the summons, but the Court found guidance as to what must be shown to merit enforcement in the statutory provisions governing IRS investigations and the IRS summons. "Reading the statutes as we do," the Court noted, "the Commissioner * * * must show that the investigation will be conducted pursuant to a legitimate purpose, that the inquiry may be relevant to the purpose, that the information sought is not already within the commissioner's possession, and that the administrative steps required by the Code have been followed—in particular, that the 'Secretary or his delegate,' after investigation, has determined the further examination to be necessary and has notified the taxpayer in writing to that effect."

Although *Powell* was speaking only of the IRS summons, the four prerequisites announced there— legitimate purpose, relevancy, lack of current possession, and adherence to agency procedures for issuance—have been applied by lower courts to administrative subpoenas generally. Lower court opinions interpreting the four *Powell* prerequisites have focused primarily on challenges to the government's allegation of a legitimate purpose (see § 17.04), but they have also lent additional content to the other prerequisites.

The agency's statement of purpose typically refers to the investigation of possible violations of designated statutory provisions (or the agency rules and regulations adopted thereunder) by specified individuals or entities in the course of activities that may be described in a fairly general fashion. Relevancy is then determined by assessing the possible relationship of the documents requested to this subject of investigation. The relevancy requirement is met, according to a frequently quoted standard, if the subpoenaed documents "might throw light" upon the subject of the investigation. *Foster v. United States* (2nd Cir.1959).

The third *Powell* prerequisite, that the information sought must not already be within the possession of the government, has been considered primarily in the context of a IRS summons calling for the production of records previously examined by IRS agents. Courts have held that the prerequisite of "possession" means actual physical possession, and is not satisfied by previous knowledge of the contents. *United States v. Texas Heart Institute* (5th Cir.1985).

The content of the fourth prerequisite, compliance with administrative procedures for issuance of the subpoena, varies with the statutes applicable to the particular agency and the rules adopted thereunder. One common requirement is that the administrative subpoena be issued with the approval of a person in a specified position within the agency—the requirement to which the *Powell* Court referred. In the case of the IRS, where the subpoena is issued to a third party record-keeper, § 7609(a) of the Internal Revenue Code requires the IRS to provide notice to the taxpayer, who may then intervene. The Fifth Circuit has suggested that violation of § 7609(a) does not necessarily bar enforcement of the summons (as where, for example, the taxpayer learned of the summons without a § 7609(a) notice and subsequently was allowed to intervene). *United States v. Texas Heart Institute*. On the other hand, the First Circuit has held indispensable compliance with § 7609(f), which authorizes a special third party record-keeper summons that does not identify the taxpayer-target (a "John Doe" summons) only if issued by a judicial officer after a showing of reasonable basis. *United States v. Gertner* (1st Cir. 1995). That provision, the First Circuit argued, provides a protection that cannot be supplied by an after-the-fact determination that the John Doe summons would have issued if it had been properly presented to a court. Compare *United States v. Ritchie* (6th Cir.1994) (suggesting a contrary conclusion).

§ 17.04 Legitimate Purpose Challenges

In discussing the prerequisites for enforcement, the *Powell* Court noted that a "court may not permit its process to be abused" and that "such an abuse would take place if the summons had been issued for an improper purpose, such as to harass the taxpayer or to put pressure on him to settle a collateral dispute, or for any other purpose reflecting on the good faith of the particular investigation." This language is sometimes described to as permitting a "bad faith" challenge to the subpoena that stands apart from the *Powell* prerequisites, but it actually does no more than recognize one possible ground for challenging the agency's allegation of legitimate purpose.

Challenges to purpose typically allege improper motivation and typically are grounded on one of the two illustrations offered in *Powell*. As for vindictive investigations, i.e. investigations designed to punish a person who exercised her/his rights, they clearly are improper, but that does not mean that an agency shift to a more adversary stance in response to the exercise of a right is necessarily vindictive. *United States v. Texas Heart Institute* (5th Cir.1985) (where statute of limitations for civil actions is about to run and taxpayer will not voluntarily extend it, bad faith is not shown by informing taxpayer that case will be transferred to the Criminal Investigation Division, not subject to the same statute of limitations). In *SEC v. Wheeling–Pittsburgh Steel Corp.* (3d Cir.1981), the Third Circuit recognized that improper motivation need not spring from the agency, but could also be the product of third party influence, there the alleged political coercion imposed by a competitor and a legislator.

The *Powell* Court noted that "the burden of showing an abuse of the court's process is on the taxpayer." Most lower courts have held that the government bears the initial burden of demonstrating a lawful purpose by submission of the agency's formal order of investigation (where used), or the affidavit of the responsible agency official, setting forth a purpose that is within the agency's statutory domain. The subpoenaed party then has the burden of asserting and proving that the subpoena is actually motivated by an improper purpose. In *United States v. Gertner* (1st Cir.1995), the First Circuit suggested that perhaps the burden on a subpoenaed party should be only to "create a substantial question in the court's mind regarding the validity of the government's purpose," and then the ultimate burden of proof should shift back to the government as the plaintiff in the enforcement action. Under either view, the subpoenaed party faces a significant burden, as it does not have an automatic right to discovery, enforcement proceedings being summary in nature. Federal Rules of Civil Procedure, Rule 81.

§ 17.05 Criminal Referrals and Continuing Investigations

In *United States v. LaSalle National Bank* (S.Ct. 1978), the Supreme Court considered the extent to which an IRS summons could be employed to obtain evidence for use in a criminal prosecution. The Court noted that the IRS statutory scheme has "interrelated criminal and civil elements," and in authorizing investigations, Congress had not sought to compartmentalize investigations of actions that could have both civil and criminal consequences. Accordingly, the IRS could utilize its summons to investigate possible tax fraud even when it was apparent that the evidence uncovered could lead to a criminal prosecution. On the other hand, Congress had refrained from giving the IRS summons authority "for purely criminal investigations," as to do so would have "broaden[ed] the Justice Department's right of criminal litigation discovery" and "infring[ed] on the role of the grand jury as a principal tool of criminal accusation." As a practical matter, such an invasion of discovery limits and the grand jury's role was most likely to occur when the IRS summons was used after a case had been referred to the DOJ for criminal prosecution. With referral, the IRS lost its capacity to settle the civil case, "interagency cooperation * * * is to be expected," and it would be "unrealistic" to attempt to build an "information barrier" that would keep a continued IRS investigation to determine civil liability from producing criminal discovery. Accordingly, a prophylactic standard would be adopted prohibiting any post-referral use of the IRS summons. To ensure that this standard was not circumvented, the Court also recognized a challenge based on a purposeful delay in referral for the sole purpose of collecting evidence for criminal prosecution. This objection, however, had to be based upon the "institutional posture" of the IRS, rather than the motivation of the individual agent. A subpoenaed party opposing enforcement on this ground would have to show "delay in submitting a recommendation to the Justice Department when there is an institutional commitment to make the referral", thereby evidencing that the IRS was acting "merely * * * to gather additional evidence for the prosecution."

In 1982, Congress amended the statutory provision on IRS summonses (Internal Revenue Code § 7602) by adding subsections (b) and (c). Subsection (b) states that the purposes for which the IRS summons may be used "include the purpose of inquiring into any offense connected with the administration or enforcement of the internal revenue laws." Subsection (c) then provides that "no summons may be issued * * *, and the Secretary may not begin an action * * * to enforce any summons, with respect to any person if a Justice Department referral is in effect with respect to such person." Lower courts have disagreed as to whether this

legislation establishes a single bright-line cutoff of
actual referral and thereby rejects any claim of
institutional bad faith in delaying referral. Compare
Hintze v. IRS (4th Cir.1989), with *Pickel v. United
States* (3d Cir.1984).

Lower courts have refused to extend the rationale
of *LaSalle National Bank* to preclude post-referral
issuance of administrative subpoenas by administrative agencies other than the IRS. In some instances, the agency has been given the authority to
investigate both criminal and civil violations, and
important enforcement responsibilities require that
the agency be allowed to continue its civil investigation and bring it to a prompt close even while the
DOJ is acting on the agency's referral and pursuing
a criminal investigation. *SEC v. Dresser Industries*
(D.C.Cir.1980) (noting that "unlike the IRS, which
can postpone collection of taxes for the duration of
parallel criminal proceedings without seriously impairing the public, the *SEC* must often act quickly,
lest the false or incomplete statements of corporations mislead investors and infect the markets").
Also, because the agency's subpoena authority is no
broader than that of a grand jury, the courts see no
potential for broadening the prosecution's "discovery rights" so long as the criminal investigation is
still before the federal grand jury (i.e., the referral
has not yet resulted in an indictment), as the grand
jury could give the prosecution access to the same
material. So too, while agency investigations may
not be subject to secrecy provisions of the type
imposed by the grand jury, the courts do not see

that as undercutting the independence or effectiveness of the grand jury investigation. Indeed, where the agency has the authority to investigate both civil and criminal violations, courts have even upheld a "joint investigation" strategy that selects the post-referral agency summons over the grand jury subpoena to obtain evidence both agency and grand jury desire, with the agency then sharing its evidence with the grand jury. *United States v. Educational Development Corp.* (3d Cir.1989).

§ 17.06 Staff Misconduct

In *Powell*, the Supreme Court noted: "[I]t is the court's process which is invoked to enforce the administrative summons and a court may not permit its process to be abused." While the *Powell* Court made that statement in the course of discussing the district court's authority to refuse to enforce a subpoena issued for an improper purpose, several lower courts have held that it also supports refusing to enforce a subpoena that is the product of flagrant staff misconduct. Illustrative is *SEC v. ESM Government Securities, Inc.* (5th Cir.1981), where ESM alleged that an SEC investigator deceived ESM in gaining access to its records (the investigator pretended to be interested only in gaining a basic education on the government securities market, while ESM was actually his investigative target), and that the information he obtained through that deception led to the issuance of the challenged subpoena. The Fifth Circuit concluded that if ESM's allegations were true—that the "SEC inten-

tionally or knowingly mislead ESM about the purposes of its review of ESM's files", that "ESM [was]
in fact mislead," and that the subpoena as to the
particular documents requested was "a result of the
SEC's allegedly improper access"—then enforcement of the subpoena as to those documents would
be denied "as an abuse of process." The Fifth
Circuit reasoned that "fraud, deceit, or trickery" by
government agents could constitute "grounds for
refusing enforcement," as the district court's obligation in "determining whether to enforce * * * [is
to] evaluate the seriousness of the violation [by the
staff] under all the circumstances, including the
government's good faith and the degree of harm
imposed by the unlawful conduct."

In contrast to *ESM*, the Fifth Circuit in *United
States v. Barrett* (5th Cir.1988), rejected its holding
in an earlier case that a district court, having found
that IRS agents had violated Code provisions re-
stricting public disclosure of information on individual taxpayers, could condition enforcement of the
subpoena on future compliance with those Code
provisions. The Fifth Circuit here reasoned that,
given the summary nature of the enforcement proceedings, the district court should limit its inquiry
to the four *Powell* prerequisites, especially since the
Internal Revenue Code contains a separate provision authorizing a civil action for damages where
IRS agents unlawfully disclosed taxpayer return
information. The Ninth Circuit has taken a contrary provision, holding that the district court may
condition enforcement on compliance with disclo-

sure restrictions, and the Supreme Court was equally divided when it considered the conflict between the circuits. *United States v. Zolin* (S.Ct.1989).

Staff misconduct has also served as the grounding for defense challenges to the government's use in the criminal prosecution of evidence obtained through that misconduct. Insofar as the staff's misconduct lies simply on its violation of agency regulations, that will not justify suppression of the evidence. In *United States v. Caceres* (S.Ct.1979), the Supreme Court rejected a judicial suppression remedy for such "internal" standards, noting that such a remedy could have "a serious deterrent impact" on agency formulation of additional standards. On the other hand, insofar as the misconduct constitutes deception that may be characterized as having undermined a consensual relinquishment of Fourth Amendment rights, suppression can be founded on the exclusionary rule of the Fourth Amendment.

§ 17.07 The Role of Counsel

Unlike the grand jury witness, the witness subpoenaed to testify in an agency proceeding may be accompanied by counsel. Indeed, that right is recognized in the Administrative Procedures Act [APA § 6(a), 5 U.S.C. § 555(b)] as well as many agency regulations dealing specifically with investigations. Very often those agency regulations also will define the role of counsel. Thus, Rule 203.7 of the SEC's Rules Relating to Investigation states that the witness' right to counsel is a right to have the attorney "(1) advise such person before, during and after the conclusion of such examination, (2) question such person briefly at the conclusion of the examination to clarify any of the answers such person has given, and (3) make summary notes during such examination solely for the use of such person." 17 C.F.R. 203.7(c). The objective of such provisions is to preclude counsel from converting the agency's taking of testimony into a trial, with counsel offering objections and arguments, and requiring the staff examiner to explain the basis and relevance of each and every question.

In some instances, agency regulations seek to deter multiple representation by the same counsel. Thus, SEC Rule 203.7(c) allows counsel to make summary notes solely for the use of the witness counsel is then representing. Also, SEC Rule 203.7(b) provides that "all witnesses shall be sequestered, and unless permitted in the discretion of the officer conducting the investigation, no witness or the counsel accompanying any such witness shall be permitted to be present during the examination of any other witness called in such proceeding." 17 C.F.R § 203.7(b). While such provisions do not absolutely prohibit multiple representation, they can take away from a witness whose counsel has appeared with a previous witness the assistance of that counsel of choice during the witness' appearance before an examiner. However, that potential has been narrowed substantially by the D.C. Circuit's ruling that use of a sequestration provision to exclude the witness' counsel of choice contravenes the Administrative Procedure Act's guarantee of counsel unless the exclusion is based on "concrete evidence" that the agency investigation will be "obstructed or impeded" by the same counsel appearing with more than one witness. *Professional Reactor Operator Society v. United States Nuclear Regulatory Commission* (D.C.Cir.1991).

CHAPTER EIGHTEEN
PARALLEL PROCEEDINGS

§ 18.01 Introduction

With violations of regulatory statutes and administrative rules so often also creating criminal liability, administrative agency proceedings (both investigations and enforcement actions) may readily overlap in subject matter with criminal proceedings (both investigations and prosecutions). So too, with white collar offenses frequently also constituting common law torts and violations of statutes creating private causes of action (e.g. civil RICO), civil actions may readily overlap in subject matter with criminal proceedings. Where the civil or administrative proceedings and the criminal proceedings appear likely to produce such an overlap, they are commonly described as "parallel proceedings." Whether brought simultaneously or seriatim, parallel criminal and civil/administrative proceedings require the participants in those proceedings to give consideration to the bearing of one proceeding upon the other. That is especially true for the "dual target"—i.e., the person who is or anticipates being a defendant in a criminal prosecution (or at least the target of a criminal investigation) and who is or anticipates being a defendant in a civil or administrative proceeding (or at least the target of an administrative agency investigation).

Where the dual target must respond first in a civil suit or administrative proceeding, consideration must be given to whether that response will be available to the prosecutor in the parallel criminal proceeding (see § 18.02), and if so, what benefits will that give to the prosecutor. Depending upon the nature of the dual target's response, a prosecutor could gain from that response: (1) incriminating evidence or leads to incriminating evidence; (2) recorded statements that can be used to impeach the target and the target's witnesses should they vary from those statements in their testimony in the criminal case, and that can provide, in any event, a useful springboard at an early date for preparing cross-examination; and (3) notice of the target's likely defense well in advance and in far greater depth than the notice that could be obtained through criminal discovery. Should these benefits for the prosecutor be likely, the dual target may seek to delay being required to respond until after the criminal proceeding reaches a conclusion (see § 18.03). If that should fail, the dual target may consider exercising the privilege against self-incrimination to limit the content of the response (see § 18.04).

Where the dual target must respond first in a criminal investigation, a major potential peril of cross-proceeding discovery is that opponents in a subsequent civil action or administrative proceeding will be able to obtain the product of the govern-

ment's criminal investigation. Of special significance here is the reach of grand jury secrecy (see
§ 18.05) and the conditions under which materials
covered by grand jury secrecy can be transferred to
potential opponents in parallel civil and administrative actions (see §§ 18.06, 18.07). When required to
respond initially to a criminal prosecution, the dual
target must consider not only the cross-proceeding
discovery that will be given to opponents in any
subsequent parallel civil or agency actions by going
to trial, but also the possibility that the prosecution
could end in a guilty verdict that will bar the target
from contesting critical issues in those other proceedings (see § 18.08).

§ 18.02　Prosecution Discovery From Parallel Proceedings

What is disclosed at trial in a civil proceeding is
open to the public, including, of course, the prosecutor. As for the documents recording disclosures
made in civil discovery (e.g., deposition transcripts,
interrogatories), these too ordinarily are public documents, freely open to inspection after being filed
with the clerk. And even where local rule allows the
documents of discovery not to be filed, an opposing
party would be free to deliver that material to the
prosecutor, and if the opposing party resisted a
prosecutorial request, the grand jury could subpoena that material.

Under Rule 26(c)(6) of the Federal Rules of Civil
Procedure, the district court may issue an order
that discovery material remain under seal where

such an order would serve to "secure the just, speedy, and inexpensive determination" of the suit by "encouraging full disclosure of all relevant evidence." *Martindell v. ITT* (2d Cir.1979). The Second Circuit in *Martindell* held that where such a protective order was issued because critical witnesses otherwise would have relied on their self-incrimination privilege to refuse to provide deposition testimony, the order prevailed over a grand jury subpoena for the record of their deposition testimony. However, three other circuits have rejected this view, concluding that the grand jury subpoena always "trumps a district court's protective order." In re *Grand Jury Subpoena Served on Meserve & Hughes* (9th Cir.1995). They reason, inter alia, that: (1) the grand jury has need for such deposition testimony even if it can gain the witness' testimony by granting immunity because it must determine whether the immunized testimony is truthful, and (2) allowing the protective order to prevail over the subpoena constitutes, in effect, a judicial grant of immunity as to that deposition testimony, which is contrary to executive branch authority to control immunity grants (see § 19.12).

Statutes governing agency investigations commonly treat information acquired through agency investigating subpoenas as "confidential," rather than as matter of public record. However, they also allow for disclosures in the public interest, which clearly encompasses disclosure to a prosecuting authority. Indeed, agency regulations often encourage staff to inform the Department of Justice or U.S.

Attorney's office of agency investigations in which they might have an interest long before a formal referral is made. *United States v. Fields* (2d Cir. 1978).

Undoubtedly the most restrictive provisions on the sharing of agency files with federal prosecutors are those containing in § 6103 of the Internal Revenue Code. That section establishes a general prohibition against IRS disclosure of "return information" (which includes both information "furnished to or collected by" the IRS) and "taxpayer return information" (the narrower category of tax returns and other information furnished by the taxpayer). That prohibition is subject to several exceptions allowing for disclosure to other governmental officials for specified purposes. Apart from emergency situations, the broadest of those exceptions allow for disclosure (with the approval of the Secretary of the Treasury) to the Department of Justice for the purposes of investigating or preparing a proceeding relating to the administration of the tax laws. More stringent conditions are imposed for disclosure to government agents and prosecutors involved in the enforcement of criminal laws other than those of tax administration. Here, the Secretary may disclose return information other than taxpayer return information "to the extent necessary to apprise the head of the appropriate Federal agency" of the possible violation of the criminal law. Upon request of a federal prosecutor, the Secretary is required to disclose "return information (other than taxpayer return information)" for use in an ongoing criminal enforcement proceeding, or ongoing investigation that may result in such a proceeding (including a grand jury investigation), upon a showing of "the specific reason or reasons why such disclosure is, or may be, relevant to such proceeding or investigation." More complete disclosure, including taxpayer return information, must be authorized by an "ex parte order [issued] by a federal district court or magistrate" upon a finding that: "(i) there is reasonable cause to believe, based upon information believed to be reliable, that a specific criminal act has been committed, (ii) there is reasonable cause to believe that the return or the return information is or may be relevant to a matter relating to the commission of such act, and (iii) the return or return information is sought exclusively for use in a Federal criminal investigation or proceeding concerning such act, and the information sought to be disclosed cannot reasonably be obtained, under the circumstances, from another source."

§ 18.03 Delaying the Parallel Civil or Administrative Proceeding

In *United States v. Kordel* (S.Ct.1970), the Supreme Court rejected the defendants' contention that they had been denied due process by a sequence of events that included the government's initial filing of an in rem action against two food products produced by the corporation of which they were officers, notification shortly thereafter that the FDA was recommending their criminal prosecution, denial of their request to stay the civil action

or extend their time for answering interrogatories
until after the disposition of the anticipated criminal proceedings, and the subsequent use in the
criminal prosecution of their answers to those interrogatories. Though recognizing that individuals who
are the targets of parallel civil and criminal proceedings face certain perils when required to respond to the civil action in advance of the criminal
proceeding (although compulsory incrimination was
not one of these perils, since they could exercise the
privilege against self-incrimination in the civil action), the Court concluded that there was no constitutional mandate that dual targets be relieved of
those perils by the issuance of a stay of the discovery in the civil proceeding. To mandate an automatic stay of the civil proceedings "would stultify enforcement of Federal law" by requiring government
agencies "invariably to choose either to forego recommendation of criminal prosecution once it seeks
civil relief or to defer civil proceedings pending
ultimate outcome of a criminal trial."

The *Kordel* Court held open, however, the possibility that certain circumstances might produce a
due process violation either in denying a stay or in
allowing the government to use in a criminal case
the fruits of its civil discovery. It noted: "We do not
deal here with a case where the Government has
brought a civil action solely to obtain evidence for
its criminal prosecution or has failed to advise the
defendant in its civil proceeding that it contem-
plates his criminal prosecution; nor with a case
where the defendant is without counsel or reason-

ably fears prejudice from adverse pretrial publicity or other unfair injury; nor with any other special circumstances that might suggest the unconstitutionality or even the impropriety of this criminal prosecution."

Although a stay may not be constitutionally mandated, the federal district court, under Fed.R.Civ.P. 26(c), has discretion to grant a stay, as does an administrative agency. In determining whether to grant a stay requested by a dual target, courts and agencies tend to apply a balancing test, weighing (1) the harm that will be suffered by the moving party from the failure to grant the stay, (2) the interest of the opposing party in proceeding expeditiously (including any prejudice it might suffer through the delay), (3) the concerns of interested persons who are not a party to the litigation (including, in particular, the "public interest"), and (4) the interests of the court in maximizing judicial efficiency.

Courts have noted that the "strongest case" for deferring civil proceedings comes when the parallel criminal proceeding has reached the indictment stage. At that point, the likely period of deferment is more predictable and ordinarily shorter than the deferment granted during an ongoing criminal investigation. Because the prosecutor cannot use the grand jury to gather further evidence once the indictment is issued (see § 16.08), there is greater concern that the prosecutor will use the civil proceeding (at least where the government is a party) to gain discovery not available through the Rules of Criminal Procedure. Also, with the government having made a firm commitment to prosecute, the defendant is under greater pressure to accept even the consequence of a default that will accompany reliance on the self-incrimination privilege (see § 18.04), rather than risk possibly assisting the prosecution in the criminal case through his presentation in the civil case. Even with these considerations working in favor of a post-indictment deferment, however, the stay will not be granted if the alleged civil violations are ongoing and threaten continued injury to the public.

The defense may prefer to go forward with the civil action, rather than seek a stay, when the government is the opposing party and the defense concludes that the civil discovery process will produce more benefit than harm as a result of what it will learn about the case the government is likely to present in the criminal prosecution. Here, it is the government who often will be seeking to stay the civil case. Courts have tended to grant such requests on the ground that administrative policy gives priority to the public interest in law enforcement. Where the criminal defendant brought the civil action against the government, there often is concern that the action was brought simply to obtain such discovery.

§ 18.04 Asserting the Self–Incrimination Privilege

A person may claim the privilege against self-incrimination in a civil case or administrative proceeding if the person's testimony realistically could provide the government with a link in the chain of evidence needed to prosecute for a crime (see § 19.02). In the civil case, the privilege may be claimed not only as to questions posed at trial or in depositions, but also as to interrogatories, requests for admissions, and subpoenas to produce documents (see § 20.02). The privilege is not available to entities (see § 20.07), so the entity that is the defendant or plaintiff in a civil action cannot rely on the privilege to refuse to answer interrogatories. Should the officer of the entity designated to answer them refuse on the ground that the answers would tend to incriminate the officer personally, the burden lies on the entity to find some other agent who can provide the answers.

The exercise of the privilege by a civil plaintiff or defendant is not without costs. If the party claiming the privilege thereby finds herself unable to present evidence supporting her side of the case, the consequence is likely to be a summary judgment. Moreover, courts may take remedial action because the party claiming the privilege has disadvantaged the opposing party by depriving that party of a useful source of evidence. Since an individual has a right to claim the privilege and since litigants do not have a right to discovery of privileged materials, courts have emphasized that any such remedy should be aimed at repairing the disadvantage rather than punishing the exercise of the privilege. *SEC v. Graystone Nash Inc.* (3d Cir.1994). Ordinarily, the entry of a dismissal or a default judgment would be viewed as punishment, but it may be justified in extreme cases, as where the exercise of the privilege results in a wholesale denial of discovery. A more common remedy in both civil and administrative actions is to bar the admission of evidence where the party's exercise of the privilege kept from the opposing party the means of challenging that evidence. *Gutierrez-Rodriguez v. Cartagena* (1st Cir. 1989).

Perhaps the most common response to the exercise of the privilege, in both civil and administrative proceedings, is to allow the finder of fact to draw an adverse inference as to the information not received (see § 19.09). Thus, where a defendant in a civil case exercises the privilege in responding to interrogatories, the plaintiff can ask the jury to assume that the answer not given would have been that most unfavorable to the defendant. Ordinarily, when a non-party witness invokes the privilege, no adverse inference may be drawn. However, where the witness is so closely connected to the party as to be "within its control" (e.g., officers of an entity) and has particular knowledge of its activities, an adverse inference may be drawn against that party.

§ 18.05 Grand Jury Matter

Insofar as information obtained by the prosecution during a criminal investigation is governed by the Rule 6(e)(2) provision on grand jury secrecy (see § 16.09), the prosecution can only share that information with potential litigants in parallel proceedings where the conditions prescribed in 6(e)(3) are met (see §§ 18.06, 18.07). When the information is not governed by Rule 6(e)(2), the prosecution ordinarily is free to share the information if it deems sharing to be in the public interest (which will almost invariably be the case where the criminal process has reached its end and the information would be useful to other government offices in bringing a parallel civil or administrative action).

Rule 6(e)(2) applies to all "matter occurring before the grand jury." That phrase is a term of art, not to be construed literally as encompassing only events actually taking place before the grand jury. *Fund for Constitutional Government v. National Archives* (D.C. Cir.1981) ("in order to effectuate" the "broad objectives" of grand jury secrecy, the Rule 6(e)(2) reference to "matter occurring before the grand jury" must be read "to encompass not only the direct revelation of grand jury transcripts, but also the disclosure of information which would reveal 'the identities of witnesses or jurors, the substance of testimony, the strategy or direction of the investigation, the deliberations or questions of the jurors, and the like' "). Thus, "grand jury matter" will include an office interview given by a subpoenaed witness in lieu of a grand jury appearance, a prosecution memorandum describing documents or testimony that was presented to the grand jury, and an expert's report to the prosecutor that served as the basis for the experts' final conclusion, which alone was given to the grand jury.

On the other hand Rule 6(e)(2) does not apply to material generated independently of the grand jury even though similar material was later presented to the grand jury. Thus, where FBI agents independently obtain in interviews with possible witnesses information that is relevant both to an ongoing grand jury investigation and an administrative investigation, they may disclose that information to the administrative agency even though the persons interviewed subsequently testified before the grand jury (and presumably conveyed the same information in that testimony). *In re Grand Jury Subpoena (U.S. v. Under Seal)* (4th Cir.1990). So too, where the prosecutor learns of the existence of a document through sources independent of the grand jury, and desires to acquire that document in a fashion that will permit sharing it with an administrative agency without having to meet the requirements of Rule 6(e)(3), the prosecutor may achieve that end by obtaining the document through process other than a grand jury subpoena (e.g., by use of a search warrant or by requesting that the agency utilize its own subpoena power to obtain the document). *United States v. Educational Development Network*, discussed in § 17.05.

Even where documents were obtained by grand jury subpoena and were presented to the grand jury, they may not be treated as grand jury matter in all possible disclosure situations. Consider, for example, the situation in which the document in question was preexisting (i.e., it was not prepared for the purpose of complying with the subpoena), the prosecutor did not return the document to the subpoenaed party after presenting it to the grand jury, a civil litigant or government agency was aware of the document and sought to obtain it from the subpoenaed party, that party then responded that the document had been subpoenaed by the grand jury and was currently in the possession of the prosecutor, and the civil litigant or government agency then sought to obtain the document from the prosecutor. A handful of federal court decisions have adopted a standard that would require the third party in such a situation to seek court ordered disclosure under Rule 6(e)(3), as they view the government's disclosure to a third party of any document presented to the grand jury as an otherwise prohibited disclosure of "matter occurring before the grand jury." However, most federal courts have adapted standards that would hold disclosure in this type of situation not to fall within Rule 6(e)(2), under at least some circumstances. *United States v. Dynavac* (9th Cir.1993) (surveying different positions).

§ 18.06   The "Preliminary To" Requirement

Under Rule 6(e)(3), grand jury matter may be disclosed to others under six basic exceptions to grand jury secrecy. Four of those exceptions relate to disclosure to implement criminal law enforcement. See Rule (6)(e)(3)(A)(1) (disclosure to U.S. Attorneys and other DOJ attorneys for use in enforcing federal criminal law); Rule (6)(e)(3)(A)(ii),(B) (disclosure to personnel, including agency personnel, designated by the prosecutor as needed to assist in the criminal investigation, with such personnel specifically prohibited from "utilizing that grand jury material for any purpose other than assisting the attorney for the government in the performance of such attorney's duty to enforce federal criminal law"); Rule (6)(e)(3)(C)(ii) (disclosure to another federal grand jury); Rule (6)(e)(3)(C)(iv) (disclosure to state prosecution official for the purpose of enforcing state criminal law). A fifth exception is limited to a criminal defendant seeking dismissal of the indictment against him. See § 16.10. Thus the only provision possibly authorizing disclosure to a prospective litigant in a parallel civil or administrative action is Rule (6)(e)(3)(C)(i)—providing for disclosure "directed by a court preliminary to or in connection with a judicial proceeding."

Where the parallel proceeding is a civil action, and is already underway, it will meet the "in connection with" standard of Rule (6)(e)(3)(C)(i). Where the civil action is readily anticipated, that is sufficient under the "preliminary to" standard. The major hurdle arises where the proceeding first anticipated is an administrative proceeding, for Rule (6)(e)(3)(C)(i) refers only to a "judicial" proceeding. As the Supreme Court noted in *United States v. Baggot* (S.Ct.1983), this limitation "reflects a judgment that not every beneficial purpose, or even every valid government purpose, is an appropriate reason for breaching grand jury secrecy." Rather, only "uses related fairly directly to some identifiable litigation" in a court were thought to merit such a breach.

Baggot held that disclosure for use in an IRS audit of civil tax liability did not fall within the "preliminary to" requirement since the IRS's calculation and collection of any amount determined to be due did not require judicial intervention. The mere possibility that the taxpayer might challenge the agency's non-judicial means of enforcing its determination would not make the agency proceeding "preliminary to a judicial proceeding." On the other side, where the administrative proceeding requires a judicial determination for enforcement (as in attorney disbarment), disclosure to assist the agency in its proceedings ordinarily would be within the Rule. The same is true where judicial review is not mandatory, but still plays "a significant role" in the "operation of the regulatory/statutory scheme." *In re Grand Jury 89–4–72* (6th Cir.1991). Even then, however, the agency investigation may be at such a preliminary stage, far removed from a substantial likelihood of a finding that would require judicial enforcement, that disclosure could not yet be viewed as preliminary to a judicial proceeding. *Baggot* specifically left open what was needed in this regard, although noting that the possibility the individual might consent to the agency's proposed sanction should not be sufficient to negate the anticipated judicial proceeding.

§ 18.07 Particularized Need

Disclosure under Rule (6)(e)(3)(C)(i) also requires that the party seeking disclosure establish a "particularized need"—i.e., establish that "the need for disclosure is greater than the need for continued secrecy, and that th[e] request is structured to cover only material so needed." *Douglas Oil Co. of California v. Petrol Stops Northwest* (S.Ct.1979). The Supreme Court and the circuit courts have pointed to a variety of factors that should be weighed by a district court in the balancing required by the particularized need standard.

Initially, the court should look to the status of the investigation that produced the requested grand jury material. The need for secrecy clearly is greatest while the grand jury is still gathering evidence and considering whether to indict. Once the grand jury is finished with the matter, the need for secrecy declines and the movant's burden in establishing a particularized need declines. As the Supreme Court noted in *Douglas Oil*, however, the value of grand jury secrecy is only "reduced," not "eliminated," by the termination of the investigation, for consideration must be given to the long term impact of disclosure, extending beyond the particular case. Frequent authorization of disclosure will undercut the effectiveness of the promise of secrecy in gaining the cooperation of grand jury witnesses.

Another factor weighed is whether the third party seeks disclosure that might subject grand jury witnesses to "retribution or social stigma." One of the considerations that the Supreme Court found to weigh against disclosure to a participant in a civil antitrust suit was that witnesses in an antitrust investigation often are employees of the target companies, or their customers, competitors or suppliers, and might face discharge or other forms of retaliation if their testimony were disclosed to their employers. *United States v. Procter & Gamble* (S.Ct. 1958). On the other hand, if there already has been substantial disclosure of the grand jury materials to the investigated companies (as where the companies were indicted and gained the witness's statements in the course of criminal discovery), disclosure to the other parties in the parallel civil suit is less likely to cause concern.

Another important consideration is the narrowness of the disclosure requested. Under a standard of "particularized" need, a request for broad disclosure will almost certainly work against the petitioner, as it did in *Procter & Gamble,* where the Court characterized the rejected request as seeking "wholesale discovery." As the Supreme Court has noted, the "typical showing of particularized need arises when a civil litigant seeks to use the grand jury transcript at the trial to impeach a witness, to refresh his recollection, to test his credibility and the like." The disclosure there "can be limited to those portions of a particular witness' testimony that bear upon his * * * direct testimony at trial." *Douglas Oil.* In addition, such requests are less likely to be based on a speculative judgment as to need, while the use involved serves the important interest of ensuring that the factfinder is not misled. In assessing need even as to fairly limited disclosure, however, the court also must take into consideration the availability of alternative means (such as civil discovery) that might produce the same information. The fact that disclosure will avoid the significant expense and delay of the alternative means is not in itself sufficient to establish the requisite need.

Where the request for disclosure comes from a governmental agency, many courts have required a somewhat lesser showing of particularized need. The Supreme Court has rejected the contention that a government agency can justify disclosure simply by showing the relevancy of the requested material, but it has also said that the balancing process may be somewhat different for disclosure to government bodies as opposed to private parties. The Court has noted in particular that "the district court may weigh the public interest, if any, served by disclosure to a government body—along with the requisite particularized need—in determining whether the need for disclosure is greater than the need for continued secrecy." *Illinois v. Abbot & Associates* (S.Ct.1983). Thus, where the contemplated disclosure was to civil attorneys within the government for the purpose of deciding whether to file a civil action, the district court could properly take into account the likelihood that the disclosure would "sav[e] the Government, the potential defendants, and witnesses, the pains of costly and time consuming depositions and interrogatories which might later have turned out to be wasted if the Government decided not to file a civil action after all." *United States v. John Doe, Inc. I* (S.Ct.1987). Accordingly too, while the governmental agency's capacity to obtain the same information through its own investigative authority is a consideration weighing against the need for disclosure, that factor cannot be treated as a per se bar against authorizing disclosure. Indeed, that authority may strengthen the case for disclosure as it responds to another concern noted by the Court—that the use of grand jury materials by other government agencies not "threaten to subvert the limitations applied outside the grand jury context on the Government's powers of discovery and investigation." *United States v. John Doe, Inc. I.*

§ 18.08 Collateral Estoppel

A defendant who goes to trial in a criminal case must consider the dual perils of disclosure and collateral estoppel as they relate to subsequent parallel civil and administrative actions. The trial puts on the public record the prosecution's case and the defendant's defense, making them available to prospective opponents in the parallel proceedings. Information that was protected by grand jury secrecy becomes available to all when the prosecution presents that information through its witnesses and documents at trial.

Of course, the prosecution's evidence may fail to convince the criminal jury, but that does not necessarily mean that it will fail to convince the finder of fact when duplicated (or improved upon) in the parallel proceeding, where there is a lower standard of proof. Even if the parallel civil proceeding involves precisely the same issue and is brought by the government, that lower proof standard means the acquitted defendant cannot use the doctrine of collateral estoppel. *United States v. One Assortment of 89 Firearms* (S.Ct.1984). On the other hand, should the defendant be convicted by trial or by guilty plea, in the subsequent civil or administrative action, collateral estoppel will treat that conviction as conclusive as to any issue determined by the criminal case. In some instances, this will mean that the only issue left to be resolved in the civil action is that of damages.

A criminal conviction based on a plea of *nolo contendere*, however, is treated differently. Although a plea of *nolo contendere* supports a conviction, it technically is not an admission of guilt (defendant saying, in effect, "I do not contest"). Accordingly, a defendant who has pleaded *nolo contendere* is not estopped from denying in a subsequent civil proceeding the facts on which the criminal charge was based, and the conviction based on a *nolo* plea is not evidence that the defendant committed the crime. *Hudson v. United States* (S.Ct. 1926).

For a criminal defendant more concerned about the consequences of anticipated parallel proceedings than the consequences of a conviction (often the case for an entity), the preferred strategy may be to enter a plea of *nolo contendere* rather than provide discovery and risk both a conviction and collateral estoppel by contesting guilt at trial. The *nolo contendere* plea, however, can be entered only with the approval of the district court. Moreover, Rule 11(b) of the Federal Rules of Criminal Procedure directs the court to accept such a plea "only after due consideration of the views of the parties and the interest of the public in the effective administration of justice." The plea is more likely to be accepted where the government does not object, but that lack of objection may require negotiated concessions by the defendant relating to restitution and other remedial orders (see § 23.06).

CHAPTER NINETEEN

THE SELF–INCRIMINATION PRIVILEGE: TESTIMONY

§ 19.01 Applicability of the Privilege

The Fifth Amendment's self-incrimination clause provides that "no person * * * shall be compelled in any criminal case to be a witness against himself." It was not until more than a century after the Amendment's adoption that the Supreme Court, in *Counselman v. Hitchcock* (S.Ct.1892), put to rest the possibility that this Fifth Amendment privilege was available only to a defendant refusing to be compelled to testify in the defendant's own criminal case. *Counselman* held that the "criminal case" phrasing refers to the eventual use of the testimony, not the nature of the proceeding in which the testimony is compelled. The Fifth Amendment, *Counselman* concluded, applies to a subpoenaed witness "in any proceeding" where compelled to give testimony that could be used against the witness in a subsequent criminal case. Since the prohibition is against the compulsion, the witness could object at the point of compulsion, even though it could not be said with certainty that the witness later would be prosecuted, and that the testimony sought in the current proceeding would then be introduced, making the individual "a witness against himself." A realistic potential for such use was sufficient and that potential could exist in any type of proceeding in which a witness was compelled to testify. Thus, the privilege became available not only to the grand jury witness (the precise issue in *Counselman*), but also to persons compelled by subpoena to testify in civil suits and in administrative proceedings (see §§ 17.01, 18.04).

§ 19.02   Potential for Incrimination

The Fifth Amendment privilege is available, of course, only if the compelled testimony carries the potential of later being used against the witness as a defendant in a criminal case. This requires a content that potentially would be harmful to a criminal defendant. Although that covers a great deal, it is not without limits. Thus, the Supreme Court has noted that content is incriminating only as it relates to criminal liability, *Ullman v. United States* (S.Ct.1956) (civil disabilities and social stigma, no matter how severe, are not sufficient), and that the potential incriminating character must relate to the witness' own criminal liability, not the criminal liability of others, *Rogers v. United States* (S.Ct.1951). Moreover, the potential for criminal incrimination must be "real and appreciable," not "imaginary and unsubstantial." *Brown v. Walker* (S.Ct.1896).

A witness' assertion of the privilege does not, in itself, establish that the witness' testimony would have this potentially incriminating quality. As *Hoffman v. United States* (S.Ct.1951), stressed, "it is for the court to say whether [the witness'] silence is justified, and to require him to answer 'if it clearly appears to the court that he is mistaken.'" *Hoffman* also indicated, however, that courts are to give the witness every benefit of the doubt in reviewing an assertion of the privilege. "The privilege," the Court noted, applies "not only to answers that would in themselves support a conviction but likewise * * * those which would furnish a link in the chain of evidence needed to prosecute the claimant." The witness must have "reasonable cause" to believe that her/his testimony would have this potential, but cannot be expected to "prove * * * [that] hazard in the sense in which a claim is usually required to be established in court," as that would "compel * * * [the witness] to surrender the very protection which the privilege is designed to guarantee." Accordingly, to sustain the witness' claim, "it need only be evident from the implications of the question, in the setting in which it is asked, that a responsive answer to the question or an explanation of why it cannot be answered might be dangerous because injurious disclosure could result."

The *Hoffman* case also provides a fine illustration of the need for the court to look to all surrounding circumstances and to imagine the worst in the witness' possible responses in determining whether there is a "real and appreciable" possibility that the witness' testimony will furnish that "link in the chain of evidence" sufficient to make it incriminating. The Supreme Court there ruled that

the district court had erred in holding the privilege
inapplicable to questions concerning the witness'
current occupation and his contacts with a person
who was a fugitive witness. Since the lower court
was aware that the grand jury was investigating
racketeering, it should have recognized that questions concerning Hoffman's current occupation
might require answers relating to violations of various gambling laws. It also should have recognized
that the answers to questions concerning Hoffman's contacts with the fugitive witness could have
referred to efforts to hide that witness, which
would be criminal.

Although *Hoffman* suggests that witness claims
of the privilege will usually be sustained without
requiring any specific explanation of the possibili-
ties for incrimination, special settings may impose
that burden upon the witness. One such setting is
the questioning of the witness regarding criminal
acts for which the witness already has been convicted (assuming that the conviction is "final", so the
double jeopardy will bar any reprosecution for that
offense). Here, the usual assumption is that the
individual "no longer has the privilege against self-
incrimination as he can no longer be incriminated
by his testimony about the crime." *Reina v. United
States* (S.Ct.1960). However, as illustrated by *Malloy v. Hogan* (S.Ct.1964), the privilege may be available even as to such questioning under some circumstances. *Malloy* found error in a lower court's
rejection of a self-incrimination claim by a witness
who had pled guilty to a gambling charge and was

now being asked about the circumstances surrounding his arrest and plea. The Court noted that the questions were obviously designed to determine the identity of the witness' employer, and "if this person were still engaged in unlawful activity, disclosure of his identity might furnish a link in a chain of evidence sufficient to connect the [witness] with a more recent crime for which he still might be prosecuted."

In re Morganroth (6th Cir. 1983), presented another setting in which a court may assume that the self-incrimination claim is not based on a realistic threat. The witness there had previously testified in separate proceedings about the same transactions that were the subject of the current questions. The district court held that the privilege did not apply to questions identical to those asked earlier, and the Sixth Circuit affirmed, concluding that the witness had failed to furnish sufficient information to establish a reasonably grounded risk of incrimination. Both the questions propounded and the witness' answers to these questions in the earlier proceedings had an entirely "innocent" content, and the Sixth Circuit rejected the witness' claim that the risk of incrimination per se existed because answers truthful in light of his current memory of events could be inconsistent with his earlier testimony, and thus lead to a perjury prosecution. To require no more to sustain an assertion of the privilege, the court reasoned, would give every witness who had happened to testify previously on an overlapping subject matter the capacity, no matter how innocuous the questions asked, to become, in effect, the "final arbiter" of the validity of his self-incrimination claim.

§ 19.03   Incrimination Under the Laws of Another Sovereign

For many years, American courts took the position that the self-incrimination privilege protected only against incrimination under the laws of the sovereign which was compelling the witness' testimony. Thus, if a witness in a federal proceeding was granted immunity against federal prosecution, he could not refuse to testify on the ground that his answers might be incriminating under the laws of a state or a foreign nation. In *Murphy v. Waterfront Commission* (S.Ct.1964), the Supreme Court rejected this "separate sovereign" doctrine as applied to state and federal incrimination. Noting that the doctrine would allow a witness to be "whipsawed into incriminating himself under both state and federal law," the Court concluded that the "policies and purposes" of the Fifth Amendment require that the privilege protect "a state witness against incrimination under federal as well as state law and a federal witness against incrimination under state as well as federal law."

Should *Murphy* be read as making the privilege available where testimony will be incriminating only in a foreign country? As *Murphy* noted, where a witness in a federal proceeding claims potential state incrimination, the federal government has the authority to grant the witness immunity that extends to state proceedings, which permits it to compel the witness' testimony. As for the states, *Murphy* held that where a state granted immunity to a witness, the federal government would be prohibited from making any use of the testimony given under that immunity, so that the state immunity, like the federal, would operate upon both sovereigns (see § 19.11). In contrast, neither the federal government nor the states have the authority to grant immunity against foreign prosecution. Elimination of the dual sovereignty doctrine here would place the state and federal systems in a position where they could not supplant the privilege and compel the testimony with a grant of immunity.

In *Zicarelli v. New Jersey Investigation Commission* (S.Ct.1972), the Supreme Court suggested that it was an open issue as to whether a witness fully immunized under federal and state law could nevertheless plead the privilege because the government could not prevent "either prosecution or use of his testimony by a foreign sovereign." The Court also noted that even if the privilege should apply to incrimination under foreign law, it would be available only when the witness could show that he would be in "real danger" of foreign prosecution. Simply relying upon a "remote and speculative possibility," would not be sufficient. Lower courts faced with self-incrimination claims based on potential foreign prosecution have commonly relied on this limitation to deny the claims without reaching the ultimate issue left open in *Zicarelli*. They have concluded that the witness failed to make the necessary showing of likely foreign prosecution with respect to either or both the applicability of foreign law to the witness' activities and the interest of foreign authorities in the enforcement of that law against a person in the witness' situation. Several courts have reasoned that where the witness is to be questioned in a federal grand jury proceeding, the requirements of grand jury secrecy render the possibility that incriminating testimony will be "funneled to foreign officials" too "remote and speculative" to present the "real and substantial fear" required by *Zicarelli*. In contrast to the above rulings, the Fourth Circuit faced the issue head on and held that incrimination under the laws of a foreign sovereign is sufficiently distinguishable from the state/federal issue considered in *Murphy* to leave operative in this context the separate sovereign limitation. *United States v. (Under Seal)* (4th Cir.1986).

§ 19.04   Compelling the Grand Jury Target to Appear

The self-incrimination privilege has long been held to prohibit the prosecution from forcing a defendant to take the stand as a witness at his own trial and to then invoke the privilege as to specific questions; the defendant's privilege protects him from even being called to testify. Should the prosecutor similarly be prohibited from forcing the "target" of an investigation to appear before the grand jury, or is the Fifth Amendment satisfied by simply allowing the target-witness, like any other witness, to refuse to respond to individual questions where his answer might be incriminating? Federal courts have concluded that the target should be treated no differently than any other witness. "The obligation to appear," the Supreme Court has noted, "is no different for a person who may himself be the subject of the grand jury inquiry." *United States v. Dionisio* (S.Ct.1973). The defendant's right of silence grew out of the early common law rule on the incompetency of parties to testify, which had bearing only on the trial.

Internal Justice Department guidelines provide a series of standards relating to subpoenaing targets (see USAM §§ 9–11.250, 9–11.254). A target is defined as "a person as to whom the prosecutor or grand jury has substantial evidence linking him to the commission of a crime, and who, in the judgment of the prosecutor is a putative defendant." A target who refuses to appear voluntarily may be subpoenaed, but only with the approval of both the grand jury and federal prosecutor. In deciding whether to subpoena the target, consideration is to be given both to the importance of the target's anticipated testimony and the availability of alternative sources of information. If the target is subpoenaed, but then gives advance notice of an intention to claim the privilege, the target ordinarily should be excused from appearing. The grand jury and prosecutor can jointly insist upon appearance, however, where justified by consideration of the importance of the testimony and the possible inapplicability of the privilege. Also, while not constitutionally compelled to do so (see § 19.06), federal prosecutors are directed to advise witnesses who are known targets of their target status.

§ 19.05 Invocation of the Privilege

A witness in any type of proceeding ordinarily must invoke the privilege on a question by question basis. A blanket objection is not satisfactory, although a court may terminate questioning along a certain line when the witness indicates that she intends to assert the privilege as to all questions relating to that particular topic. Above all, the witness must refuse to testify and note that her refusal is based on the privilege. The witness bears the responsibility for recognizing that the privilege would apply to her testimony and invoking it by refusing to give that testimony. Should the witness simply testify, the privilege is lost as to that testimony (and often more, see § 19.07), even though her failure to assert the privilege may have been the product of ignorance or confusion regarding the existence and application of the privilege. This consequence occasionally has been described as a product of waiver, but the Supreme Court has recognized that it is not sustained by the traditional standard for waiver of constitutional rights (requiring a "knowing and intelligent" relinquishment of the right). *Garner v. United States* (S.Ct.1976). Rather, the invoke-or-forfeit standard rests on an analysis of the element of compulsion that was summarized by Justice Frankfurter in an oft-quoted passage from his dissent in *United States v. Monia*

(S.Ct.1943): "The Amendment speaks of compulsion. It does not preclude a witness from testifying voluntarily in matters which may incriminate him. If, therefore, he desires the protection of the privilege, he must claim it or, he will not be considered to have been 'compelled' within the meaning of the Amendment."

§ 19.06   Advice as to Right

In *Miranda v. Arizona* (S.Ct.1966), the Supreme Court held that the Fifth Amendment bars admission of a statement obtained by police through custodial interrogation of a suspect where the police have failed to advise the suspect of various rights relating to the self-incrimination privilege. The *Miranda* mandated advice, which has come to be known as the "*Miranda* warnings," includes informing the suspect of the right to "remain silent." In *United States v. Mandujano* (S.Ct.1976), the defendant argued that the rationale of *Miranda*, rather than that of *Monia*, should govern the testimony of a grand jury witness who was a "putative defendant," in that the witness was being questioned about an event for which the government already had probable cause to charge him. In the absence of appropriate warnings, Mandujano argued, his failure to invoke the privilege was irrelevant, and his grand jury testimony should be viewed as compelled (as in *Miranda*) rather than as voluntary (as in *Monia*). Because Mandujano had committed perjury in his grand jury testimony (which would not be excused even if his testimony had been compelled), the Supreme Court was able to affirm his perjury conviction without ruling on whether a "putative defendant" called before a grand jury has to be advised of his right to assert the privilege. However, six justices did speak to the need for self-incrimination warnings.

Chief Justice Burger's plurality opinion, speaking for four members of the Court, flatly rejected extension of *Miranda* to the grand jury setting. *Miranda*, he noted, applied only to the special setting of custodial interrogation. The position of a subpoenaed grand jury witness could hardly be compared to that of the arrestee subjected to police questioning in the "hostile" and "isolated" setting of the police station. See also *Minnesota v. Murphy* (S.Ct. 1984) (Court majority notes "we have never held that [*Miranda* warnings] must be given to a grand jury witness").

Chief Justice Burger added that since Mandujano had been advised of his right to exercise the privilege against self-incrimination, there was no need to decide whether even that limited advice—less complete than the full set of *Miranda* warnings—was constitutionally required. However, the Chief Justice also stated that a grand jury witness' exercise of the privilege, whether or not a prospective defendant, should be governed by the compulsion analysis of *Monia*, and that analysis does not *require* that any warning be given (although judges and hearing officers often will advise a witness of the right to exercise the privilege when the question posed clearly appears to call for incriminating information). Justice Brennan, joined by Justice Marshall, viewed the Chief Justice reliance upon *Monia* as indicating no warning would be needed and expressed disagreement with that position.

Justice Brennan's opinion in *Mandujano* did not stop with requiring warnings as to the privilege alone. In his view, the Fifth Amendment also required the prosecution to inform a witness who was a putative defendant that "he was currently subject to possible criminal prosecution for the commission of a stated crime." In *United States v. Washington* (S.Ct.1977), the Court rejected (over Justice Brennan's dissent) the contention that the Fifth Amendment requires some form of notification of "target" status. The witness there had been given full *Miranda*-type warnings, but had not been told that he was a primary suspect in the theft of a motorcycle as a result of his possession of the stolen motorcycle. The Court reasoned that a failure to give a potential defendant a target warning simply did not put the witness at a "constitutional disadvantage." His status as a target "neither enlarge[d] nor diminish[ed]" the scope of his constitutional protection. He "knew better than anyone else" whether his answers would be incriminating, and he also knew that anything he did say, after failing to exercise the privilege, could be used against him. The "constitutional guarantee," the Court noted, ensures "only that the witness be not *compelled* to give self-incriminating testimony."

Although the Supreme Court in *Washington* again found it unnecessary to decide whether a target witness has to be informed of the right to refuse to answer incriminating questions, that issue has largely been mooted by the Department of Justice guidelines on the questioning of grand jury witnesses. Under those guidelines, all witnesses who are either a "target" or a "subject" of the grand jury investigation are informed of several rights by a form attached to the grand jury subpoena (see USAM § 9–11.150). That form advises the witness of; (1) the general subject of investigation (e.g., "illegal gambling"); (2) the right "to refuse to answer any question if a truthful answer to the question would incriminate you"; (3) that any testimony given could be used against the witness by the grand jury or in a "subsequent legal proceeding"; and (4) that the witness will be given a reasonable opportunity to consult with retained counsel (see § 16.11). Since a "subject" is defined in the guidelines as "a person whose conduct is within the scope of the grand jury's investigation", the requirement that the advice be furnished to subjects as well as targets ensures coverage of virtually all persons in a position where possible incrimination reasonably could be anticipated. Of course, as USAM § 9–11.150 is merely an internal guideline, the failure to comply with it does not give the witness a right to a judicial remedy. *United States v. Gillespie* (7th Cir.1992) (also concluding warnings are not constitutionally required). As noted in § 19.03, the Department of Justice guidelines also call for target warnings, although *Washington* made clear that such warnings are not constitutionally mandated.

§ 19.07 Separate Proceedings

When a witness testifies as to particular activities in one proceeding, that does not prohibit the witness from claiming the privilege and refusing to testify as to the same activities in another proceeding (assuming the witness' testimony would be incriminating). The privilege is "proceeding specific," so that testifying in one proceeding does not relinquish the privilege as to the same information in a second proceeding. On occasion, however, there may be a question as whether separate hearings are necessarily separate proceedings. Thus, the D.C. Circuit has held that a witness who testifies before a grand jury, having been advised of the privilege and having decided not to invoke it, may not thereafter claim it if called to testify as a witness at the trial on the indictment issued by that grand jury. *United States v. Miller* (D.C.Cir.1990). But other circuits have taken a contrary position, concluding that the grand jury inquiry and the trial are separate proceedings.

§ 19.08 Scope of the Testimonial Forfeiture

When a witness testifies, she relinquishes the privilege in that proceeding not only as to her testimony, but often also as to further information on the subject of her testimony. *Rogers v. United States* (S.Ct.1951), is the leading case on the scope of such testimonial "forfeiture" or "waiver." The witness there testified before a grand jury that, as treasurer of the Communist Party of Denver, she had been in possession of party records, but had subsequently delivered those records to another person. She refused, however, to identify the recipient of the records, asserting that would be incriminating. A divided Supreme Court affirmed her contempt conviction, holding the privilege inapplicable. The Court noted that Rogers had already incriminated herself by admitting her party membership and past possession of the records; disclosure of her "acquaintanceship with her successor present[ed] no more than a 'mere imaginary possibility' of increasing the danger of prosecution." A witness would not be allowed to disclose a basic incriminating fact and then claim the privilege as to "details." To uphold such use of the privilege would "open the way to distortion of facts by permitting a witness to select any stopping point in her testimony."

Although *Rogers* often is described as posing great danger for the witness who answers even seemingly "innocuous questions," the decision actually is fairly limited. Lower courts have held, for example, that where a witness' initial admission related to only one element of an offense, that did not constitute a waiver as to questions that might require her to admit other elements of the offense. The fact that the second question asks for further detail as to the same event does not in itself establish that the privilege is not available. Indeed, most of the reported cases finding a forfeiture as to further information have involved, as did *Rogers*, a witness' refusal to name others in a setting suggesting that the witness actually was concerned about incriminating those persons rather than herself.

§ 19.09 Penalties and Burdens

The Fifth Amendment, the Supreme Court has noted, guarantees to the witness both the "right * * * to remain silent until he chooses to speak in the unfettered exercise of his own will, and to suffer no penalty * * * for such silence." *Malloy v. Hogan* (S.Ct.1964). *Griffin v. California* (S.Ct.1965), presents the classic illustration of the prohibition against governmental action that penalizes the exercise of the privilege. At issue there was the constitutionality of the prosecutor's adverse comment on the defendant's failure to take the stand and give testimony, thereby offering no explanation of incriminating circumstances peculiarly within his knowledge. In an earlier ruling, *Grunewald v. United States* (S.Ct.1957), the Court had held that a defendant who testified at trial could not be impeached by reference to the fact that he had exercised his privilege against self-incrimination when questioned about some of the same circumstances before the grand jury. But that ruling was not constitutionally based, as it rested largely on the lack of inconsistency between exercising the privilege in the earlier proceeding (thereby asserting that his answers were potentially incriminatory) and providing testimony at trial that denied guilt and offered innocent explanations for the circumstances in question. In *Griffin*, the prosecution argued that drawing an adverse inference from defendant's failure to come forward and testify on critical facts "peculiarly within the accused's knowledge" was entirely logical and something the jury would do even if the prosecution did not ask it to do so. The Court responded, however, that the critical factor was the prosecution's attempt, with the trial court's acquiescence, to use the defendant's exercise of the privilege as evidence of his guilt. That was a characteristic "of the inquisitorial system of criminal justice, which the Fifth amendment outlaws." Adverse comment on the defendant's exercise of the privilege constituted "a penalty imposed by courts for exercising a constitutional privilege," which "cuts down on the privilege by making its assertion costly," and therefore violates the self-incrimination clause itself.

Spevack v. Klein (S.Ct.1967), and its progeny provide a line of "penalty" cases of special relevance to the field of white collar crime. *Spevack* held that the state could not utilize the exercise of the privilege as the basis for disbarring a lawyer who had refused on self-incrimination grounds to produce documents subpoenaed in a state bar disciplinary proceeding. Disbarment here was being used as a penalty and therefore violated the Fifth Amendment. The Court reasoned that "in this context, 'penalty' is not restricted to fine or imprisonment," but extends to "the imposition of any sanction which makes assertion of the Fifth Amendment 'costly' ", and therefore certainly includes "the threat of disbarment," which entails "the loss of professional standing, professional reputation, and of livelihood." Relying on *Spevack*'s analysis of prohibited penalties, the Supreme Court subsequently held invalid: state statutes that required the dismissal of police officers and other government employees who refused to waive their privilege against self-incrimination in an official inquiry relating to their employment, *Gardner v. Broderick* (S.Ct. 1968), and *Uniformed Sanitation Men Association v. Commissioner of Sanitation of New York* (S.Ct. 1968); a state statute that required disqualification of a contractor from doing business with the state for five years should the contractor refuse to waive the privilege before a grand jury investigating transactions with the state, *Lefkowitz v. Turley* (S.Ct.1973); and a state statute that imposed a five year bar on holding office in a political party should an officeholder refuse to waive the privilege before a grand jury investigating possible misuse of his office, *Lefkowitz v Cunningham* (S.Ct.1977).

As illustrated by *Baxter v. Palmigiano* (S.Ct. 1976), not all burdens resulting from the exercise of the privilege are deemed penalties and therefore prohibited by the Fifth Amendment. In *Baxter*, a prison inmate summoned before a disciplinary board on a charge of causing a disturbance was told that the charge against him involved a potential criminal violation, and that he therefore had a right to remain silent, but that the board would be entitled to draw an adverse inference from that silence in resolving the disciplinary charge. The Supreme

Court held that drawing an adverse inference in this setting did not penalize the exercise of the self-incrimination privilege. Unlike *Griffin*, the inference here was not being drawn in a criminal case. Unlike, the *Spevack* line of cases, the state here did not automatically impose a sanction upon the person who exercised the privilege. A prison inmate who remained silent was not automatically found guilty of a disciplinary infraction. The disciplinary board simply was allowed to give his silence whatever "evidentiary value was * * * warranted by the facts surrounding the case."

The *Palmigiano* Court noted that its ruling was "consistent with the prevailing rule that the Fifth Amendment does not forbid adverse inferences against parties to civil actions when they refuse to testify in response to probative evidence offered against them." *Palmigiano* has been viewed by the lower courts as also lending support for the imposition of various other adverse consequences within a civil suit that may attach to a party's invocation of the privilege (see § 18.04).

What if the state threatens to impose a penalty upon the exercise of the privilege and the individual, rather than risk that sanction, provides testimony? Exactly that happened in *Garrity v. New Jersey* (S.Ct.1967), where police officers, after being warned that they would be discharged if they did not forgo the privilege and give testimony relating to ticket-fixing, gave incriminating testimony. The Supreme Court held that testimony could not be used against them at trial because it was not given voluntarily.

§ 19.10 Immunity: Constitutional Grounding

In *Brown v. Walker* (S.Ct.1896), a sharply divided Court concluded that precluding reliance on the privilege by granting a witness immunity from criminal prosecution was entirely consistent with the purposes of the Fifth Amendment privilege, as illustrated by historical practice. That practice, the majority noted, established that the Fifth Amendment could not be "construed literally as authorizing the witness to refuse to disclose any fact which might tend to incriminate, disgrace, or expose him to unfavorable comments." The history of the Amendment made clear that the privilege's objective was only to "secure the witness against criminal prosecution." Thus, the English adopted an immunity procedure, known as providing "indemnity" against criminal prosecution, soon after the privilege against compulsory self-incrimination became firmly established, and a similar practice was followed in the colonies. So too, the self-incrimination privilege had been held inapplicable where the witness' compelled testimony would relate only to an offense as to which he had been pardoned or as to which the statute of limitations had run. The privilege also had been held not to apply where the witness' response might tend to "disgrace him or bring him into disrepute" but would furnish no information relating to a criminal offense. Such rulings implicitly sustained the constitutionality of the immunity procedure. Since the immunity grant removed the only danger against which the privilege protected the witness, the witness could no longer claim that he was being compelled to be "a witness against himself" in a "criminal case."

§ 19.11   The Constitutionally Required Scope of the Immunity

In *Counselman v. Hitchcock* (S.Ct.1892), the Court struck down a federal immunity statute that granted protection only against the prosecution introducing the witness' immunized testimony into evidence in a subsequent prosecution of the witness. The Court stressed that the statute failed to afford protection against derivative use of the witness' testimony. Thus, the statute "could not, and would not, prevent the use of his testimony to search out other testimony to be used in evidence against him." At the conclusion of its opinion, however, the Court spoke in terms of even broader protection than prohibiting derivative use. "To be valid," it noted, an immunity grant "must afford absolute immunity against future prosecution for the offense to which the question relates." This statement was taken as indicating that a valid immunity grant must absolutely bar prosecution for any transaction noted in the witness' testimony. Accordingly, Congress adopted a new immunity statute providing for such "transactional immunity."

The transactional immunity statute provided that a witness directed to testify or produce documentary evidence pursuant to an immunity order could not be prosecuted "for or on account of any transaction, matter, or thing concerning which he may testify or produce evidence." This provision was upheld in *Brown v. Walker*, and for many years it was assumed that immunity had to be transactional. Even so, it was recognized that transactional immunity was subject to two major limitations, inherent in any type of immunity grant. First, the witness may still be prosecuted for perjury committed in the immunized testimony. Second, the immunity does not extend to an answer totally unresponsive to the question asked. Thus, the witness could not gain immunity from prosecution for all previous criminal acts by simply including a reference to these transactions in her testimony even though they had nothing to do with the subject about which she was questioned.

In *Murphy v. Waterfront Commission* (S.Ct.1964), the Court first upheld immunity that was not as broad in scope as the traditional transactional immunity. *Murphy*, as discussed in § 19.03, held that the self-incrimination privilege extended to possible incrimination under both federal and state law. Accordingly, to be constitutionally acceptable, the immunity granted to a witness had to provide adequate protection against both federal and state prosecutions. If that protection had to encompass transactional immunity, the state immunity provisions would necessarily fail. Congress could use its legislative authority to preempt state prosecutions, but the states lacked authority to prohibit federal prosecutions. The Court held, however, that the immunity grant need not absolutely bar prosecution in the other jurisdiction. It was sufficient that the witness was guaranteed that neither the witness' testimony nor any fruits derived from that testimony would be used against the witness in any criminal prosecution.

Following *Murphy*, Congress adopted a new immunity provision for federal witnesses, replacing transactional immunity with a prohibition against use and derivative use as to both federal and state prosecutions. The statute provided that "no testimony or other information compelled under the [immunity] order (or any information directly or indirectly derived from such testimony or other information) may be used against the witness in any criminal case, except a prosecution for perjury, giving a false statement, or otherwise failing to comply with the order." In *Kastigar v. United States* (S.Ct.1972), a divided Court upheld the new federal provision. The "broad language in *Counselman*," which suggested the need for transactional immunity, was discounted as inconsistent with the "conceptual basis" of the *Counselman* ruling. The crucial question, as *Counselman* noted, was whether the immunity granted was "coextensive with the scope of the privilege against self-incrimination." Both the immunity upheld in *Murphy* and the traditional Fifth Amendment remedy of simply excluding from evidence the compelled statement and its evidentiary fruits (as exemplified by coerced confession cases) indicated that the privilege did not require an absolute bar against prosecution. A prohibition against use and derivative use satisfied the privilege by placing the witness "in substantially the same position as if * * * [the witness] had claimed his privilege."

The *Kastigar* majority rejected the argument, relied upon by the dissenters, that the bar against derivative use could not be enforced so effectively as to ensure that the witness really was placed in the same position as if he had not testified. The statute's "total prohibition on use," it noted, "provides a comprehensive safeguard, barring the use of compelled testimony as an 'investigatory lead,' and also barring the use of any evidence obtained by focusing investigation on a witness as a result of his compelled disclosures." Appropriate procedures for "taint hearings" would ensure that this prohibition was made effective. Once a defendant demonstrates that he previously testified under a grant of immunity, the prosecution must carry "the burden of showing that [its] evidence is not tainted by establishing that [it] had an independent, legitimate source for the disputed evidence." This requirement, the Court noted, would provide the immunized witness with "protection commensurate with that resulting from invoking the privilege itself."

§ 19.12 The Federal Immunity Provisions: 18 U.S.C. §§ 6000–6005

Chapter 601 of the Federal Criminal Code (18 U.S.C. §§ 6000–6005) sets forth the immunity provisions commonly relied upon in federal white collar cases. Section 6002 defines the scope of the immunity. The immunity is restricted to a witness who refuses, "on the basis of his privilege against self-incrimination, to testify or provide other information in a proceeding before or ancillary to" (1) a federal court, (2) a federal grand jury, (3) an "agency of the United States", (which covers a series of agencies, e.g., the S.E.C., specified in the definitions section, § 6001), and (4) Congressional Committees. Once granted pursuant to court order, the witness is compelled to testify and "no testimony or other information compelled under the order (or an information directly or indirectly derived from such testimony or other information) may be used against the witness in any criminal case, except in a prosecution for perjury, giving a false statement, or otherwise failing to comply with the order."

The immunity order for a witness in a grand jury or agency proceeding is issued by the district court, but that court does not assess the justification for granting immunity. Its sole function is to assure that the procedural prerequisites of § 6003 and § 6004 are met. The executive branch has the sole responsibility for determining whether or not immunity should be granted to a particular witness who otherwise would exercise the self-incrimination privilege. The basic procedural prerequisites of § 6003 (governing grand jury witnesses) are: (1) the prosecution's request for the issuance of an immunity order must have been approved by one of several high-level Justice Department officials specified in the statute; and (2) the prosecutor must state in the request that, "in his judgment," (i) the "testimony or other information * * * [sought from the witness] may be necessary to the public interest," and (ii) the witness "has refused or is likely to refuse to testify or provide other information on the basis of his privilege against self-incrimination." In the case of a witness called before an administrative agency, the agency must be one of those listed in § 6001, the agency must gain approval of the Attorney General, and it must have "in its judgment" reached the same conclusions as to the public interest and the witness' reliance on the privilege as are required for the prosecutor when obtaining a § 6003 immunity order.

Once granted immunity, the witness can be ordered to respond to all questions within the scope of the immunity order. A witness refusing to respond faces contempt sanctions, absent some legal justification for refusing to respond (e.g., the attorney-client privilege). Self-incrimination is no longer a valid justification for refusing to respond, as the immunity grant supplants the privilege as to both state and federal prosecution. Witnesses sometimes claim that they fear physical retaliation by associates, but the lower courts have invariably found that a true case of duress is not presented, as the threat must be of a "palpable, imminent danger." *In re Grand Jury Proceedings of December 1989 (Freligh)* (7th Cir.1990).

The immunity order under § 6002 is proceeding specific. Thus, *Pillsbury v. Conboy* (S.Ct.1983), held that where a witness had given immunized testimony in a grand jury proceeding and later was called to testify in a civil case and asked there whether he had testified previously to the contents of his immunized testimony, he could assert the privilege against self-incrimination. The Supreme Court majority reasoned that it need not decide whether an affirmative answer would itself be excludable in a subsequent criminal prosecution as the fruit of immunized grand jury testimony. The witness could not be compelled to testify by virtue of the earlier grant of immunity, as it did not extend to the civil proceeding. The § 6002 immunity order was not intended to serve as the basis for compelling testimony except where it makes a "duly authorized assurance of immunity at the time" (i.e., the proceeding in which the order is obtained).

§ 19.13 Prosecuting the Immunized Witness

Unlike transactional immunity, use/derivative-use immunity does not absolutely preclude later prosecuting an immunized witness for criminal activities touched upon in the immunized testimony. To sustain such a prosecution, however, the government must establish, under a preponderance of evidence standard, that the evidence upon which it relies was not derived from the defendant's immunized testimony, but came instead from a "legitimate source wholly independent of the compelled testimony." *Kastigar v. United States* (§ 19.11). The primary hearing on this issue—commonly called a taint hearing—" 'may be held' pre-trial, post-trial, [or] mid-trial (as the evidence is offered)," at the discretion of the trial court. *United States v. North*

(D.C.Cir.1990). Many courts favor a pretrial hearing on the ground that the defendant should not be forced to trial unless the government can show that its evidence is not tainted. One byproduct of such a hearing is to give the defense valuable pretrial discovery that would otherwise not be available, as the government identifies each item of evidence it intends to use and cites its independent source.

Some courts have suggested that the government cannot possibly sustain its *Kastigar*-burden if the evidence shows that "but for" the immunized testimony, the government would not have come into possession of its evidence. Others suggest that a causal connection can be so attenuated—particularly where critical steps in uncovering the evidence were taken by non-governmental actors—that the evidence will be considered not to have been derived from the immunized testimony even though that testimony was the catalyst for the initiation of the process that eventually brought the evidence to the government's attention. *United States v. Helmsley* (2d Cir.1991). Courts generally agree that the government is most likely to meet its *Kastigar*-burden when it can show that its evidence was collected before the witness was ever given immunity. Thus, the Department of Justice's guidelines direct prosecutors to follow the practice of preparing a memorandum prior to the grant of immunity listing all evidence against the witness then known to exist and designating its source and date of receipt. USAM § 9–23.330. Where that evidence consists, however, of witnesses who testified before the grand jury and those witnesses subsequently learn of the defendant's immunized testimony before testifying at trial, their testimony at trial may be tainted by virtue of the immunized testimony having further shaped their memory of events. *United States v. North.*

Although *Kastigar* spoke primarily of immunity grant protection against the government using the compelled testimony as evidence or as an investigatory lead to other evidence, it also used broader language that several courts have read as establishing a prohibition against the government's "tactical" or "nonevidentiary" use of the compelled testimony. The theory here is that the government must be placed in the same position that it would have been if the witness (now defendant) had never testified, so all uses of the testimony are prohibited. *United States v. McDaniel* (8th Cir.1973). Other courts have suggested that certain "nonevidentiary" uses are so tangential to the strength of the prosecution's case as to be consistent with *Kastigar*'s protection. Thus, the prosecution should not be banned from utilizing the compelled testimony in deciding whether to indict or whether or not to offer the defendant a plea bargain. *United States v. Byrd* (11th Cir.1985). Because of concern about claims of possible nonevidentiary use where the trial prosecutor was familiar with the immunized testimony, prosecutors often seek to insure that the portion of the staff working on the criminal prose-

cution be cut off from any possible exposure to the
defendant's immunized testimony.

§ 19.14 Immunity Agreements

Where the witness is willing to testify in exchange for immunity, the prosecutor may prefer to
provide immunity through an agreement (whereby
the witness agrees to testify in exchange for a
promise of non-prosecution) rather than an immunity grant. Use of an immunity agreement, rather
than statutory immunity, permits the prosecutor to
tailor the scope of the immunity to the needs of the
case. Thus, a prosecutor may believe that an infor-
mal grant of transactional immunity will be more
effective in gaining witness cooperation. In other
situations, the immunity provided by statute may
be more than the witness requires or the prosecutor
is willing to give; an immunity agreement may be
limited to barring prosecution only as to certain
aspects of the transaction. For the witness, an immunity agreement has an advantage primarily
where the agreement grants broader immunity than
would be available by statute. Very often, however,
the witness will go along with narrower agreement
immunity because the prosecution simply will not
offer statutory immunity. Federal courts have frequently upheld the use of immunity agreements,
viewing them as similar in nature to plea agreements that are conditioned on the defendant providing testimony against others. *United States v. Pelletier* (2d Cir.1990). This means that the recalcitrant

witness who wants to back away from an agreement cannot be compelled to testify, *United States v. Winter* (1st Cir.1981), but once the witness provides the testimony he promised to give, the government will be required to honor its side of the agreement. *United State v. Pelletier*.

CHAPTER TWENTY

THE SELF–INCRIMINATION PRIVILEGE: DOCUMENTS

§ 20.01 *Boyd v. United States* and "Content Protection"

Boyd v. United States (S.Ct.1886), was the first Supreme Court case to consider the applicability of the self-incrimination privilege to compelled production of documents, and for close to a century thereafter, *Boyd* dominated Fifth Amendment analysis of the subpoena duces tecum. At issue in *Boyd* was the constitutionality of a court order requiring an importing firm organized as a partnership to produce the invoice it had received for items alleged to have been illegally imported. The Court initially concluded that the court order was the equivalent of a search and therefore was subject to the Fourth Amendment (see § 16.03). It then concluded that the search was unreasonable because it constituted a forcible compulsion that was contrary to the 5th Amendment's self-incrimination clause. Just as the Fifth Amendment prohibited "compulsory discovery by extorting the party's oath," it also prohibited discovery by "compelling the production of his private books and papers." The documentary production order was simply another form of "forcible and compulsory extortion of a man's own testimony."

Insofar as it relied upon the self-incrimination privilege, the *Boyd* ruling might well be read as limited to documents. As documents contain words, the compelled disclosure of their content could be seen as more closely analogous to the compelling of testimonial utterances than compelling the disclosure of other forms of property possessed by the subpoenaed party. Also, the Court spoke of "private" papers, which would often have been authored by the owner. However, the document at issue in *Boyd* itself was not authored by the owner and was not a confidential document relating to a personal or private matter, but a business record that had been prepared by the shipper of the items in question. Moreover, the Court spoke generally of the individual's privacy interest in the possession of personal property as to which the public had no entitlement (such entitlement existing, the Court noted, only where a third-party had a superior right, as with stolen property, or the state had a superior interest, as with records required to be kept by law). Thus, the *Boyd* approach to the Fifth Amendment has been described as more property than privacy oriented, and *Boyd* has been described as having protected the individual "from any disclosure, in the form of oral testimony, documents, or chattels sought by legal process against him as a witness." *United States v. White* (S.Ct.1944).

Starting with *Hale v. Henkel* (S.Ct.1906), decided only two decades after *Boyd*, the Supreme Court gradually developed a series of doctrines that chipped away at the broad implications of *Boyd's* property-rights/privacy analysis of Fifth Amendment protection. The Court recognized various "exceptions" to the application of the Fifth Amendment to document production, including those for entity records (see § 20.07), required records (§ 20.06), and third party production (§ 20.05). More significantly, it adopted doctrine that rejected, at least in part, a property rights or privacy analysis of the Fifth Amendment. Building upon *Boyd*, the Court initially held that a search was unreasonable under the Fourth Amendment if it sought property that was not contraband or the fruits or instrumentalities of a crime (i.e., property that was "mere evidence" of a crime), but it later rejected that doctrine and upheld even a search for documents of the type involved in *Boyd*. *Andressen v. Maryland* (S.Ct.1976). So too, in a series of cases culminating in *Schmerber v. California* (S.Ct.1966), the Court held that privilege was limited to testimonial compulsion. Thus, *Schmerber* held that the compelled extraction of a blood sample was not subject to the privilege, notwithstanding the privacy and property interests obviously involved. The individual was not making a "communication" in providing blood, but was simply being made "the source of 'real' or 'physical' evidence." Communication was not necessarily limited to statements "compelled from a person's own lips"; it could take other forms as well, but those other forms must also convey "testimony"—i.e., reflect the "contents of the mind." *United States v. Doe* (§ 20.04).

In *Fisher v. United States* (S.Ct.1976), the Court majority concluded that all that remained of *Boyd* was a prohibition against forcing the production of private papers that had "long been a rule searching for a rationale." In light of *Schmerber*, the prohibition could not rest on the incriminating content of the document, for the court order does not direct the subpoenaed party to author the requested document, but simply to produce a document that is preexisting. Since the documents were prepared voluntarily, they "cannot be said to contain compelled testimonial evidence." The documents may contain incriminating writing, but whether the writing of the subpoenaed party or another, that writing not a communication compelled by the subpoena. Its content is no more protected than the content of physical evidence with similar incriminating content (as in *Schmerber*). As explained in § 20.02, the Court did find an element of compelling testimony implicit in the act of producing the preexisting document, and where the communicative aspect of that act— not the contents of the document—is potentially incriminating, the privilege remains as a bar to requiring production of the document.

While *Fisher* did not overturn *Boyd*, in offering the act of production as the focal point for the application of the self-incrimination doctrine, it certainly appeared to turn away from a rationale that looked to the "private" character of the subpoenaed documents. That rationale, advanced by Justices Brennan and Marshall in concurring opinions in *Fisher*, relies in large part on the content of the records, which the *Fisher* majority characterized as irrelevant. In *United States v. Doe* (S.Ct.1984), a case involving a grand jury subpoena for various business records, the lower court had sustained a claim of the privilege both upon a privacy analysis that drew from *Boyd* and upon the act-of-production analysis of *Fisher*. Affirming solely on the latter ground, the Supreme Court criticized the lower court's alternative analysis, noting that it tied the privilege to the content of the documents and that reasoning was contrary to "the reasoning underlying this Court's holding in *Fisher*." Justice O'Connor wrote separately "to make explicit what is implicit in the analysis of [the Court's] opinion; that the Fifth Amendment provides absolutely no protection for the contents of private papers of any kind. The notion that the Fifth Amendment protects the privacy of papers originated in *Boyd v. United States*, but our decision in *Fisher v. United States*, sounded the death-knell for *Boyd*." Justice Marshall, joined by Justice Brennan, expressed disagreement, noting that the *Doe* case dealt only with business records "which implicate a lesser degree of concern for privacy interests than, for example, personal diaries."

Subsequent lower court opinions have been divided in their response to contentions that a privacy analysis can still sustain the privilege even when the act of production would not do so. Many have agreed with Justice O'Connor's analysis, concluding that the rationale of *Fisher* and *Doe* precludes self-incrimination protection of the contents of a voluntarily prepared document, no matter how personal the document. *In re Grand Jury Subpoena Duces Tecum Dated Oct. 29, 1992* (2d Cir.1993). Other courts have also rejected a privacy contention, but on the ground that the papers before them did not fall in the class of "intimate papers such as private diaries and drafts of letters or essays." If the "content of papers are protected at all," they note, "it is only in rare situations, where compelled disclosure would break the heart of our sense of privacy." *In re Steinberg* (1st Cir.1988).

§ 20.02   The Act–Of–Production Doctrine

Having concluded that the application of the privilege cannot rest on the declarations contained in a preexisting voluntarily authored writing that the subpoenaed party was now compelled to produce, the *Fisher* Court looked to communicative aspects of the very act of producing the documents and concluded that such a communication could sometimes (but not always) be sufficient to invoke the privilege. The act of producing subpoenaed documents, the Court noted, "has communicative aspects of its own, wholly aside from the contents of the papers produced." Compliance with a subpoena "tacitly concedes the existence of the papers demanded and their possession or control by the [subpoenaed party]." It also would indicate that party's "belief that the papers are those described in the subpoena," and in some instances this could constitute authentication of the papers. These three elements of production—acknowledgment of existence, acknowledgment of possession or control, and potential authentication by identification—were clearly compelled, but whether they also were "testimonial" and "incriminating" would depend upon the "facts and circumstances of particular cases or classes thereof." The resolution of that question, the Court reasoned, should determine whether a particular documentary production is subject to a Fifth Amendment challenge.

The *Fisher* Court was concerned in that case with the testimonial significance of the implicit admissions as to the existence and possession of an accountant's workpapers through their compelled production. Relying upon what came to be known as the "foregone conclusion" standard, the *Fisher* Court concluded:

It is doubtful that implicitly admitting the existence and possession of the papers rises to the level of testimony within the protection of the Fifth Amendment. The papers belong to the accountant, were prepared by him, and are the kind usually prepared by an accountant working on the tax returns of his client. Surely the Government is in no way relying on the "truthtelling" of the taxpayer to prove the existence of or his access to the documents. The existence and location of the papers are a foregone conclusion and the taxpayer adds little or nothing to the sum total of the Government's information by conceding that he in fact has the papers. Under these circumstances by enforcement of the summons "no constitutional rights are touched. The question is not of testimony but of surrender."

In further explaining this forgone conclusion analysis, the Court cited by analogy its rulings holding the Fifth Amendment inapplicable to a court order requiring an accused to submit a handwriting sample. Incidental to the performance of that act, the Court noted, the accused necessarily "admits his ability to write and impliedly asserts that the exemplar is his writing." But the government obviously is not seeking this information—the "first would be a near truism and the latter self-evident"—, and therefore "nothing he has said or done is deemed to be sufficiently testimonial for purposes of the privilege." Where the existence and possession of the documents to be produced were a "foregone conclusion," the act of production was viewed by the *Fisher* Court as having the same non-testimonial character. The government in such a case obviously was not seeking the assertions of the subpoenaed party as to the facts of existence and possession, and his incidental communication as to those facts, inherent in the physical act that the government had the authority to compel, therefore would not rise to the level of compelled "testimony."

Fisher did not have before it an act of production that had a significant potential for providing authentication evidence, and therefore spoke of the foregone conclusion doctrine only as it related to establishing existence and possession of the documents. However, in *United States v. Doe* (S.Ct.

1984), the Court indicated that the foregone conclusion analysis applied as well to this potentially testimonial aspect of the act of production. *Doe* affirmed two lower court rulings finding the privilege applicable under *Fisher* analysis. The lower courts there had concluded that the government was subpoenaing records that it did not know to exist or to be in the subpoenaed party's possession or control, and apparently was relying on that party's act of production to serve as an "admiss[ion] that the records exist, that they are in his possession, and that they are authentic." The Supreme Court accepted this conclusion as resting on a "determination of factual issues." It added however, that the government was "not foreclosed from rebutting respondent's claim [of privilege] by producing evidence that possession, existence, and authentication were a 'foregone conclusion.' "

The Court in *Fisher* indicated that even if the act of production in that case had been testimonial, the privilege still would not apply because there had been no showing that the communicative aspects of production posed a "realistic threat of incrimination to the taxpayer." As to authentication, it noted that production would not provide the government with evidence that could be used to authenticate the subpoenaed workpapers since production by the taxpayer would "express nothing more than the taxpayer's belief that the papers are those described in the subpoena" and the taxpayer could not thereby authenticate as he "did not prepare the papers and could not vouch for their accuracy." As to existence and possession, "surely it was not illegal to seek accounting help in connection with one's tax returns or for the accountant to prepare workpapers and deliver them to the taxpayer." "At this juncture," the Court noted, it was "quite unprepared to hold that either the fact of the existence of the papers or their possession by the taxpayer" posed a sufficient threat to raise a legitimate self-incrimination claim.

In *Doe*, in contrast to *Fisher*, the lower courts had found that the production of the documents had a potential for incrimination. Indeed, the Supreme Court, in a revealing footnote, rejected the government's contention that even if the act of production there were viewed as having sufficient "testimonial aspects," any incrimination would be "so trivial" that the Fifth Amendment would not be implicated. Respondent Doe, the Court noted, had never conceded that the records subpoenaed actually existed or were within his possession. As respondent also noted, "even if the government could obtain the documents from another source, by producing the documents, respondent would relieve the government of the need for authentication." The potential prosecution uses of respondent's act of production, the Court noted, "were sufficient to establish a valid claim of the privilege."

What distinguished *Doe* from *Fisher* was not the character of the records involved, as the standard business records there were as innocuous on their face as the accountant's workpapers subpoenaed in *Fisher*. The potential for incrimination existed in tying the subpoenaed party to the contents of those records through his acknowledgment that he was aware of their existence and possessed them—factors that were significant to the government's case as the respondent had never conceded that the records existed or were in his control. In *Fisher*, in contrast, those issues did not exist and the taxpayer had raised no more than a blanket claim of the privilege as it related to the records as a whole. In stating that it was unprepared "at this juncture" to find a realistic threat of incrimination, the Court may have been leaving the door open for the taxpayer to make a more particularized showing of possible incrimination. Thus, a valid self-incrimination claim arguably could have been presented in *Fisher* if the taxpayer had pointed to particular records that posed a real and appreciable threat of containing incriminatory information and had indicated that the government was seeking to link the taxpayer to those potentially incriminatory records through the testimonial aspects of his act of production.

As the *Doe* decision indicates, existence and possession are not a foregone conclusion simply because the records sought are of a type typically possessed by a particular type of business. As in *Doe*, the subpoenaed party's connection to the business may be uncertain. But even when that connection is obvious, lower courts require the government to make a showing that the business in question has the particular record that is being subpoenaed. In *Fisher*, that was readily achieved because the subpoena there had been directed to the attorneys, and to raise the self-incrimination claim via the attorney-client privilege (see § 20.05), the attorneys had to establish that they received the particular records from their client. More often, the government will seek to meet its foregone-conclusion burden through a person who can testify to the documents having existed and having been in the possession of the subpoenaed party. Very often, that same person would provide authentication, thereby also meeting the foregone conclusion standard as to that potential testimonial element. Authentication also can be established as a foregone conclusion, even without such a witness, where the records are self-authenticating, or can be authenticated by a handwriting comparison or a comparison to other records in the government's possession.

§ 20.03 Act of Production Immunity

In *United States v. Doe* (S.Ct.1984), the government argued that, should the Supreme Court accept the lower court's finding that the privilege applied to the subpoena duces tecum, the Court should nonetheless order the district court to enforce the subpoena on condition that the government agree not to make use or derivative use of the act of production. Rejecting this proposal, the Court noted that the government was, in effect, offering to provide immunity for the act of production and that only could be done in accordance with the immunity statutes (see § 19.12). The Court did note, however, that the government "could have compelled respondent to produce the documents" by utilizing the federal immunity statutes, and the use/derivative-use immunity granted thereunder could be limited to the act of production. There was no need for the immunity grant to extend to the contents of the documents as such, because the privilege was based solely on the act of production and the "immunity need be only as broad as the privilege."

Concurring in *Fisher*, Justice Marshall noted that immunity tied to the act of production would nonetheless commonly serve to "effectively shield" the contents of the subpoenaed documents, as the contents would be a direct fruit of the "immunized testimony" contained in the act of production. Justice Marshall's apparent assumption was that the immunized testimonial components of the act of production ordinarily would include the implicit admissions of the existence of the document and of its possession by the subpoenaed party, and the government's discovery of the document would come through those admissions. Thus, the contents of the document would be evidence "derived" from the immunized admissions and could not be used in evidence or as a source of investigatory leads. That would not be the case if existence and possession were established as a foregone conclusion so that the only testimonial element of the immunized act of production was that of authentication, but such cases would be rare. Most often the same sources of evidence that independently establish existence and possession also independently establish authentication, so immunity is not needed.

In contrast to Justice Marshall, the Department of Justice has taken the position that immunity limited to the act of production never encompasses the document itself (including its contents) because *Fisher* held quite clearly that the document and its contents were not the source of the Fifth Amendment privilege. USAM § 9–23.215. Thus, the D.O.J. argues, the "contents may be used for any purpose because they are not privileged." It is sufficient, from this viewpoint, that government simply avoid any reference at trial or during the investigation to the production of the documents by the subpoenaed party. Of course, if the document is used against the subpoenaed party at trial, the government bears the burdens of authentication and linking the document to that person, but the D.O.J. position allows both the document itself and investigative leads furnished by the document to be used in meeting this burden.

So far, the lower courts have not ruled definitively on the proper scope of immunity tied to the act-of-production. Some opinions have stated that such immunity would not prohibit the government from using the contents to establish authentication, thereby suggesting that the result might be different as to existence and possession. *United States v. Porter* (7th Cir.1983). Other opinions, however, have contained statements suggesting that the contents of the document can be used for any purpose because *Fisher* limits the privilege only to the testimonial components of the act of production. *In re Grand Jury Proceedings (Martinez)* (1st Cir.1980).

§ 20.04   Requiring Non–Testimonial Writings

Building upon the reasoning of *Fisher, Doe v. United States* (S.Ct.1988), recognized that even a compelled writing could be nontestimonial. The Court there held that an individual could not rely on the privilege to refuse to obey a court order directing the individual to sign a form authorizing a foreign bank to release records relating to any account held by the individual. The government's purpose, it noted, was not to have the individual, by signing the form, "relate a factual assertion or disclose information." Indeed, the form was carefully drafted so that the signing party noted that he was acting under court order and did not acknowledge the existence of any account in any particular bank. The form did not constitute evidence that the requested documents existed and offered no assistance to the government in later establishing the authenticity of any records produced by the bank in response to the form. Accordingly, the Court concluded, the signed form constituted a communication, but did not constitute "testimony" for Fifth Amendment purposes. The Court was directing the individual only to perform the act of signing a directive to the bank, not to engage in "truth telling" through the directive.

§ 20.05   Third Party Production

In both *Fisher* and *Couch v. United States* (S.Ct. 1973), the owner of records had transferred the records to an independent professional, and it was that person who was subpoenaed to produce the records. In *Couch*, the taxpayer had delivered various financial records to her accountant for the purpose of preparing her income tax returns, and the IRS subsequently issued a summons directing the accountant to produce the papers. In *Fisher*, the IRS directed a summons to lawyers for production of accountant's workpapers that had been delivered to them by clients seeking legal advice. In both instances, the taxpayers sought to challenge the IRS summons as invading the taxpayer's privilege against self-incrimination. They stressed their ownership of the documents and the potential incrimination that would fall upon them though the content of the documents. The Supreme Court responded that the persons compelled to produce the documents were the professionals, not the taxpayers, and the Fifth Amendment protected only those persons who themselves were "compelled" to give testimony or perform a testimonial act. The taxpayers themselves were not required "to do anything."

Both *Fisher* and *Couch* acknowledged that "situations might exist where constructive possession is so clear or the relinquishment of possession is so temporary and insignificant as to leave the personal compulsion upon the accused substantially intact." Lower courts have since indicated that constructive possession is a concept largely limited in application to situations in which an employer seeks to raise the privilege in response to a subpoena directed to an employee who maintains the employer's records under the supervision of the employer. Moreover, to take advantage of the concept, the employer must show that he "exercised dominion" over the records and that the employee's control was restricted. *In re Grand Jury Proceedings (Manges)* (9th Cir.1984).

§ 20.06 Required Records

Where individuals engage in a regulated business, they may be required to keep certain records and to make such records open for inspection by public officials. In *Shapiro v. United States* (S.Ct.1948), the Supreme Court held that the self-incrimination privilege does not provide protection against the compelled disclosure of such records as the records had been created for the public benefit with the government reserving the right to insist upon their production. The *Shapiro* Court acknowledged that "there are limits which the Government cannot constitutionally exceed in requiring the keeping of records which may be inspected * * * and may be used in prosecuting statutory violations committed by the record-keeper himself," but it had no need to consider those limits in the context of the records before it—records of commodity sales that wholesale fresh produce dealers were required to keep in the implementation of the Wartime Emergency Price Control Act. Subsequently, in *Grosso v. United States* (S.Ct.1968), the Court characterized three elements as necessary "premises of the [required records] doctrine."

First, "the purposes of the United States' inquiry [requiring that the records be kept] must be essentially regulatory." The government's interest in the records must arise out of a regulatory scheme rather than a criminal law enforcement objective. Thus, the doctrine could not be used to impose a reporting requirement on professional gamblers, a "group inherently suspect of criminal activities." Most states make gambling a crime, and looking to the "characteristics of the activity" and "the composition of the group to which inquires are made," the Court could not say that Congress was dealing here with "an essentially non-criminal and regulatory area." *Grosso v. United States*.

Second, the information that is to be obtained by the government by "requiring the preservation of records" must be of a kind which the regulatory party has customarily kept. This reduces the burden placed upon the record keeper and often supports their regulatory relevance. "[T]hird, the records themselves must have assumed 'public aspects' which render them at least analogous to public documents." This characteristic was said to exist in *Shapiro* because the "transaction which it [the required record] recorded was one in which petitioner could lawfully engage solely by virtue of the license granted to him under the statute."

§ 20.7 The Entity Exception

Hale v. Henkel (S.Ct.1906) not only reconstructed *Boyd's* Fourth Amendment analysis (see § 16.03), but also added a major exception to the application of its Fifth Amendment analysis. *Hale* held that the self-incrimination privilege was not available to a corporation and therefore the *Boyd* ruling did not operate to bar a grand jury subpoena duces tecum requiring production of corporate records. The Court's reasoning stressed the different status of the individual and the corporation. The individual, it noted, "owes no duty to the State * * * to divulge his business, or to open his doors to an investigation, so far as it may tend to incriminate him." The corporation, in contrast, "is a creature of the State," and exercises its franchise subject to the "reserved right" of the State to compel its assistance in ensuring that it has not "exceeded its powers."

The Court in *Hale* also took special note of a concern repeatedly cited in subsequent entity cases—the enforcement needs of the government in regulating entities. If the government were precluded by the self-incrimination clause from compelling production of corporate records, "it would result in a failure of a large number of cases where the illegal combination was determinable only upon such papers." Not surprisingly in light of this concern, the Court in *Wilson v. United States* (S.Ct.1911), rejected the claim of a corporate officer possessing subpoenaed corporate records that he could refuse to produce those records because they would personally incriminate him. The State's "reserved power of visitation," the Court noted, "would seriously be embarrassed, if not wholly defeated in its effective exercise, if guilty officers could refuse inspection of the records and papers of the corporation." As the records were those of the corporation, not personal records, and were held "subject to the corporate duty," the official could "assert no personal right * * * against any demand of the government which the corporation was bound to recognize." The subpoena in *Wilson* was directed to the corporation, but *Dreier v. United States* (S.Ct.1911) held that the result was the same where the subpoena was directed to a specified individual in his capacity as corporate custodian.

In *United States v. White* (S.Ct.1944), the Court extended the *Hale* exception to entities other than corporations. *White* held that the president of an unincorporated labor union could not invoke his personal privilege to a subpoena demanding union records. The privilege against self-incrimination, the Court noted, was "designed to prevent the use of legal process to force from the lips of the accused the evidence necessary to convict him or force him to produce and authenticate any personal documents that might incriminate him," and "thereby avoid * * * physical torture and other less violent but equally reprehensible modes of compelling the production of incriminating evidence." These concerns did not apply to the entity, which lacked the qualities of human personality and therefore could not suffer the "immediate and potential evils of compulsory self-disclosure."

The *White* Court characterized the labor union as an organization with "a character so impersonal in scope of its membership and activities that it cannot be said to embody or represent the purely private or personal interests of its constituents, but rather to embody their common or group interests only." In *Bellis v. United States* (S.Ct.1974), however, the Court concluded that the entity exception remained applicable even though the entity embodied personal as well as group interests. The functional key was that the organization "be recognized as an independent entity apart from its individual members." Thus, a small law firm, organized as a partnership, was an entity for this purpose even though it "embodied[d] little more than the personal legal practice of the individual partners."

Bellis noted that "this might be a different case if it involved a small family partnership, or * * * if there were some other pre-existing relationship of confidentiality among the partners." Lower courts have viewed any such exceptions as quite narrow. Indeed, even where there is no formal partnership agreement, a structured business organization may fall within the entity exception. Thus, the entity exception was held to apply to persons who owned commercial property as tenants in common, had a separate bank account for business activities relating that to that property, and utilized as assumed name in conducting such business. *In re Grand Jury Proceedings (Shiffman)* (6th Cir.1978). On the other hand, a husband-wife professional service firm, though organized as a partnership under the Uniform Partnership Act, was held not to constitute an entity where it had no employees and no office outside the couple's home. *In re Grand Jury Subpoena* (E.D.N.Y.1985).

§ 20.08   The Entity Agent

Because the entity has no self-incrimination privilege, and the entity agent is responding in a representative capacity in producing the documents of the entity, *United States v. Wilson* (see § 20.07) and a series of other early 1900s cases held that the entity agent could not invoke the agent's personal privilege even though the content of the documents were clearly incriminating to the agent. Prior to *Fisher*, the only major open issue as to production by an entity agent was where the agent's responsibility ended. The lower courts had held, with some suggestion of approval by the Supreme Court, that the agent could be required to testify for the purpose of identifying the documents. However, once this was done, the agent could exercise his personal privilege as to further questions relating to the records (e.g., how they were prepared). In an analogous situation, the Supreme Court held that an officer of a local union, having established that he no longer possessed the subpoenaed records, could then assert the privilege as to questions concerning their disposition. *Curcio v. United States* (S.Ct. 1957). But note *United States v. Rylander* (S.Ct. 1983) (custodial agent still carries burden of establishing that he no longer had the records, which could not be carried by simply claiming the privilege).

After *Fisher* introduced the act-of-production doctrine (see § 20.01), several lower courts concluded that the entity agent should be allowed to claim the privilege as to the act of production, at least where the subpoena was directed to the particular entity official rather than to the entity itself. In *Braswell v. United States* (S.Ct.1980), a closely divided Supreme Court rejected that position. The *Braswell* majority concluded that *Fisher*'s adoption of the act-of-production doctrine had not altered the unavailability of the privilege to the entity agent. The Court's pre-*Fisher* rulings on the responsibility of the agent had not ignored the testimonial aspects of the act of production, but had correctly considered any such testimonial elements to be properly attributed to the entity rather to the agent acting on its behalf. Even where the subpoena was directed by name to a particular entity official having control of the records, rather than simply to the entity itself, that official was not performing "a personal act, but rather an act of the [entity]" in complying with the subpoena. The dissent argued that this position was to allow the law "to be captive to its own fictions," but the majority responded that *Fisher* itself had accepted this distinction in the course of analyzing the act-of-production rationale. Thus, the *Braswell* majority noted, "whether one concludes—as did the Court [in *Fisher*]—that a custodian's production of corporate records is deemed not to constitute testimonial self-incrimination or instead that a custodian waives the right to exercise the privilege, the lesson of *Fisher* is clear: A custodian may not resist a subpoena for corporate records on Fifth Amendment grounds." To rule otherwise, as the Court had noted in its earlier rulings, would "largely frustrate legitimate government regulation of such organizations" and have a "detrimental impact," in particular, on "the Governments efforts to prosecute 'white collar crime' * * * as the greater portion of evidence of wrongdoing by an organization or its representatives is usually found in the official records of that organization."

Braswell, however, added an evidentiary limitation not mentioned in the earlier cases rejecting self-incrimination claims by entity agents. Since the agent's act of production is an act of the entity and not the individual, the government "may make no evidentiary use of the 'individual act' against the individual." Illustrating this point, the Court noted that "in a criminal prosecution against the custodian, the Government may not introduce into evidence before the jury the fact that the subpoena was served upon and the corporation's documents were delivered by one particular individual, the custodian." The government would be limited to showing that the entity had produced the document and to using that act of the entity in establishing that the records were authentic entity records that the entity had possessed and had produced.

The Court added in a footnote to its discussion of this evidentiary limitation an important caveat: it was "leav[ing] open the question [of] whether the agency rationale supports compelling a custodian to produce corporate records when the custodian is able to establish, by showing for example that he is the sole employee and officer of the corporation, that the jury would inevitably conclude that he produced the records." One possible response to the sole employee situation is to direct the subpoena to the corporation and have it make production through some specially appointed third person who would serve as custodian.

CHAPTER TWENTY–ONE

SEARCHES

§ 21.01 Overview

There has been an increase in the use of searches in investigating white collar crime. This may in part be a result of the advantages to the government in employing searches as opposed to using subpoenas to secure documents. For example, searches do not provide advance notice that can result in the destruction, concealment, or alteration of documents. In addition to receiving immediate access to documents, searches offer the opportunity of discovering items not specified in the warrant that are in "plain view." The disruptive impact of a search can convey a sense of urgency and also an aggressiveness toward the prosecution of white collar crime. A search is not subject to the secrecy requirements that attach to a grand jury subpoena duces tecum.

There are, however, disadvantages to using searches to secure documents. In contrast to subpoenas, searches require a showing of probable cause. Further, the affidavit supporting the search is presumed to be open to the public (and press). The remedy for conducting an unconstitutional search can be harsher than the remedy for issuing an illegal subpoena. There are also greater administrative costs in using a search as opposed to a subpoena. Finally, warrants directed at third party nonsuspects may be precluded or severely limited by the Privacy Protection Act (42 U.S.C. § 2000aa–2000aa–12) and the guidelines adopted pursuant to the Act.

§ 21.02 Fourth Amendment Principles

The Fourth Amendment to the United States Constitution provides that, "[t]he right of the people to be secure in their persons, houses, papers, and effects against unreasonable searches and seizures, shall not be violated, and no Warrants shall issue, but upon probable cause, supported by Oath or affirmation, and particularly describing the place to be searched, and the persons or things to be seized." Most of the searches involved in white collar cases will require a warrant in that these searches seldom involve exceptions, such as "exigent circumstances," that would permit forgoing the warrant requirement. The Fourth Amendment requires for the issuance of a warrant a showing of probable cause before a "neutral and detached" magistrate. The warrant must be supported by an "oath or affirmation," and it must particularly describe what is intended to be seized.

In *Illinois v. Gates* (S.Ct.1983) the Supreme Court noted that "[p]robable cause is a fluid concept-turning on the assessment of probabilities in particular factual contexts—not readily, or often usefully, reduced to a neat set of legal rules." The magistrate issuing the warrant must conclude on the basis of a "practical, common-sense" analysis of the information presented that "there is a fair probability" that evidence of a crime will be found in the place to be searched. A magistrate's finding of probable cause is given deference by a reviewing court, but there are limits. "Sufficient information must be presented to the magistrate to allow that official to determine probable cause; his action cannot be a mere ratification of the bare conclusions of others."

Search warrants need to particularly describe the items to be seized. Search warrants for the seizure of documents often receive closer scrutiny to avoid invasions of privacy. "[T]here are grave dangers inherent in executing a warrant authorizing a search and seizure of a person's papers that are not necessarily present in executing a warrant to search for physical objects whose relevance is more easily ascertainable." *Andresen v. Maryland* (S.Ct.1976).

Ordinarily, evidence obtained in an unconstitutional search (and the fruits thereof) will be excluded from prosecution use in its case-in-chief. However, *United States v. Leon* (S.Ct.1984) recognized an exception to this "exclusionary rule" for reasonable reliance upon a search warrant that is later held to be invalid. *Leon* held: "the Fourth Amendment exclusionary rule should be modified so as not to bar the use in the prosecution's case-in-chief of evidence obtained by officers acting in reasonable reliance on a search warrant issued by a detached and neutral magistrate but ultimately found to be unsupported by probable cause." *United States v. Leon*.

Leon does not exempt from the exclusionary rule all searches based on warrants issued with insufficient probable cause or particularity in the affidavit. Knowingly or reckless falsehoods in the affidavit render the search warrant invalid and require exclusion. *Franks v. Delaware* (S.Ct.1978). *Leon's* "good faith" exception also is inapplicable "where the issuing magistrate wholly abandoned his judicial role," or the affidavit was significantly lacking in probable cause to make the belief in the affidavit totally unreasonable. "Finally, depending on the circumstances of the particular case, a warrant may be so facially deficient—i.e., in failing to particularize the place to be searched or the things to be seized—that the executing officers cannot reasonably presume it to be valid." *United States v. Leon.*

United States v. Diaz (1st Cir.1988), illustrates the application of Fourth Amendment principles in a white collar context. The First Circuit there reviewed an order suppressing corporate documents that had been seized pursuant to a warrant. The FBI had seized 37 cartons and file folders of documents during an investigation concerning bribery of a public official and an alleged scheme to defraud insurance companies. The appellate court examined the particularity of the warrant as related to the scope of the search, the duration of the alleged fraud, and whether the officer had proceeded in "good faith." It affirmed the suppression of "all bank account records,"finding that "[t]here is nothing in the affidavit to imply that any evidence of crime could be gleaned from" these records. The court noted that the affidavit seemed "to establish that the fraudulent transactions were all cash transactions." The court, however, reversed other aspects of the suppression order finding that although the "warrant was overbroad as to the other categories of documents, it was not so facially deficient that" the Special Agent "could not have reasonably and in good faith believed that it adequately authorized the search he undertook."

§ 21.03   Law Office Searches

"Law offices are not immune from search." *United States v. Mittelman* (9th Cir.1993). In *Mittelman*, the Ninth Circuit held that although "special care" should be used in executing a search warrant on a law office, "separate legal rules are not necessary for remedying such searches when they exceed the scope of the warrant." The Department of Justice has adopted explicit guidelines for executing search warrants on law offices. These guidelines have been subject to criticism by defense attorneys as being insufficient to protect the interests of an attorney's representation of a client.

§ 21.04   Regulatory Inspections

Regulatory inspections can uncover criminality that may ultimately lead to the charging of a criminal offense. Regulatory inspections also may occur during the pendency of a criminal action. In *United States v. Gel Spice Co. Inc.* (2d Cir. 1985), the Second Circuit stated that, "even if the FDA were pursing criminal enforcement of the Act at the time of the inspections in question, standing alone this does not imply or suggest that the inspections were conducted in bad faith."

The Fourth Amendment applies to regulatory searches. *Camara v. Municipal Court* (S.Ct.1967). Administrative searches, however, do not require the same level of probable cause as the search conducted as part of a criminal investigation. Courts use a "balancing test" to determine "whether a particular inspection is reasonable—and thus in determining whether there is probable cause to issue a warrant for that inspection—the need for the inspection must be weighed in terms of these reasonable goals of code enforcement." Although inspections do not have to be grounded on a general administrative scheme, the probable cause grounding may be found sufficient when an agency uses a set of criteria that provide protection against arbitrariness in the selection of the premises to be inspected.

Absent an "emergency situation" or "consent," warrants have been found necessary for housing inspections, fire department inspections, and OSHA inspections. *Marshall v. Barlow's, Inc.* (S.Ct.1978). In contrast, warrantless inspections have been permitted in some circumstances such as for mining operations under the Federal Mine Safety and Health Act, (*Donovan v. Dewey* (S.Ct.1981)), inspections of a liquor licensee, (*Colonnade Catering Corp. v. United States* (S.Ct.1970)), and inspections of a licensed firearm dealer (*United States v. Biswell* (S.Ct.1972)). The *"Colonnade-Biswell"* doctrine provides for a "reduced expectation of privacy by an owner of commercial premises in a 'closely regulated' industry." *New York v. Burger* (S.Ct.1987).

In *New York v. Burger* the Supreme Court articulated three considerations that may justify warrantless inspections in the context of regulated business: (1) "there must be a 'substantial' government interest that informs the regulatory scheme pursuant to which the inspection is made," (2) "the warrantless inspections must be 'necessary to further [the] regulatory scheme,'" (3) "'the statute's inspection program, in terms of the certainty and regularity of its application, [must] provid[e] a constitutionally adequate substitute for a warrant." This last consideration provides that "the regulatory statute must perform the two basic functions of a warrant: it must advise the owner of the commercial premises that the search is being made pursuant to the law and has a properly defined scope, and it must limit the discretion of the inspecting officers." *New York v. Burger*.

CHAPTER TWENTY–TWO

ATTORNEY–CLIENT PRIVILEGE AND WORK PRODUCT DOCTRINE

§ 22.01 Overview

The attorney-client privilege and the work product doctrine each provide counsel with the ability to better represent their client in our adversarial system of justice. The attorney-client privilege offers better communication between a lawyer and the client. The work product doctrine fosters the adversarial model by allowing counsel the ability to prepare their case without having to provide opposing counsel with their work product.

A key distinction between these two principles is that the attorney-client privilege is a privilege that prevents others from receiving the confidential information. In contrast, information obtained "in anticipation of litigation," may be obtained despite the work product doctrine when a compelling need exists. Courts also find distinctions when examining the general rules of each of these two principles. For example, waiver of the attorney-client privilege will not always serve as a waiver of the work product doctrine.

In addition to the attorney-client privilege and work-product doctrine, professional rules of attorneys may mandate nondisclosure of confidential communications. *A.B.A. Model Rules of Professional Conduct, Rule 1.6.* Other privileges may also apply. Several states have recognized an accountant/client privilege. There is also some limited recognition of a "self-evaluation" or "self-criticism" privilege, allowing "individuals and businesses to candidly assess their compliance with regulatory and legal requirements without creating evidence that may be used against them by their opponents in future litigation." *In Reichhold Chemicals v. Textron et al.* (N.D. Fla. 1994).

§ 22.02 Attorney–Client Privilege

Federal Rules of Evidence, Rule 501 provides that, "the privilege of a witness, person, government, State, or political subdivision thereof shall be governed by the principles of the common law as they may be interpreted by the courts of the United States in the light of reason and experience." The attorney-client privilege is a common law privilege. "Its purpose is to encourage full and frank communication between attorneys and their clients and thereby promote broader public interests in the observance of law and administration of justice." *Upjohn Company v. United States* (S.Ct.1981). The privilege is held by the client and not the attorney. The privilege protects confidential communications between privileged parties where the purpose of the communication was for legal advice. Although the privilege protects the attorney from having to disclose confidential communications of the client, it ordinarily does not extend to other aspects of the lawyer-client relationship. For example, the identity of a client will in many instances not be protected by the attorney-client privilege. *In re Grand Jury Investigation No. 83–2–35* (6th Cir.1983). The attorney-client privilege applies to both individuals and corporations.

In *Upjohn Company v. United States,* the Supreme Court examined the attorney-client privilege in the context of a corporation that was conducting an internal investigation of "questionable payments" made to foreign government officials. As part of their investigation, attorneys for the corporation distributed a questionnaire and conducted interviews that would elicit information that would enable counsel to give legal advice. Although the Court "decline[d] to lay down a broad rule or series of rules to govern all conceivable future questions in this area," they did "conclude that the attorney-client privilege protects the communications involved in this case from compelled disclosure." The Supreme Court did not accept the "control group" test used by the lower court, finding that "[m]iddle-level—and indeed lower-level—employees can, by actions within the scope of their employment, embroil the corporation in serious legal difficulties, and it is only natural that these employees would have the relevant information needed by corporate counsel if he is adequately to advise the client with respect to such actual or potential difficulties." The attorney-client privilege is limited, however, in that the Court explicitly notes that "[t]he privilege only protects disclosure of communications; it does not protect disclosure of the underlying facts by those who communicated with the attorney." *Upjohn Company v. United States*.

Although the attorney-client privilege has been found applicable to corporations, it is there limited by the corporation's fiduciary responsibility to its shareholders. In finding the privilege inapplicable where shareholders could not obtain the information sought from another source, the Sixth Circuit held that, "[w]hen a corporation asserts the privilege in an action by its shareholders, it is entitled to prevent disclosure of such information only if the policy underlying the privilege requires withholding evidence when balanced against the rights of shareholders and the fundamental responsibility of every person to testify." *A.J. Fausek v. White* (6th Cir. 1992). Various factors, such as the number of shareholders involved, the percentage of the stock they hold, the nature of their claim, and the nature of the communication are weighed in striking that balance. *Garner v. Wolfinbarger* (5th Cir.1970).

§ 22.03 Work Product Doctrine

The work-product doctrine emanates from the Supreme Court decision in *Hickman v. Taylor* (S.Ct. 1947) where the Court found that "it is essential that a lawyer work with a certain degree of privacy." The Court in *Hickman* refused to allow "an attempt, without purported necessity or justifica-

tion, to secure written statements, private memo-
randa and personal recollections prepared or formed
by an adverse party's counsel in the course of his
legal duties." The work-product doctrine protects
materials prepared by an attorney (or investigators
other staff acting at the attorney's direction), where
acting for the client "in anticipation of litigation."
Although the work product doctrine generally protects the required disclosure of such information, it
is limited in that a sufficient showing of need will
permit the release of the material. Federal Rules of
Civil Procedure, Rule 26(b)(3) incorporates the principles enunciated in *Hickman*. It has also been
found to protect materials prepared by the lawyer's
representative.

Courts analyzing the work-product privilege di-
vide the materials into two distinct groups: "fact
work-product" and "opinion work-product." The
work product privilege may not apply to "fact work
product" where there is a "substantial need and an
inability to secure" the material in an alternative
manner "without undue hardship." *In re Grand
Jury Proceedings, United States v. Under Seal* (4th
Cir.1996). Courts are more reluctant to override the
privilege in the case of "opinion work-product" in
that the impressions and opinions of the lawyer are
being protected. See also Federal Rule of Civil Procedure 26(b)(3)(directing courts to protect against
disclosure of attorney mental impressions, conclusions, opinions, or legal theories in ordering discovery).

In examining the work-product doctrine in *Upjohn Company v. United States*, the Court noted that "upon a showing of substantial need and inability to obtain the equivalent without undue hardship," work-product material may be subject to disclosure. The requisite need and hardship to permit disclosure is case specific. An unavailable witness, as through the death of the witness, may serve as a requisite need justifying disclosure of work-product items. Disclosure, however, does not necessarily authorize disclosure of the attorneys' "mental impressions and legal theories." Courts use a balancing test to determine whether the need of party for the information is outweighed by the need to protect the work product from disclosure.

§ 22.04 Waiver of Attorney–Client Privilege and Work Product Doctrine

Disclosure of the communication to a third party, even when inadvertent, can result in a waiver of the attorney-client privilege. Courts have divided however, as to whether selective disclosure to the government will serve as a waiver of the attorney-client privilege for other parties. This seriously impacts the disclosure of the results of internal corporate investigations to the government, notwithstanding the incentives the government may offer for voluntary self-reporting. To protect the privilege, some counsel will enter into a confidentiality agreement with the government.

Defendant in *United States v. Bilzerian* (2d Cir. 1991) sought to present a defense of "his good-faith attempt to comply with the securities laws," by testifying that he "thought his actions were legal." He objected, however, to cross-examination as to what his lawyer had told him about the legality of his actions. The Second Circuit found that "[h]is conversations with counsel regarding the legality of his schemes would have been directly relevant in determining the extent of his knowledge and, as a result, his intent." Noting that the "attorney-client privilege cannot at once be used as a shield and a sword," the court found that "the privilege may implicitly be waived when defendant asserts a claim that in fairness requires examination of protected communications."

Waiver of the work-product doctrine occurs when there is a disclosure to an opposing party. Inadvertent disclosures do not necessarily serve to waive the entire work product. As with the attorney-client privilege, courts are divided as to whether a voluntary disclosure to the government constitutes a waiver of the work-product doctrine. In *In re Steinhardt Partners, L.P.* (2d Cir. 1993), the Second Circuit held that voluntary submission to the SEC of a memorandum served as a waiver of the work-product doctrine. The court noted, however, that "[e]stablishing a rigid rule would fail to anticipate situations in which the disclosing party and the government may share a common interest in developing legal theories and analyzing information, or situations in which the SEC and the disclosing party have entered into an explicit agreement that the SEC will maintain the confidentiality of the disclosed materials."

In *United States v. Nobles* (S.Ct.1975), the Supreme Court addressed a case in which defense counsel in a criminal case sought to present a defense investigator to testify as to statements previously made to the investigator by witnesses. Counsel, however, did not consent to the production of the entire report. The district court ruled that without the production of the report, the defense witness could not testify. The Supreme Court found that presentation of the investigator can serve as a waiver of the work-product doctrine. The Court stated that, "[r]espondent can no more advance the work-product doctrine to sustain a unilateral testimonial use of work-product materials than he could elect to testify in his own behalf and thereafter assert his Fifth Amendment privilege to resist cross-examination on matters reasonably related to those brought out in direct examination."

Where the disclosure of the information is as a result of government misconduct, a court has found that defense counsel did not voluntary waive the work product privilege and that sanctions could be imposed against the prosecutor. In *United States v. Horn* (D.N.H.1992), prosecutors obtained copies of documents selected by defense counsel during their review of materials in the course of the discovery process. A New Hampshire District Court found "that the defendants have been and will continue to be prejudiced by the government's misconduct in improperly copying and reviewing the documents in question because they provided an important insight into defense tactics, strategy, and problems." Although the court denied the defense request to dismiss the case, the court's remedies included ordering the government to provide witness summaries, a list of exhibits, removal of the lead prosecutor, and limiting the use of certain documents at trial.

§ 22.05 Crime Fraud Exception

The attorney-client privilege and work-product doctrine have been found inapplicable where the information given the attorney is for the purpose of furthering a crime or fraud. Mere evidence of a crime or fraud, however, does not trigger the crime fraud exception. "[T]he exception applies only when the Court determines that the client communication or attorney work product in question was itself in furtherance of the crime or fraud.... Second, the crime-fraud exception applies only where there is probable cause to believe that the particular communication with counsel or attorney work product was intended in some way to facilitate or to conceal the criminal activity." *In re Richard Roe, Inc.* (2d Cir.1995).

Even though an attorney does not have knowledge of the client's fraudulent activity, courts have applied the crime fraud exception. *In re Grand Jury Proceedings* (9th Cir.1996). Courts have also found the work-product doctrine inapplicable where it is in furtherance of a crime or fraud, despite the material being "opinion work product." However, because both the lawyer and the client have an independent interest in work product protected materials, an "innocent lawyer" may assert the privilege to protect her own thought processes on her own behalf notwithstanding client fraud. *In re Special September 1978 Grand Jury (II)* (7th Cir.1980).

In *In re Grand Jury Investigation (Schroeder)* (11th Cir.1987), the Eleventh Circuit used a two-prong test to determine whether the crime fraud exception applies. "First, there must be a prima facie showing that the client was engaged in criminal or fraudulent conduct when he sought the advice of counsel, that he was planning such conduct when he sought the advice of counsel, or that he committed a crime or fraud subsequent to receiving the benefit of counsel's advice. Second, there must be a showing that the attorney's assistance was obtained in furtherance of the criminal or fraudulent activity or was closely related to it."

In deciding whether to permit an *in camera* review of the evidence " 'the judge should require a showing of a factual basis adequate to support a good faith belief by a reasonable person,' that in camera review of the materials may reveal evidence to establish the claim that the crime-fraud exception applies .." *United States v. Zolin* (S.Ct.1989). "[T]he decision whether to engage in *in camera* review rests in the sound discretion of the district court."

§ 22.06   Joint Defense Agreements

Parties with common interests occasionally enter into joint defense agreements. The purpose in entering into these agreements is to extend the attorney-client privilege to communications resulting from the sharing of information. "A joint defense privilege protects communications between an individual and an attorney for another when the communications are 'part of an on-going and joint effort to set up a common defense strategy.'" *In the Matter of Bevill, Bresler & Schulman Asset Management Corporation* (3d Cir.1986)(*citing Eisenberg v. Gagnon* (3d Cir.1985)). The agreements allow the defendants to share strategies, information, and to jointly hire experts. This can be particularly helpful in white collar crime cases. Courts have permitted a joint defense privilege for communications made both before and after an indictment. *Continental Oil Co. v. United States* (9th Cir.1964).

There is some uncertainty, however, as to the extent that the joint agreement will truly protect the information exchanged. Issues arise as to whether the parties have truly entered into an agreement and if so, the scope of that agreement. "The burden to establish the applicability of the privilege is upon the defendants." *United States v. Moss* (6th Cir.1993). To establish a joint defense privilege, "the party asserting the privilege must show that (1) the communications were made in the course of a joint defense effort, (2) the statements were designed to further the effort, and (3) the privilege has not been waived." *In the Matter of Bevill, Bresler & Schulman Asset Management Corporation, supra.*

Issues can also arise when a party to the agreement chooses to cooperate with the government. The prevailing view is that one party to a common defense agreement cannot unilaterally waive the privilege for the other parties, so other parties can still claim the privilege to defeat process that would require them to reveal communications that were made in the interests of the joint defense. *In the Matter of a Grand Jury Subpoena Duces Tecum Dated November 16, 1974* (S.D.N.Y.1975). A risk involved in entering into these agreements may include the potential for the government filing a motion to disqualify counsel when one of the parties to the agreement becomes a government witness. *United States v. Anderson* (W.D.Wash.1992).

In *In re Grand Jury Subpoenas, 89–3 and 89–4, John Doe 89–129* (4th Cir.1990), the Fourth Circuit used the term "common interest rule" to describe the joint defense privilege. The court noted that the "rule applies not only to communications subject to the attorney-client privilege, but also to communications protected by the work-product doctrine."

*

PART FOUR

PUNISHMENT

CHAPTER TWENTY–THREE

SANCTIONS

§ 23.01 Introduction

An indeterminate sentencing system was the norm in the United States federal criminal system for nearly the past one hundred years. Although a judge had the outside restrictions of the maximum sentence specified in the statutory offense, coupled with basic Eighth Amendment prohibitions against cruel and unusual punishment, an enormous latitude was afforded to a judge in deciding a convicted defendant's term of imprisonment, fine, or imposition of probation. Discretion was also given to parole officers in making their parole determinations.

This indeterminate sentencing system was premised upon a goal of rehabilitation. By giving broad discretion to the court and parole officer, they were able "to make their respective sentencing and release decisions upon their own assessments of the offender's amenability to rehabilitation." *Mistretta v. United States* (1989).

This "outmoded rehabilitation model" was designated a failure by a 1983 Senate Report. The report noted two significant consequences of the indeterminate sentencing model: judicial disparity in sentences and uncertainty in time to be served by a defendant. *Mistretta v. United States*. To correct these perceived problems, Congress passed the Sentencing Reform Act of 1984.

This Act created a Sentencing Commission charged with the duty of establishing determinative sentencing guidelines. The guidelines mandate the imposition of sentences within set ranges as computed via a grid system that considers the defendant's offense level in conjunction with the offender's criminal history. Although the guidelines are not advisory, they also do not endorse a strict determinative sentencing system with no judicial discretion.

On November 1, 1991, the United States Sentencing Commission adopted guidelines for sentencing organizations. These guidelines provide fines, probation, and in some instances restitution. The sentencing guidelines for organizations permit reductions for self-reporting and for effective programs to prevent and detect violations.

In addition to sentences mandated pursuant to federal sentencing guidelines, white collar criminals often are subject to collateral proceedings in the civil arena. Some white collar offenders have faced a loss of license or exclusion from participating in government contracts. For example, lawyers have found their convictions used as a basis for suspension and disbarment from the legal profession. Convicted defense contractors have in some cases been precluded from obtaining future government contracts.

§ 23.02   Federal Sentencing Commission

The Sentencing Reform Act of 1984 creates a United States Sentencing Commission. This Commission "is established as an independent commission in the judicial branch of the United States ..." (28 U.S.C. § 991(a)). The Commission is composed of seven voting members appointed by the President, "with the advice and consent of the Senate," and two nonvoting ex-officio members. The Attorney General, or a designee of the Attorney General, is a non-voting ex-officio member of the Commission. At least three of the members of the Commission are required to be federal judges, and not more than four members of the Commission may be from the same political party. (28 U.S.C. § 991). The Sentencing Reform Act of 1984 directs the Commission to devise sentencing guidelines for the imposition of criminal sentences in federal court. (28 U.S.C. § 994). The Act also abolishes the Parole Commission.

Seven factors are set forth as considerations in imposing a sentence. These factors include, "the nature and circumstances of the offense and the history and characteristics of the defendant, ... any pertinent policy statement issued by the Sentencing Commission ..., and the need to avoid unwarranted sentence disparities among defendants with similar records who have been found guilty of similar conduct." (18 U.S.C. § 3553(a)). A court is instructed that a sentence shall be sufficient "but not greater than necessary to comply with the [following] purposes, ... the need for the sentence imposed (A) to reflect the seriousness of the offense, to promote respect for the law, and to provide just punishment for the offense; (B) to afford adequate deterrence to criminal conduct; (C) to protect the public from further crimes of the defendant; and (D) to provide the defendant with needed educational or vocational training, medical care, or other correctional treatment in the most effective manner."

Congressional legislation instructs the Commission to "insure that the guidelines reflect the inappropriateness of imposing a sentence to a term of imprisonment for the purpose of rehabilitating the defendant ..." (28 U.S.C. § 994(k)). The Commission is also instructed that the guidelines should reflect sentences other than imprisonment when the defendant is a first offender engaging in non-violent and non-serious offenses. Consideration for imprisonment should, however, be given when the offender engages in a crime of violence that results in serious bodily injury. (28 U.S.C. § 994(j)).

The Sentencing Commission is an ongoing body charged with the duty to periodically "review and revise" the guidelines. (28 U.S.C. § 994(o)). The

§ 23.03   *FEDERAL SENTENCING GUIDELINES*   **401**

Commission is authorized to promulgate and submit to Congress amendments to the guidelines. "Such an amendment or modification shall be accompanied by a statement of the reasons therefor and shall take effect on a date specified by the Commission, which shall be no earlier than 180 days after being so submitted and no later than the first day of November of the calendar year in which the amendment or modification is submitted, except to the extent that the effective date is revised or the amendment is otherwise modified or disapproved by Act of Congress." (28 U.S.C. § 994(p)). Sentences are calculated by reference to the guidelines in effect at the time of the sentencing, but where the guidelines applicable at the time of the commission of the crime were more lenient, defendant may challenge application of the current guidelines on ex post facto grounds.

§ 23.03   Federal Sentencing Guidelines

The Sentencing Guidelines commence with a policy statement that includes an explanation of the methodology used in formulating the guidelines. This policy statement notes the extensive study and use of existing empirical data in formulating the guidelines. It states that the guidelines are intended "toward the achievement of a more honest, uniform, equitable, proportional, and therefore effective sentencing system." (Chapter One, Part A, Guidelines).

The policy statement preceding the actual guidelines explains the Commission's struggle with deciding if a real offense or charge offense sentencing system was more appropriate. A real offense system looks to the actual conduct engaged in by the defendant, without regard to the charges brought. A charge offense system examines the conduct that forms the elements of the offense upon which the defendant is convicted. The Commission's guidelines compromises these two positions by commencing with a charge offense system, in initially determining the base level offense, and modifying this result to consider some of the actual conduct. For example, the defendant's role in the offense and quantitative amounts involved in the offense are used to adjust the base level.

Section 1B1.1 of the guidelines provides a general overview of how to use the guidelines. It offers a step-by-step approach to determining a defendant's sentence. Section 1B1.3 of the guidelines describes the relevant conduct that a court may consider in determining the applicable guideline range. This includes "all acts and omissions ... that occurred during the commission of the offense, in preparation for that offense or in the course of attempting to avoid detection or responsibility for that offense," and "all acts or omissions" similarly defined as to other offenses that "were part of the same course of conduct or common scheme or plan as the offense of conviction." In interpreting the "other offense" portion of this definition, the Supreme Court in *United States v. Watts* (S.Ct.1997) held that "a jury's verdict of acquittal does not prevent the sentencing court from considering conduct underlying the acquitted charge, so long as that conduct has been proved by a preponderance of the evidence."

In computing a defendant's sentence under the sentencing guidelines, a grid is used. On the horizontal axis there are 43 offense levels. On the vertical axis there are six criminal history categories.

Computation of a sentence can be commenced by determination of the offense level. One starts by taking the conviction and matching it to the base offense levels as specified in the guidelines. For example, the crime of mail fraud (18 U.S.C. § 1341) is located in 2F1.1 of the guidelines and carries a base offense level of six. If the mail fraud pertains to a public official and involves the deprivation of the intangible right to honest services (18 U.S.C. § 1346) then the guideline is located in 2C1.7 and commences with a base level of ten.

Within each guideline are adjustment factors that reflect the "real offense" as measured by all "relevant conduct.". For example, in the fraud guideline found in 2F1.1, adjustments are made for the amount of loss involved. Thus, to the base level of six, there is an increase in level by adding eighteen when the loss is more than eighty million dollars. Other specific offense characteristics that can increase the base level of fraud include "more than minimal planning," "a scheme to defraud more than one victim," "the conscious or reckless risk of serious bodily injury," and "substantially jeopardizing the safety and soundness of a financial institution."

Chapter three of the guidelines provides general adjustment factors used in determining the offense level (also with reference to all relevant conduct). The first three factors considered are victim-related adjustments, role in the offense adjustments, and obstructive conduct. For example, where the "defendant knew or should have known that a victim of the offense was unusually vulnerable due to age, physical or mental condition, or that a victim was otherwise particularly susceptible to the criminal conduct," the guidelines authorize an increase by two levels. (3A1.1).

An aggravating role in the offense, as specified in the guidelines, can increase the offense level. (3B1.1). Likewise, a mitigating role serves to decrease the offense level. (3B1.2). "If the defendant abused a position of public or private trust, or used a special skill, in a manner that significantly facilitated the commission or concealment of the offense," there is an increase by two levels. (3B1.3). An increase by two levels is also provided when a defendant "willfully obstructed or impeded, or attempted to obstruct or impede, the administration of justice during the investigation, prosecution, or sentencing of the instant offense," (3C1.1) or "recklessly created a substantial risk of death or serious bodily injury to another person in the course of fleeing from a law enforcement officer." (3C1.2).

The Supreme Court recently held that it is constitutional for a court to enhance a defendant's sentence "if the court finds the defendant committed
perjury at trial." This obstruction of justice en-
hancement, pursuant to 3C1.1, was found not to
infringe on the defendant's constitutional right to
testify. *United States v. Dunnigan* (S.Ct.1993).

Also contained in chapter three of the guidelines
is the method for applying multiple counts in factoring the base level. Base levels applicable to each
count are not added together. Rather, the most
serious count is examined and relevant-conduct increases in this level of offense are provided to
reflect the increase in harm. Closely related counts
are grouped together. (3D1.1). Thus, when a prosecutor uses separate charges for essentially the same
conduct, conduct graded by the aggregate of the
same type of harm (e.g., financial loss), or conduct
that is part of the same transaction or common
scheme, the counts will be grouped together for
purposes of determining the base level. (3D1.2).

A final adjustment provided in chapter three of
the guidelines offers a defendant a reduction for an
acceptance of responsibility. "If the defendant clearly demonstrates acceptance of responsibility for his
offense," the guidelines authorize a reduction by
two levels. Amendments to the guidelines, effective
1992, provide for an additional one level decrease in
certain circumstances. One such instance is when
the offense level is sixteen or greater prior to the
initial two level decrease for acceptance of responsibility and the "defendant has assisted authorities in

the investigation or prosecution of his own misconduct by ... timely notifying authorities of his intention to enter a plea of guilty, thereby permitting the government to avoid preparing for trial and permitting the court to allocate its resources efficiently." (3E1.1).

The number ascertained after taking the initial base level and factoring in the applicable adjustments reflects the number on the vertical axis. It is next necessary to determine the numerical value of the defendant's criminal history. Chapter four of the guidelines pertains to a defendant's criminal history and criminal livelihood. The six categories of criminal history on the horizontal axis of the sentencing grid, represent groupings of points accumulated for a defendants' prior sentences and for the defendants' commission of the act "while under any criminal justice sentence, including probation, parole, supervised release, imprisonment, work release, or escape status." The greater the criminal history, the greater the points attributed to the defendant.

The point on the grid at which the offense level of a defendant meets the defendant's criminal history level is the sentencing range for that defendant. It defines the period of time of a defendant's sentence. For example, an offense level of 19 with a criminal history category II results in a sentencing range of 33 to 41 months.

Below a certain point on the grid, a court has the option for alternatives to prison. Chapter five of the sentencing guidelines specifies the rules for probation, supervised release, restitution, fines, assessments, forfeitures, and costs of prosecution. Sentencing options, such as community confinement or home detention, are also described in this chapter.

Once the grid point total is calculated, a departure—i.e., a sentence above or below that prescribed in the grid—may be considered. A judge is precluded from departing from the sentencing range on the grid unless there is a basis for departure under subsection K of chapter five. Noteworthy in subsection K is the permissibility of departure upon a motion of the government stating that defendant provided substantial assistance to authorities. (5K1.1).

The Supreme Court considered a defendant's right to challenge the failure of a prosecutor to file a 5K1.1 motion requesting the district court reduce a sentence for substantial assistance to the government. The Court viewed the discretion normally accorded to prosecutors in decisions as applicable to the decision of a prosecutor on whether to file a substantial assistance motion under 5K1.1. Thus, claims that the defendant provided substantial assistance which the government refused to recognize, or generalized claims of the prosecutor acting on improper motive in refusing to file a 5K1.1 motion, will not merit a remedy for the defendant. The Court did state, however, that "a defendant would be entitled to relief if a prosecutor refused to file a substantial-assistance motion say, because of the defendant's race or religion." *Wade v. United States*

(S.Ct.1992). A sentencing judge is not bound, however, to accept a government motion for departure premised upon substantial assistance. *United States v. Mariano* (1st Cir.1993).

Departure from the guidelines is also permissible when "there exists an aggravating or mitigating circumstance of a kind, or to a degree, not adequately taken into consideration by the Sentencing Commission in formulating the guidelines that should result in a sentence different from that described." (18 U.S.C. § 3553(b)). Certain factors are considered encouraged while others are considered discouraged bases for departure. (5K2.0 et. seq.) In deciding whether to depart from the guidelines, courts need to consider the following four questions: "(1)What features of this case, potentially, take it outside the Guidelines' 'heartland' and make of it a special, or unusual, case? (2) Has the Commission forbidden departures based on those features? (3) If not, has the Commission encouraged departures based on those features? (4) If not, has the Commission discouraged departures based on those features?" *Koon v. United States* (S.Ct.1996) (*citing United States v. Rivera* (1st Cir.1993)).

Forbidden factors (e.g., race or socio-economic status) cannot be used as a basis for departure. Encouraged factors (e.g., diminished capacity) can be used as a basis for departure if the applicable guidelines have not taken the factor into account. If the factor is a discouraged factor (e.g., family responsibilities), or an encouraged factor taken into account by a guideline, the court should depart only when "the factor is present to an exceptional degree or in some other way makes the case different from the ordinary case where the factor is present." Factors that are omitted from the guidelines can be a basis for departure if the court determines that the case is outside the "heartland" "after considering the 'structure and theory of both relevant individual guidelines and the Guidelines taken as a whole.' " This will, however, not be a frequent occurrence. In determining whether a departure is proper, an appellate court "should ask whether the sentencing court abused its discretion." *Koon v. United States* (S.Ct.1996).

Section 5G1.1 provides that if Congress has specified a statutory minimum or maximum sentence for the applicable crime, then that minimum or maximum sentence authorized by Congress shall control over the guideline range. When a defendant provides substantial assistance, the government has the option of filing a motion pursuant to 18 U.S.C. § 3553(e) requesting the court depart below the statutory minimum. The Supreme Court has held that a government motion pursuant to 5K1.1 does not authorize a court to depart below the statutory minimum absent a specific government request pursuant to 18 U.S.C. § 3553(e). *Melendez v. United States* (S.Ct.1996).

In addition to providing the methodology for determining a sentence, the guidelines also provide procedural structure to the plea agreement and sentencing process. For example, the commentary to the guidelines provides that "[t]he Commission believes that use of a preponderance of the evidence standard is appropriate to meet due process requirements and policy concerns in resolving disputes regarding application of the guidelines to the facts of a case." (6A1.3, Commentary).

A substantial number of the appellate criminal decisions issued in the past few years have included arguments concerning the sentencing guidelines (e.g., different methods of determining "loss" in a fraud case). In examining these cases, it is evident that ambiguities in the guidelines have resulted in substantial litigation. Differing interpretations among the circuits have also complicated this area. In some instances, however, the Sentencing Commission has amended guidelines to clarify and foreclose the continual litigation of these issues.

Williams v. United States (S.Ct.1992), involved a district court's upward departure as a result of the defendant's criminal history category not taking account of two convictions and several prior arrests. The appellate court found the district court's use of the two old convictions, that were outside the criminal history category of the defendant, to be a valid basis for departure under the sentencing guidelines. The use of the prior arrests, however, were found to be improper. Despite the invalidity of one of the basis for departure used by the trial court, the Seventh Circuit affirmed the sentence.

In ruling in *Williams*, the Supreme Court noted the impropriety of an appellate court substituting its judgment for the trial court solely on the basis of the reasonableness of a sentence, after ruling that the lower court had used an improper factor in determining the defendant's sentence. If the appellate tribunal determines that the sentence was imposed "either in violation of law or as a result of an incorrect application of the Guidelines," a remand is appropriate. (18 U.S.C. § 3742(f)(1)). It is only required under § 3742(f)(1), however, "if the sentence was 'imposed as a result of an incorrect application' of the Guidelines." If the appellate court concludes that the departure is not a result of an error in interpreting the guidelines, but is a sentence that is an unreasonably high or low departure from the relevant guideline range, a remand is also proper. (18 U.S.C. § 3742(f)(2)). A remand is not, however, required every time a district court considers an erroneous factor in sentencing. The Court stated that "in determining whether a remand is required under § 3742(f)(1), a court of appeals must decide whether the district court would have imposed the same sentence had it not relied upon the invalid factor or factors."

The sentencing guidelines have been criticized by many judges and defense attorneys. Some individuals also complain that there is a lack of flexibility in rendering a sentence, as well as the complexity of the process. Reports by the Sentencing Commission on initial impressions to the guidelines support the view that sentencing disparity is being reduced through the implementation of the guidelines. This view, however, is not uniformly accepted.

In *United States v. Harrington* (D.C.Cir.1991), Circuit Judge Harry T. Edwards stated in a concurring opinion that "[W]e also have come to understand that the Guidelines do not, by any stretch of the imagination, ensure uniformity in sentencing." Prosecutorial discretion in charging, the plea bargaining process, and the characterizations placed upon the defendant by the probation officer are three ways that serve to circumvent the uniformity.

§ 23.04 Constitutionality of the Guidelines

The federal sentencing guidelines were initially met with many cases contesting their constitutionality. Lower courts resolving these issues ruled inconsistently with some finding the guidelines valid and others holding them unconstitutional. In 1988 the Supreme Court accepted on certiorari the case of *Mistretta v. United States*, to consider the constitutionality of the guidelines as promulgated by the United States Sentencing Commission. In granting the petition for certiorari the Court noted the " 'imperative public importance' of the issue" and the "disarray among the Federal District Courts."

The *Mistretta* case, in upholding the guidelines, resolved two key constitutional attacks on the guidelines. The first argument questioned the propriety of delegating the promulgation of guidelines for every federal offense to an independent sentencing commission. The second argument questioned the constitutionality of the Act in light of the separation of powers doctrine.

Justice Blackmun, writing the opinion for the majority, found Congress' delegation of authority to the Sentencing Commission to be "sufficiently specific and detailed to meet constitutional requirements." Although the Court admitted that the Commission was given significant discretion, it noted that "[d]eveloping proportionate penalties for hundreds of different crimes by a virtually limitless array of offenders is precisely the sort of intricate, labor-intensive task for which delegation to an expert body is especially appropriate."

The Court also rejected Mistretta's claim of a violation of separation of powers. Examined by the Court was the effect of the Sentencing Commission being placed in the judicial branch, having federal judges serve on the Commission, and the giving of the power to appoint and remove members of the Commission to the President. The Court found the Act's placement of the Commission within the judicial branch justified "since substantive judgment in the field of sentencing has been and remains appropriate to the Judicial Branch, and the methodology of rulemaking has been and remains appropriate to that Branch."

The Court also validated the Act's placement of federal judges on the Sentencing Commission. The Court held that the judges were not serving pursuant to their authority as Article III judges, but rather in an administrative capacity resulting from their Presidential appointment. The Court stated that, "the Constitution, at least as a *per se* matter, does not forbid judges from wearing two hats; it merely forbids them from wearing both hats at the same time." The mixed nature of the Commission did not violate the Constitution, since the Sentencing "Commission is not a court and exercises no judicial power ... the Act does not vest Article III power in nonjudges or require Article III judges to share their power with nonjudges."

Mistretta also claimed that by having the President appoint and remove the members of the Commission, the Judicial Branch was being prevented from performing its constitutional functions. The Court found that the appointment power of the President would not corrupt the integrity of the Judiciary. Likewise the removal power, limited to good cause, would pose no risk of preventing "the Judicial branch from performing its constitutionally assigned function of fairly adjudicating cases and controversies."

Mistretta has not foreclosed defendants from questioning the constitutionality of the guidelines. In light of *Mistretta,* however, it is less common to see constitutional arguments centered on a violation of separation of powers. Many of the arguments are now premised upon alleged violations of a defendant's due process rights. For example, the Eleventh Circuit, in the case of *United States v. Hernandez* (11th Cir.1991), rejected defendant's claim that the guidelines violated her due process rights under the fifth amendment by granting to prosecutors, as opposed to judges, the ability to determine a sentence when they move or fail to move for departures under the guidelines.

§ 23.05   Criminal and Civil Fines

Statutory provisions set forth the factors a court should consider in imposing a fine. (18 U.S.C. § 3572) For example, a court should consider "the defendant's income, earning capacity, and financial resources," as well as the burden of the fine on the defendant and others associated with the defendant. 18 U.S.C. § 3571 specifies the maximum fines that can be imposed against individuals and organizations. For example, in determining an individual's maximum fine permitted upon conviction of a felony, one looks to not more than the greatest of the "amount specified in the law setting forth the offense," a fine based on gain or loss as computed under the statute, or an amount not to exceed $250,000.

Civil proceedings brought by the government, after completion of a criminal action, can raise issues of collateral estoppel when the issue being litigated in the civil proceeding has previously been litigated in the criminal action. Parallel civil and criminal actions by the government also raise questions of double jeopardy. In *United States v. Halper* (S.Ct. 1989), the Supreme Court accepted for review a case involving a civil action brought by the government that was premised upon the same conduct upon which the defendant had been criminally punished.

In *Halper* the defendant was convicted of 65 counts of violating the false claims statute (18 U.S.C. § 287) and 16 counts of mail fraud. He received a two year sentence of imprisonment and a fine of $5,000. The government then proceeded against the defendant on a civil case claiming violations of the civil False Claims Act. (31 U.S.C. §§ 3729–3731). The facts of the criminal action were incorporated into the civil suit and served as the basis for granting the government summary judgment. The District Court, however, refused to award the government the statutory penalty of $130,000. The court found that "in light of Halper's previous criminal punishment, an additional penalty this large would violate the Double Jeopardy Clause."

The Supreme Court in reviewing this matter held that, "under the Double Jeopardy Clause a defendant who already has been punished in a criminal prosecution may not be subjected to an additional civil sanction to the extent that the second sanction may not fairly be characterized as remedial, but only as a deterrent or retribution." The Court in *Halper* remanded the case to permit the government the opportunity to show that "the District Court's assessment of its injuries was erroneous."

The Court emphasized the limited effect of its ruling. It noted that the decision did not preclude the government from proceeding on the full civil penalty against a defendant who had not been criminally punished for the same conduct. It also authorized the government to proceed against the defendant for the full civil penalty, as well as the authorized criminal penalties, in a single proceeding. Finally, the *Halper* Court stated that its decision did not preclude private civil parties from bringing actions for damages against a defendant who was criminally prosecuted for the same conduct. "The protections of the Double Jeopardy Clause are not triggered by litigation between private parties."

Halper does not, however, apply to civil forfeitures. In *United States v. Ursery* (S.Ct.1996), the Supreme Court held that civil forfeitures do not constitute "punishment" for purposes of the Double Jeopardy Clause without regard to whether the forfeiture is disproportionate to the harm suffered by the government. Civil forfeitures, the Court noted, serve a unique nonpunitive function of disgorgement. The fact that they may be limited by the Eighth Amendment prohibition against excessiveness does not mean that they also are so "punitive" as to constitute "punishment."

§ 23.06 Sentencing Guidelines for Organizations

Federal sentencing guidelines for organizations became effective on November 1, 1991. These guidelines provide the rules applicable for computing fines against organizations. These rules are applicable only to organizations. Thus, individual agents of an organization that are convicted for criminal conduct, are sentenced under the general federal sentencing guidelines for individuals. Not all offenses are subject to the fines provisions of the organization guidelines. For example, environmental offenses are omitted.

An overview of the guidelines is provided in Part A. (8A1.2). Part B of the guidelines provides the sentencing requirements and options relating to restitution, remedial orders, community service, and the necessity to provide notice to victims. For example, "community service may be ordered as a condition of probation where such community service is reasonably designed to repair the harm caused by the offense." (8B1.3).

Part C describes the considerations for determining a fine. When the organization operated for primarily a criminal purpose, or primarily by criminal means, the guidelines state that the fine should be sufficient to divest the organization of all its net assets. (8C1.1). Organizations that are not criminal in nature, that have committed offenses listed in the organization guidelines are subject to fines as computed under these rules. Inability to pay, however, can eliminate or reduce a fine. (8C2.2).

In computing the fine, one commences by taking the offense level as listed in the guidelines for individuals and adjusting that figure as designated in the applicable guideline for individuals (see § 17.03). Multiple counts use the combined offense level as designated in the individual guidelines. (8C2.3). The base fine is then calculated by taking the amount corresponding to the offense level on a table located in the organization guidelines. (8C2.4(d)). If, however, the pecuniary gain to the organization from the offense, or the "pecuniary loss from the offense caused by the organization, to the extent the loss was caused intentionally, knowingly, or recklessly," is greater, that figure becomes the base fine. If the calculation of the pecuniary gain or loss will unduly complicate the process, then that amount should not be used in computing the fine. Further, if special instructions exist in the individual guidelines that reflect consideration of organizational fines, that special instruction should be applied.

The organization's culpability score is next determined by starting with a level of five points and adding or subtracting points based upon actions that reflect upon the organization's culpability. The level of authority and size of the organization can increase the culpability score. Points are also added when the organization is involved in or tolerates criminal activity, has a history of criminal activity, violates a judicial order, or obstructs justice. In contrast, points are subtracted when the organization has an effective program to prevent and detect violations or self-reports, cooperates, or accepts responsibility for the criminal conduct. (8C2.5). These latter guidelines provide increased incentives for an organization to plead guilty and cooperate with the government.

The Commentary to 8A1.2 notes that "[a]n effective program to prevent and detect violations of law means a program that has been reasonably designed, implemented, and enforced so that it generally will be effective in preventing and detecting criminal conduct." A failure to prevent criminal conduct "by itself, does not mean that a program was not effective." The "hallmark" of an effective program is the exercise of "due diligence." The guidelines commentary provide seven steps that should be taken by an organization for "due diligence." (8A 1.2, Commentary, Application Note 3(k)). The "[e]ntry of a plea of guilty prior to the commencement of trial combined with truthful admission of involvement in the offense and related conduct ordinarily will constitute significant acceptance of responsibility.... unless outweighed by conduct of the organization that is inconsistent with such acceptance of responsibility." (8C2.5, Commentary, Application Note 13).

The ascertained culpability score corresponds to minimum and maximum multipliers found in a table in the organization guidelines. (8C2.6). To determine the applicable fine range, one multiplies the previously determined base fine by the minimum multiplier and the base fine by the maximum multiplier. This provides the minimum and maximum guideline range. The judge imposing the fine then has ten factors to consider in determining where within the range the actual assessed fine should be. These factors include, "the need for the sentence to reflect the seriousness of the offense, promote respect for the law, provide just punishment, afford adequate deterrence, and protect the public from further crimes of the organization." The judge should consider the vulnerability of the victim, as well as the collateral civil consequences of a conviction. In addition to the ten specified factors for consideration by the court in determining the fine within the range, the guidelines also permit the court to "consider the relative importance of any factor used to determine the range." (8C2.8).

The organization guidelines contain a disgorgement provision that instructs a court to add to the fine "any gain to the organization from the offense that has not and will not be paid as restitution or by way of other remedial measures." (8C2.9). As with the individual guidelines, the organization guidelines also provide for upward and downward departures. For example, upward departures may be warranted when there is a death or bodily injury, or foreseeable risk of death or bodily injury. (8C4.2). Other examples of instances that may warrant an upward departure are threats to the market, national security, or environment. Similarly, upward departures can be given if the mandatory program to prevent and detect violations of law was implemented in response to a court order. (8C4.10). Upon a motion of the government alleging substantial assistance to authorities, a court may depart downwards from the guidelines. (8C4.1).

The guidelines set forth situations in which probation is to be given, (8D1.1), and the applicable terms, (8D1.2), and conditions of the probation. (8D1.3). Recommended conditions of probation are also specified. (8D1.4). The guidelines also account for violations of conditions of probation, (8D1.5), special assessments statutorily placed on organizations, (8E1.1), forfeiture, (8E1.2), and assessment of costs. (8E1.3).

§ 23.07 Licenses and Program Exclusion

Professional licenses are usually issued by individual states. These jurisdictions often adopt rules for the acquisition and maintenance of the license. For example, in most states a lawyer must pass a bar examination and character and fitness review for admission into the bar. When the attorney later violates the provisions set forth in the ethical mandates of that state, the attorney is subjected to bar disciplinary action. This discipline can include punishments such as a reprimand, suspension, or disbarment.

Conviction of a felony offense usually has severe implications on a professional license. The American Bar Association Model Rules of Professional Conduct, explicitly state that it is professional misconduct for a lawyer to "commit a criminal act that reflects adversely on the lawyer's honesty, trustworthiness or fitness as a lawyer in other respects." (Rule 8.4 (b)). In the Comments to this Rule, it is noted that illegal conduct "such as offenses involving fraud and the offense of willful failure to file an income tax return," reflect adversely on one's fitness to practice law. Thus, white collar offenses committed by attorneys may subject the attorney to disciplinary action by the bar, court, or the state agency charged with the enforcement of the disciplinary rules.

Discipline for felony convictions is not limited to attorneys. Many states provide for disciplinary action in other professional codes. For example, in

Georgia a doctor "convicted of a felony in state or any other state, . . . ," may be subject to discipline. According to the Georgia statute, conviction is not limited to a finding by a judge or jury of guilt or the defendant entering a guilty plea. Rather, it includes a plea of nolo contendere in a criminal proceeding. Ga.Code Ann. § 43–34–37 (1992).

Those practicing before the Securities Exchange Commission (SEC) have been disciplined, including temporary or permanent suspension to practice before the Commission, when they have violated a provision of federal securities law. In *Touche Ross & Co. v. Securities and Exchange Commission* (2d Cir.1979), the right of the SEC to conduct administrative proceedings against an accounting firm, for the purpose of determining whether the accountants should be censured or suspended from practicing before the Commission, was questioned. The administrative proceeding in the *Touche Ross* case was commenced to determine whether the accountants had "engaged in unethical, unprofessional or fraudulent conduct in their audits" of the financial statements of two companies. The accounting firm brought this action to obtain an injunction stopping the SEC's administrative proceeding against them. The District Court granted the SEC's motion dismissing the complaint.

In affirming the right of the SEC to proceed administratively, the Second Circuit in *Touche Ross* noted that rules permitting these actions had existed for over forty years and had been the basis for disciplinary actions against professionals such as accountants and attorneys. The court noted that "Rule 2(e) thus represents an attempt by the SEC essentially to protect the integrity of its processes. If incompetent or unethical accountants should be permitted to certify financial statements, the reliability of the disclosure process would be impaired." The court found that the accounting firm would be required to exhaust its administrative remedies before the Commission prior to bringing a civil action in court.

In addition to discipline relating to a license, or discipline with respect to a right to practice before an agency, criminality can exclude an individual or company from continuing to participate in a government program. This has had significant ramifications for defense contractors convicted for fraud. Government regulation "specifically permits an agency to debar a contractor if it has been convicted of, or is subject to a civil judgment for, inter alia, fraud in connection with obtaining a government contract, a violation of the antitrust laws, or bribery, or for '[a]ny other cause of so serious or compelling a nature that it affects the present responsibility of a government contractor ...' "*Robinson v. Cheney* (D.C.Cir.1989).

Health care providers may suffer collateral consequences when they engage in criminal acts. Specifically there is the possibility of exclusion from Medicare and Medicaid programs. "In 1977, Congress enacted the Medicare–Medicaid Antifraud and Abuse Amendments requiring the Secretary to suspend any physician or 'other individual practitioner' convicted 'of a criminal offense related to such physician's or practitioner's involvement' in the Medicare and Medicaid programs." *Greene v. Sullivan* (E.D.Tenn.1990).

An attorney representing an individual charged with a white collar offense needs to be particularly aware of the collateral consequences to the individual. Considerations such as civil suits, license suspensions, program debarment, and benefit exclusions, may impact the course taken in the litigation.

*

INDEX

ACCESSORIES
See Principals & Accessories

ADMINISTRATIVE AGENCY INVESTIGATIONS
    See also Immunity
    Generally, 282–297
Attorney–Client Privilege, 283
Attorneys, 295–297
Criminal referrals, 290–293
Fourth Amendment, 283–285, 295
Immunity, 345–347
Legitimate purpose challenges, 288–290
Parallel proceedings, 290–293
Powell requirements, 285–288
Staff misconduct, 293–295
Subpoenas, 282–283
Summons enforcement, 212, 283, 285–288

ANTITRUST
    Generally, 3
Conspiracies, 54–56

ATTORNEY–CLIENT PRIVILEGE
    Generally, 384–395
Administrative subpoenas, 283
Client identity, 211–212
Confidential communications, 211–212, 385–387
Crime Fraud Exception, 392–393

427

ATTORNEY–CLIENT PRIVILEGE—Cont'd
Currency Reporting Crimes, 210–212
Defense Agreements, 393–395
Distinctions with Work Product Doctrine, 384
Last Link Doctrine, 211
Legal Advice Exception, 211
Section 6050I, pp. 210–212
Self–Evaluation Privilege, 385
Self–Incrimination, 363
Special circumstances, 210–212
Waiver, 389–392

ATTORNEYS
See also Attorney–Client Privilege; Law Office Searches
Administrative agency investigations, 295–297
Advice of counsel, 188
Currency Reporting Crimes, 210–212
Grand jury, 278–281
Licenses, 337–338, 399, 422
Multiple representation, 280–281
Sentencing, 299, 422

ATOMIC ENERGY ACT
See Environmental Crimes

BADGES OF FRAUD
See Tax Offenses

BANK FRAUD
Generally, 72–73
Check kiting, 73
Justice department priority, 3
Penalty, 72

BANK SECRECY ACT
See also Currency Reporting Crimes
Generally, 198–212
Collective Knowledge, 28–29, 209
Constitutionality, 201–202
Domestic financial institutions, 200, 203–206
Exporting and importing monetary instruments, 200–208
Financial institutions, 200, 203–205
History, 198–200
Knowledge, 208–209
Penalties, 202–203
Recordkeeping requirements, 200, 205–208
Reporting requirements, 200, 205–208

BANK SECRECY ACT—Cont'd
Structuring transactions, 200, 210
Travel Act, 129
Willfulness, 202, 208–209

BANKRUPTCY CRIMES
Generally, 213–222
Bankruptcy fraud, 213–217
Concealment, 217–220
Conspiracy, 215
Elements, 216–217
Embezzlement, 213
False oath, 217–220
Fixing of fee, 214
Fraudulently, 220–222
Knowingly, 220–222
Mail fraud, 74, 215
Materiality, 219–220
Penalties, 213–214, 217
Perjury, 215, 218–219
Proceeding, 220
RICO, 215
Tax evasion, 215
Willful blindness, 221
Wire fraud, 215

BRIBERY
Generally, 110–118
Corruptly, 115–118
Elements, 112
Foreign Corrupt Practices Act, 9–10, 111
Gratuities, 112
History, 111–112
Obstruction of Justice, 95, 100
Official Acts, 115–118
Penalty, 112
Public officials, 113–115
Quid pro quo, 117–118
RICO, 139–140, 144
Speech and Debate Clause, 115
Things of value, 113

CERCLA
See Environmental Crimes

CHAIN CONSPIRACIES
See Conspiracy

CHECK KITING
See Bank Fraud

CIVIL PROCEEDINGS
See Parallel Proceedings, Sentencing

CLEAN AIR ACT
See Environmental Crimes

CLEAN WATER ACT
See Environmental Crimes

COLLATERAL CONSEQUENCES
See Parallel Proceedings, Sentencing

COLLATERAL ESTOPPEL
See Parallel Proceedings, Sentencing

COLLATERAL PROCEEDINGS
See Parallel Proceedings

COLLECTIVE KNOWLEDGE
Corporate criminal liability, 27–29, 209

COMMERCE CLAUSE
See Interstate Commerce

COMPLIANCE PROGRAMS
See Sentencing

**COMPREHENSIVE ENVIRONMENTAL RESPONSE, COMPEN-
SATION & LIABILITY ACT**
See Environmental Crimes

COMPUTER CRIMES
Generally, 3, 236–242
Accessing, 237–239, 241
Browsing in government computer, 238
Computer Fraud and Abuse Act, 236
Conspiracy, 237
Copyright, 237
Damages, 241–242
Elements, 237–241
Espionage, 237–238
Extortion, 240
History, 236–237

COMPUTER CRIMES—Cont'd
Interception devices and equipment, 237
Penalties, 238–241
Theft, 239
Trafficking of passwords, 240
Transportation of stolen property, 237
Unlawful access to stored communications, 237
Wire fraud, 236

COMPUTER FRAUD & ABUSE ACT
See Computer Crimes

CONSPIRACY
Generally, 37–56
Agreement, 40–41
Antitrust conspiracies, 54–56
Bankruptcy, 215
Chain conspiracies, 51–52
Computer crimes, 237
Defraud, 46–48
Double jeopardy, 40
Elements, 40
Environmental, 225
Inconsistent verdicts, 42–43
Intent, 48–49
Intra-corporate conspiracies, 44, 55–56
Intra-enterprise conspiracies, 54–55
Knowledge, 48–49
Offense, 46–48
Overt Acts, 50
Penalties, 40
Pinkerton Rule, 52–54
Plurality, 41–46
Prosecutorial advantages, 38–40
RICO, 144–145
Securities fraud, 79
Sherman Act, 54–56
Single or multiple conspiracies, 50–52
Tax, 182
Unlawful object, 46–48
Wharton's Rule, 45–46
Wheel and spoke conspiracies, 51–52
Withdrawal, 41

CORPORATE CRIMINAL LIABILITY
Generally, 16–36

CORPORATE CRIMINAL LIABILITY—Cont'd
Acting on behalf of a corporation, 20, 22–27
Collective Knowledge, 27–29
Dead corporations, 29–30
Elkins Act, 17–18
Entity liability, 29–30
Environmental, 19, 224
Food, Drug & Cosmetic Act, 33–36
High managerial agent, 20–24
History, 16–19
Indemnification, 36
Mergers, 29–30
Model Penal Code, 20–25
Occupational Health & Safety Administration, 19
Respondeat superior, 2–26
Responsible corporate officer, 32–36
Self–Incrimination, 369–373
Sherman Act, 27, 29
Strict liability, 16–17, 34–36
Willful blindness, 33

CORRUPTION
See Public Corruption

CRIME FRAUD EXCEPTION
See Attorney–Client Privilege; Work Product Doctrine

CRIMINAL REFERRALS
See Parallel Proceedings

CURRENCY REPORTING CRIMES
     See also Bank Secrecy Act; Money Laundering
   Generally, 198–212
Attorneys, 210–212
Collective knowledge, 28–29, 209
Form 8300, pp. 210–212
History, 198–199
RICO, 141
Section 1956, p. 199
Section 1957, p. 199
Section 6050I, pp. 198, 209–212

CUSTOMS VIOLATIONS
See False Statements

DEAD CORPORATIONS
See Corporate Criminal Liability

DEFENSE AGREEMENTS
Joint defense, 393–395

DEFENSE PROCUREMENT FRAUD
See also False Statements
Generally, 3
False statements, 161–162
Penalties, 424–425

DEFENSES
See also Entrapment
Generally, 11–15
Entrapment, 10–15

DEPARTMENT OF JUSTICE GUIDELINES
Administrative agencies, 295
Grand Jury, 246, 256
Immunity, 348
Law office searches, 381
Mail fraud, 97
Petite Policy, 7–8
RICO, 183
Searches, 378, 381
Self–Incrimination, 328, 365
Tax, 183, 190

DOCTORS
See Health Care Fraud; Physicians

DOMESTIC FINANCIAL INSTITUTIONS
See Bank Secrecy Act

DOUBLE JEOPARDY
Conspiracy, 40
False statements, 162–163
RICO, 140
Sentencing, 415–417

DUAL PROSECUTION
See Dual Sovereignty Rule

DUAL SOVEREIGNTY RULE
RICO, 140
State/Federal prosecution, 6–8

EFFLUENT LIMITATIONS
See Environmental Crimes

EIGHTH AMENDMENT
Cruel and unusual punishment, 397, 417
RICO Forfeitures, 146–147

ELKINS ACT
Corporate Criminal Liability, 17–18

ENTITY LIABILITY
See Corporate Criminal Liability

ENTRAPMENT
Defenses, 10–15
Outrageous government conduct, 15

ENVIRONMENTAL CRIMES
See also Corporate Criminal Liability; Strict Liability
Generally, 223–135
Atomic Energy Act, 224
CERCLA, 224, 227
Clean Air Act, 224, 233
Clean Water Act, 224, 228–230
Comprehensive Environmental Response, Compensation & Lia-
bility Act, 224, 227
Conspiracy, 225
Corporate criminal liability, 224
Effluent limitations, 229–230
Environmental Protection Agency, 223
False statements, 225
Federal Food, Drug & Cosmetic Act, 224
Hazardous wastes, 231
Insecticide, Fungicide and Rodenticide Act, 224
Intent, 225–227
Knowing endangerment, 229, 232
Knowledge, 226–227, 229–230, 232–235
Mail fraud, 225
Migratory Bird Treaty Act, 226
Occupational Health and Safety Act, 224
Penalties, 227, 229
Refuse Act, 224, 227–228
Resource Conservation and Recovery Act, 224, 231–235
Responsible corporate officers, 230, 235
Rivers & Harbors Appropriation Act, 224, 227–228
Safe Drinking Water Act, 224
Sentencing, 417
Strict liability, 226, 228
Toxic Substances Control Act, 224

ENVIRONMENTAL CRIMES—Cont'd
Water Pollution Control Act, 224, 228–230
Willful blindness, 226

ENVIRONMENTAL PROTECTION AGENCY
See Environmental Crimes

ESPIONAGE
See Computer Crimes

EVASION
See Tax Offenses

EXCULPATORY NO'S
See False Statements

EXPORTING AND IMPORTING MONETARY INSTRUMENTS
See Bank Secrecy Act

EXTORTION
See Hobbs Act

EXTRATERRITORIALITY
    Generally, 8–10
False declarations, 165
Fraud, 3, 9
Obstruction of justice, 94
Perjury, 165, 167
Self–Incrimination, 325–327

FALSE CLAIMS STATUTE
False statements, 150, 161–162
Mail fraud, 74
Qui tam actions, 162
Sentencing, 415–416

FALSE DECLARATIONS
    Generally, 164–180
Distinction with perjury, 165–166
Elements, 165
Extraterritoriality, 165
Falsity, 171–174
History, 164
Immigration, 164
Immunity, 166–167
Inconsistent statements, 174
Knowledge, 175
Literally true statements, 171–173

FALSE DECLARATIONS—Cont'd
Materiality, 174–175
Oath, 167–170
Organized Crime Control Act, 164–165
Penalties, 165
Recantation, 177–180
Section 1746, pp. 165, 167
Tribunals, 170–171

FALSE STATEMENTS
Generally, 149–163
Concealment, 154–156, 158
Customs violations, 162–163
Defense Procurement Fraud, 161–162
Department or agency, 159–161
Double jeopardy, 162–163
Elements, 150
Environmental, 225
Exculpatory no's, 151–154
False claims, 150, 161–162
False Statements Accountability Act, 150, 158
Falsity, 154–155
Federal Trade Commission Act, 149
History, 150
Intent, 155–158
Jurisdiction, 156–161
Knowledge, 155–158
Major Fraud Act, 161
Materiality, 158–159
Penalty, 150
Procurement fraud, 161–162
Qui tam actions, 162
Securities fraud, 78
Statements, 151
Tax offenses, 182–183
Willfulness, 155–156

FALSE TAX RETURNS
See Tax Offenses

FEDERAL SENTENCING GUIDELINES
See Sentencing

FIFTH AMENDMENT
See Self–Incrimination

FINANCIAL INSTITUTION FRAUD

FINANCIAL INSTITUTION FRAUD—Cont'd
See Bank Fraud

FINANCIAL INSTITUTIONS
See Bank Fraud; Bank Secrecy Act

FINES
See Sentencing

FOOD, DRUG & COSMETIC ACT
Corporate criminal liability, 33–36

FOREIGN CORRUPT PRACTICES ACT
Bribery of Foreign Officials, 9–10, 111

FOREIGN FINANCIAL AFFAIRS
See Bank Secrecy Act

FORFEITURE
See also Sentencing
Contract rights, 146
Eighth Amendment, 146–147
Relation Back Doctrine, 145
RICO, 145–147

FOURTH AMENDMENT
Administrative agency investigations, 283–285, 295
Documents, 352
Grand jury investigations, 247–257
Searches, 378–381

GRAND JURY INVESTIGATIONS
See also Immunity; Searches
Generally, 243–281
Advice of rights, 246, 330–334
Assistance of counsel, 278–281
Chilling effect, 261–264
Department of Justice Guidelines, 246, 256
Fourth Amendment, 247–257
Grand jury matter, 308–317
Immunity, 345–347
Indictment challenges, 273–278
Investigative advantages, 243–246
Leaks, 268–293
Misuse objections, 264–268
Multiple representation, 280–282
Overbreadth, 247–253
Parallel proceeding, 308–317

GRAND JURY INVESTIGATIONS—Cont'd
Quashing subpoenas, 257–261
Rule 6(e)(2), pp. 268–273, 308–311
Rule 17(c) objections, 264–268
Secrecy violations, 268–273
Subpoena ad testificandum, 246
Subpoena duces tecum, 246–248, 257–261
Subpoenas, 246–247

GRATUITIES
See Bribery

HAZARDOUS WASTES
See Environmental Cases

HEALTH CARE FRAUD
See also Physicians
Department of Justice priority, 3
Obstruction of justice, 95
Sentencing, 424–425
Statute, 75

HIGH MANAGERIAL AGENT
See Corporate Criminal Liability

HOBBS ACT
Generally, 118–128
Campaign contributions, 125–128
Economic fear, 125–128
Elements, 118
Extortion, 118, 123–125
History, 118
Interstate commerce, 119–123
Penalties, 119
Quid pro quo, 126–128
Robbery, 123
Under color of official right, 125–128

HONEST SERVICES
See Mail Fraud

IMMUNITY
See also Administrative Agency Investigations; Grand
Jury Investigations; Self–Incrimination
Generally, 340–351
Act of production, 363–366
Agreements, 350–351

IMMUNITY—Cont'd
Department of Justice Guidelines, 348
Derivative use, 343–344, 347–350
False declarations, 166–167
History, 340–343
Perjury, 166–167
Prosecuting immunized witness, 347–350
Scope, 341–344
Section 6000, et. seq., 344–347
Transactional immunity, 341–342
Use immunity, 343–350

INDEMNIFICATION
Corporate criminal liability, 36

INSECTICIDE, FUNGICIDE & RODENTICIDE ACT
See Environmental Crimes

INSIDER TRADING
See Securities Fraud

INTERCEPTION OF DEVICES AND EQUIPMENT
See Computer Crimes

INTERNATIONAL
See extraterritoriality

INTERSTATE COMMERCE
Commerce clause, 4
Federal jurisdiction, 3–6
Hobbs Act, 6, 119–123
RICO, 138–139
Travel Act, 129–131
Wire fraud, 5, 71

JOINT DEFENSE AGREEMENTS
See Defense Agreements

JURISDICTION
See also Extraterritoriality; False Statements; International;
        Interstate Commerce
Dual Sovereignty Rule, 6–8
Federal/State, 6–8

LAST LINK DOCTRINE
See Attorney–Client Privilege

LAW OFFICE

LAW OFFICE—Cont'd
Searches, 381

LAWYERS
See Attorney–Client Privilege; Attorneys;

LEGAL ADVICE EXCEPTION
See Attorney–Client Privilege

LICENSES
　　Generally, 399, 422–425
Attorneys, 337–338, 399, 422
Mail fraud, 65
Physicians, 422–425
Securities, 423–424
Sentencing, 399, 422–425

MAIL FRAUD
　　Generally, 57–75
Bank fraud, 72–73
Bankruptcy, 74, 215
Department of Justice Guidelines, 74
Elements, 58
Environmental, 225
False Claims Statute, 74
False Pretenses Theory, 60–61
Federal Trade Commission Act, 74
Fraudulent intent, 60–61
Health Care Fraud, 75
History, 57–58
Honest services, 61–63
In furtherance, 65–71
Intangible property, 64–65
Intangible rights, 61–63
Intent to deceive, 60
Jenkins Act, 74
Landum–Griffin Act, 74
Licenses, 65
Lulling, 69
National Stolen Property Act, 74
Penalties, 58–59
Postal power, 4
Public Corruption, 61–63
RICO, 141, 183
Right to Control Theory, 60–61
Scheme to defraud, 58–59

MAIL FRAUD—Cont'd
Securities violation, 59, 74, 78–79
Sentencing, 403, 410
Tax offenses, 74–75, 183
Telemarketing fraud, 59
Truth In Lending Act, 74
Willful blindness, 60
Wire fraud, 71–72

MAJOR FRAUD ACT
False statements, 161

MATERIALITY
Bankruptcy fraud, 219–220
False statements, 158–159
Perjury and false declarations, 174–175
Tax, 196

MEDICAL FRAUD
See Health Care Fraud

MERGERS
See Corporate Criminal Liability

MIGRATORY BIRD TREATY ACT
See Environmental Crimes

MISAPPROPRIATION THEORY
See Securities Fraud

MODEL PENAL CODE
Corporate Criminal Liability, 20–25
Personal Liability, 31

MONEY LAUNDERING
See also Currency Reporting Crimes
Department of Justice priority, 3
Section 1956, p. 199
Section 1957, p. 199
Travel Act, 129

NOLO CONTENDERE
Parallel Proceedings, 318–319

OATHS
See False Declarations; Perjury

OBSTRUCTION OF JUSTICE
Generally, 91–109

OBSTRUCTION OF JUSTICE—Cont'd
Antitrust Civil Process Act, 92
Assault on process server, 91
Bribery, 95, 100
Congressional proceedings, 92
Corruptly, 92, 98–101
Court orders, 92
Demonstrating, 91
Due administration of justice, 97, 103–106
Elements, 97–98
Endeavors, 99, 101–102
Extraterritorial jurisdiction, 94
Federal agencies, 92–93
Federal audit, 95
Financial institutions, 95
Force, 98
Health care investigations, 95
History, 91, 97
Influencing a juror, 91
Intent, 99–101, 105–106
Intimidation or harassment of witnesses, 92–96, 106–109
Jurors or court officers, 97–98
Jury deliberations, 91–92
Jury questions, 101
Knowledge, 105–106
Nexis, 104–105
Penalties, 95–97
Pending proceeding, 103–106
Perjury, 104–105
Resistance to an extradition agent, 91
RICO, 141
Securities fraud, 79
Self–incrimination, 101
State and local law enforcement, 92
Tax, 182
Theft of record, 91
Threats, 98–99
Victim and Witness Protection Act, 92–97, 106–109
Witness tampering, 92–97, 106–109

OCCUPATIONAL HEALTH & SAFETY ADMINISTRATION (OSHA)
Corporate criminal liability, 19
Environmental, 224

ORGANIZATIONS
See Corporate Criminal Liability; Sentencing

ORGANIZED CRIME
See False Declarations; Perjury; Racketeer Influenced and Corrupt Organization Act; Travel Act

OUTRAGEOUS GOVERNMENT CONDUCT
See Entrapment

PARALLEL PROCEEDINGS
Generally, 8, 290–293, 298–319
Administrative agency investigations, 290–293, 298–319
Collateral estoppel, 8, 317–319
Criminal referrals, 290–293
Delaying parallel proceedings, 303–306
Dual target, 298–300
Environmental, 223
Grand jury matter, 308–311
Nolo contendere, 318–319
Particularized need, 313–317
Preliminary to, 311–313
Prosecution discovery, 300–303
Rule 6(e)(2), pp. 308–311
Securities fraud, 76
Self–Incrimination, 306–308, 334
Sentencing, 398, 415
Stays, 8, 303–306
Taxpayer return information, 302–303

PAROLE
See Sentencing

PERJURY
Generally, 164–180
Bankruptcy, 215, 218–219
Distinction with false declarations, 165–166
Elements, 165
Extraterritoriality, 165, 167
Falsity, 171–174
History, 164
Immigration, 164
Immunity, 166–167
Jury questions, 173
Knowledge, 175
Literally true statements, 172–173
Materiality, 174–175

PERJURY—Cont'd
Oath, 167–170
Obstruction of justice, 104–105
Organized Crime Control Act, 164–165
Penalties, 165
Section 1746, pp. 165, 167
Securities fraud, 79
Sentencing, 405
Tax, 164, 183, 194–197
Tribunals, 179–171
Two witnesses, 175–177
Willfulness, 175

PERSONAL LIABILITY IN A CORPORATE SETTING
Generally, 30–36
Following orders, 32
Model Penal Code, 31
Responsible corporate officers, 32–36
Self–Incrimination, 373–376

PETITE POLICY
State/Federal prosecution, 8

PHYSICIANS
See also Health Care Fraud; Sentencing
License, 422–425

PINKERTON RULE
See Conspiracy

PRINCIPALS & ACCESSORIES
General criminal law principles, 11
Securities fraud, 76

PROCUREMENT FRAUD
See Defense Procurement Fraud; False Statements

PUBLIC CORRUPTION
See also Bribery; Hobbs Act
Extortion, 118, 128
Mail fraud, 61–63
State and federal, 6–7
Travel Act, 128–131
White collar crime, 3

PUNISHMENT
See Sentencing

QUI TAM ACTIONS
False Statements, 162

**RACKETEER INFLUENCED AND CORRUPTION ORGANIZA-
TION ACT (RICO)**
  Generally, 132–148
  Associations in fact, 135–138
  Bankruptcy, 215
  Bribery, 139–140, 144
  Civil, 134, 147–148
  Conspiracy, 144–145
  Continuity plus relationship, 141–143
  Contract rights forfeiture, 146
  Currency reporting crimes, 141
  Department of Justice Guidelines, 183
  Drug offenses, 141
  Dual Sovereignty Rule, 140
  Economic motive, 135
  Eighth Amendment, 146–147
  Elements, 133–134
  Enterprise, 134–138
  Entity-person, 137–138
  Federal offenses, 139–141
  Forfeiture, 145–147
  Government enterprises, 135–136
  History, 132
  Interest forfeiture, 145–146
  Interstate commerce, 138–139
  Joint and several liability, 146
  Mail fraud, 141, 183
  Nexus, 143–144
  Obstruction of justice, 141
  Operation or management, 143–144
  Organized crime, 132
  Pattern of racketeering, 139–143
  Penalties, 134, 145–147
  Predicate Acts, 139–143
  Proceeds, 146
  Prohibited conduct, 133
  Relation Back Doctrine, 145
  State offenses, 139–140
  Tax offenses, 183
  Travel Act, 129
  Treble damages, 147
  Unlawful debt, 133–134

RACKETEER INFLUENCED AND CORRUPTION ORGANIZA-TION ACT (RICO)—Cont'd
Wire fraud, 141

RECANTATION
See False Declarations

REFUSE ACT
See Environmental Crimes

REGULATORY INSPECTIONS
See Administrative agency investigations; Searches

REHABILITATION
See Sentencing

RESOURCE CONSERVATION AND RECOVERY ACT (RCRA)
See Environmental Crimes

RESPONDEAT SUPERIOR
See Corporate Criminal Liability

RESPONSIBLE CORPORATE OFFICER
Corporate criminal liability, 32–36
Environmental crimes, 230, 235

RICO
See Racketeer Influenced and Corrupt Organization Act

RIVERS AND HARBORS APPROPRIATION ACT
See Environmental Crimes

SAFE DRINKING WATER ACT
See Environmental Crimes

SEARCHES
See also Administrative Agency Investigations; Grand
Jury Investigations
Generally, 377–383
Advantages, 377
Department of Justice Guidelines, 378, 381
Disadvantages, 377–378
Department of Justice Guidelines, 378, 381
Exclusionary Rule, 379–381
Fourth Amendment, 378–381
Good faith, 380
Grand jury investigations, 247–251
History, 377
Law office searches, 381

SEARCHES—Cont'd
Plain view, 377
Privacy Protection Act, 378
Probable cause, 377–379
Regulatory inspections, 381–383

SECTION 1956 AND 1957
See Currency Reporting Crimes; Money Laundering

SECTION 6050I
     See also Attorneys, Currency Reporting Crimes
  Generally, 209–212
Attorney–Client Privilege, 210–212
Client identity, 211–212
Confidential communications, 211–212
Form 8300, pp. 210–212
Last Link Doctrine, 211
Legal Advice Exception, 211
Special circumstances, 210–212
Summons enforcement, 212
Tax, 193

SECURITIES FRAUD
  Generally, 76–90
Aiding & Abetting, 76
Conspiracy, 79
False Statements, 79
Good faith, 80–81
Insider trading, 82–90
Insider Trading Sanctions Act, 78
Insider Trading and Securities Fraud Enforcement Act, 78
Investigation, 76
Licenses, 423–424
Mail fraud, 78–79
Mens rea, 79–82
Misappropriation theory, 86–90
No knowledge proviso, 77, 82
Obstruction of justice, 79
Penalties, 77–78
Principles & accessories, 76
Securities Act, 77–78
Securities Exchange Act, 77–78, 111
Securities Exchange Commission, 76
Willful blindness, 79–80
Willfulness, 76–77, 79–82
Wire fraud, 79

SELF–INCRIMINATION
See also Immunity; Parallel Proceedings
Generally, 320–376
Act of production, 357–366
Administrative agency subpoenas, 283
Adverse inferences, 336–337, 339
Advice of rights, 330–334
Attorney–Client Privilege, 363
Compelling targets, 327–329
Content protection, 352–357
Custodians, 373–376
Department of Justice Guidelines, 328, 365
Documents, 352–376
Entity agent, 373–376
Entity exception, 369–373
Exculpatory no's, 151–154
Extraterritoriality, 325–327
Foreign sovereigns, 325–327
History, 320–321
Immunity, 340–351, 363–366
International, 325–327
Invocation of privilege, 329–330
Obstruction of justice, 101
Penalties, 337–340
Potential for incrimination, 321–325
Required records, 368–369
Separate proceedings, 334
Subjects, 333
Targets, 327–329, 333
Testimony, 320–351, 360–361
Third party production, 366–368
Waiver, 334–336
Writings, 366

SENTENCING
Generally, 397–425
Attorneys, 299, 422
Civil fines, 415–417
Civil forfeitures, 417
Collateral estoppel, 415
Community service, 418
Compliance programs, 398, 419–420
Constitutionality, 412–414
Debarment, 424–425
Defense contractors, 424

SENTENCING—Cont'd
Departures, 407–411
Double jeopardy, 415–417
Effective Program, 398, 419–420
Eighth Amendment, 397, 417
Environmental, 417
False Claims Statute, 415–416
Federal Sentencing Commission, 398–401, 412–414
Federal Sentencing Guidelines, 398, 401–412, 417–421
Fines, 415–417
Guidelines, 398, 401–412
Health care providers, 424–425
History, 397–399
Individual guidelines, 401–412
Licenses, 399, 422–425
Mail fraud, 403, 410
Minimum/maximums, 409
Multiple counts, 405
Organization guidelines, 417–421
Parole, 399
Parallel proceedings, 398, 415
Perjury, 405
Physicians, 422–425
Plea-agreements, 409–410
Rehabilitation, 397–398
Securities practitioners, 423–424

SHERMAN ACT
See Conspiracy; Corporate Criminal Liability

STAYING OF PROCEEDINGS
See Parallel Proceedings

STRICT LIABILITY
Corporate criminal liability, 16–17, 34–36
Environmental crimes, 226, 228

STRUCTURING TRANSACTIONS
See Bank Secrecy Act

SUBPOENA
See Administrative Agency Investigations; Grand Jury Investigations

SUMMONS ENFORCEMENT
See Administrative Agency Investigations

TAX OFFENSES
Generally, 181–197
Advice of counsel, 188
Badges of fraud, 185, 191
Bank deposit method, 192–193
Bankruptcy, 215
Cash expenditures method, 192–193
Conspiracy, 182
Delivering a fraudulent return, 181
Department of Justice Guidelines, 183, 190
Direct proof, 191–193
Disclosure of information, 182
Elements, 183–189, 190, 193–194
Evasion, 181, 189–191
Extortion, 182
Failure to collect tax, 181
Failure to file return, 181, 193–194
Failure to obey summons, 182
Failure to supply withholding information, 181
False statements, 183
False statements to purchasers or lessors, 182
False tax return, 181, 194–197
Furnishing fraudulent statement, 181
Good faith, 186–189
Indirect proof, 192–193
Knowledge, 187–189
Mail fraud, 74–75, 183
Materiality, 196
Methods of proof, 191–195
Mistake of law, 187
Obstruction, 182
Penalties, 190, 193, 194–195
Perjury, 183, 194–197
RICO, 183
Section 6050I, p. 193
Summons enforcement, 212, 283, 285–288
Supplying false withholding information, 181
Tax deficiency, 190, 191–193
Tax payer return information, 302–303
Tax preparer, 196–197
Taxing powers, 4
Willfulness, 183–189, 190–191, 193–194

TELEMARKETING FRAUD
Department of Justice priority, 3

TELEMARKETING FRAUD—Cont'd
Mail fraud, 59

TOXIC SUBSTANCES CONTROL ACT
See Environmental Crimes

TRAFFICKING OF PASSWORDS
See Computer Crimes

TRANSACTIONAL IMMUNITY
See Immunity

TRAVEL ACT
Generally, 128–131
Bank Secrecy Act, 129
Business enterprise, 131
Elements, 129
History, 128–129
Interstate commerce, 129–131
Money Laundering, 129
Organized crime, 128–129
Public Corruption, 128–131
RICO, 129

USE IMMUNITY
See Immunity

VICTIM AND WITNESS PROTECTION ACT
See Obstruction of Justice

WATER POLLUTION CONTROL ACT
See Environmental Crimes

WHARTON'S RULE
Conspiracy, 45–46

WHEEL AND SPOKE CONSPIRACIES
See Conspiracy

WHITE COLLAR CRIME
Definition, 1–3

WILLFUL BLINDNESS
Bankruptcy, 221
Corporate criminal liability, 33
Environmental crimes, 226
Mail Fraud, 60
Securities Fraud, 79–80

452 *INDEX*
References are to Pages

WILLFULNESS
Bank Secrecy Act, 202, 208–209
False statements, 155–156
Perjury, 175
Securities fraud, 76–77, 79–82
Tax, 183–189, 190–191, 193–194

WIRE FRAUD
   See also Mail Fraud
   Generally, 71–72
Bankruptcy, 215
Commerce clause, 72
Computer crimes, 236
Elements, 71
International, 9
Interstate commerce, 5, 71–72
RICO, 141
Securities fraud, 79

WITNESS TAMPERING
See Obstruction of Justice

WORK PRODUCT DOCTRINE
   Generally, 384, 387–395
Crime Fraud Exception, 392–393
Defense agreements, 393–395
Distinctions with Attorney–Client Privilege, 384
Waiver, 389–392

†